Principles of Marketing

James Spiers
Arizona State University

KENDALL/HUNT PUBLISHING COMPANY
4050 Westmark Drive   Dubuque, Iowa 52002

Cover image courtesy of PhotoDisc

Copyright © 2004 by Kendall/Hunt Publishing Company

ISBN 0-7575-1272-0

All rights reserved. No part of this publication may be reproduced, stored in a retrieval system, or transmitted, in any form or by any means, electronic, mechanical, photocopying, recording, or otherwise, without the prior written permission of the copyright owner.

Printed in the United States of America
10 9 8 7 6 5 4 3 2 1

Contents

Syllabus	v
Notes	1
Articles	229
The Role of Marketing: Theory, Practice, and Conceptual Conflict *Banton Machiette & Abhijit Roy*	231
Product Policy and Its Origins *A. P. Sloan, Jr.*	299
Strategies for Mature and Declining Markets *Walker, Boyd, & Larréché*	307
Social Relations and Japanese Business Practices *Bradley M. Richardson & Taizo Ueda*	341
Illustrations	349
Map of United States	350
Map of California	351
Alternative Shapes for Territories	352
Circle	352
Cloverleaf	352
Wedge	352

Principles of Marketing Exams

	Date of Exam	**Score**
Exam #1		
Exam #2		
Exam #3		
Final		
Extra Credit #1		
#2		
#3		
#4		
#5		
#6		

Total (Drop lowest exam)

900+	=	A
800–899	=	B
700–799	=	C
600–699	=	D
<600	=	F

Section 1

Notes

Marketing—What Is It?

- **Bringing buyers and sellers together**
- **Exchange process**
    —When two or more parties exchange or trade something of value
- **Intangible goods**

A Definition of Marketing

> **The process of planning and executing the conception, pricing, promotion, and distribution of ideas, goods, and services to create exchanges that will satisfy individual and organizational objectives.**

Ethical Issues in Sales and Sales Management

Corporate codes of conduct

Compliance with the law

Honesty and integrity

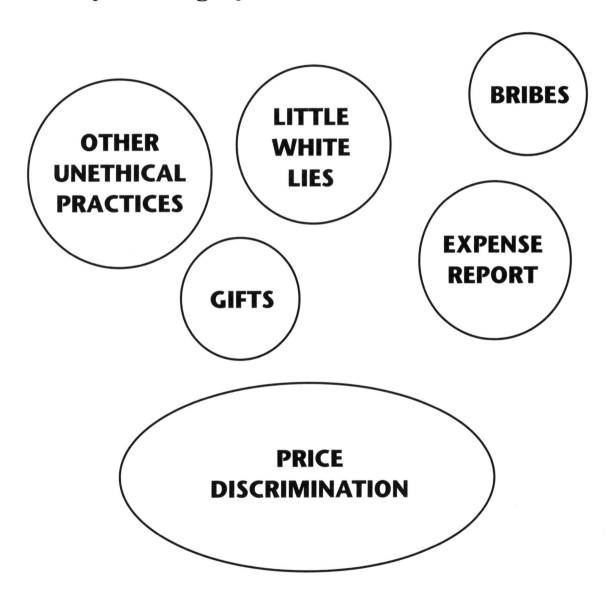

Integrity

We make a living by what we get

N

We make a life by what we give

Four Types of Utility

1. **Ownership**
2. **Place**
3. **Form**
4. **Time**

The Card Game

Four Ps
Objectives
Win–Lose

Common Interview Questions
Plus, What the Interviewer Is Really Asking

[handwritten: tell weakness and what you're doing to correct it]

- Could you tell me about your two greatest weak points?
  - The interviewer wants to see if you can show that what some might designate as a weakness is actually a strength. This shows your **selling ability.**

- What other companies are you interviewing with?
  - The interviewer wants to know if you are focused. They want to hear that you are interviewing with companies within the same industry as their own. If you tell them you are interviewing with a wide spectrum of companies, they may conclude you have not decided what career you really want.

- Could you describe a situation where you had an impact on a group?
  - The interviewer wants to know about your leadership skills. Tell him/her about a situation where you led a group with some success.

- Could you describe two of the biggest problems you have recently faced and how you handled them?
  - The interviewer wants to know your **decision-making** process. Tell him/her how you analyzed the problem and arrived at an effective decision.

- What are your five- and ten-year career goals?
  - The interviewer wants to know if your career ambitions fit with his/her company's career path. Find out the company's career path, so that the goals match.

- How was your achievement in school (work) measured?
  - The interviewer really wants to know your **commitment to achieve.** Tell him/her not only about how it was measured, but how you excelled.

- Could you give me an example of how you overcame an obstacle to achieve a goal?
  - The interviewer wants to know about your **flexibility.** Tell him/her about a time when you were flexible or creative in solving a problem.

- How do you schedule your time and set priorities?
  - The interviewer wants to know about your **organizational ability.** Tell him/her in detail how you do this. Use your calendar or schedule to show them.

- Could you please sell me this pen? Or, can you tell me how you would handle an objection?
  - The interviewer wants to know if you know **how to sell.** Study a sales model so that you can be persuasive throughout the process. A perceptive sales interviewer will recognize the model and understand that you have had some sales training.

[handwritten: 5 p's - Proper prior preparation prevents poor performance]

What Is a Market?

- **The word *market* has many uses (fish market, stock market, supermarket).**
- **Markets consist of people or groups with <u>purchasing power</u>.**
- **These people are willing and able to exchange their resources for <u>something else</u>.**

value to them

authority is important too
— under 21 cannot buy drinks even though they have purchasing power ($) + are willing to exchange resources for beer

Orientations Toward Marketing

Focus	Means	Goals	Illustrative Comments
Product Orientation			
Manufacturing *(Focus on themselves)*	Making high-quality products	Produce as much product as possible	"You can have any color you want as long as it's black." "Make the best product you can and people will buy it." "I know people want my kind of product."
Sales Orientation			
Selling existing products *(Focus on themselves)*	Aggressive sales and advertising efforts	Maximize sales volume	"You don't like black? I'll throw in a set of glassware." "Sell this inventory no matter what it takes." "Who cares what they want? Sell what we've got."
Marketing Orientation			
Fulfilling actual and potential customer needs and wants *(Focus on customers)*	Customer orientation, profit orientation, and integrated marketing	Make profits through customer satisfaction	"Find out what customers want before you make the product." "Maybe people don't want the 'best' product. Find out what they do want." "I'm going to find out what the people want."

You take care of customers; they'll take care of you.

Evolution of Marketing

1. **Production Era** — Depression
2. **Sales era** — WWII
3. **Marketing era** → start of personal relationships (not just salesman but a problem solver)
4. **Relationship marketing**

Needs and Wants

Needs
- **The consumer's unsatisfactory conditions that led him or her to actions that will make the conditions better**

marketing is different if it's needs or wants — different approaches

Wants
- **Desires to obtain more satisfaction than is absolutely necessary to improve unsatisfactory conditions.**

SWOT Analysis

Helps Match Opportunities to the Organization

Economy could be a threat
Natural Disaster
Government
Taxes △ price

Activities of Marketing

Producer → Wholesaler → Retailer → Consumer

Exchange – Buying + Selling

Logistical – Transporting + Storing goods/services

Facilitating – Financing, Risk-taking, Providing information, Standardizing + Grading

- Financing: Facilitates exchange
- Risk-taking: Holding inventory (title) → risky
- Providing information: understanding the markets (consumer + industrial)
- Standardizing + Grading: Sorting (size/quality)

The Target Market and Marketing Mix Variables

Group(s) of potential customers toward which a firm directs its marketing mix(es)

↑ some companies sell more than one type of product

The Marketing Mix Variables

Decisions on 4 p's are based on Target Market

Planning Focus

Management Level	Planning Focus	Marketing Questions
Top Management	Corporate Plans	What is our organizational mission? How do we organize our business?
Middle Management	Strategic Business unit (i.e., division or product)	What is our competitive strategy for growth? What is our competitive advantage?
Operational Management	Operational Plans for tactical execution	How can we best support the competitive strategy? What are our schedules for weekly operations?

Handwritten notes:
- create marketing plans + marketing objectives (pointing to Operational Management)
- Top/Middle Mgt. (next to "How can we best support the competitive strategy?")
- By a building on the east → sun behind you when coming in morning, leaving in evening.

Societal Marketing Concept

- **Adoption of Marketing Concept** — we take care of customers → they take care of us.
- **Considering the needs of society as a whole**
  - Environment
  - Health
  - Safety ⟶ Boosts price

Strategic Marketing Concept

Corporate mission is to
- **Seek sustainable competitive advantage**
- **Meet customer needs**

Marketing Myopia

- **Shortsightedness by business firms that causes management to define their business too narrowly**

  causes business to miss out on opportunities

Marketing Myopia Examples

Myopic Description: *(Small vision)*

Broad Description: *(Large Vision)*

- Railroad company
- Electricity company
- Television network

- Transportation company
- Power company
- Entertainment provider

Filtering of Corporate Strategy

Strategic corporate planning
- Define organization mission
- Establish strategic business units
- Anticipate change

Marketing planning for SBUs
- Set marketing objectives
- Develop marketing strategy
- Formalize marketing plan

Operational marketing plans

They make it happen

The Strategic Marketing Process

1. **Identifying and evaluating opportunities** *SWOT analysis*
2. **Analyzing market segments and selecting target markets**
3. **Planning a market position and developing a marketing mix strategy** *4 p's*

4. **Executing the plan**

5. **Controlling efforts and evaluating the results**

Typical Marketing Plan

Don't memorise — Just understand the concepts

I. Market Review
II. Problems and Opportunities
III. Marketing Objectives — *need to be measurable* — *How do we support objectives — have a timeframe — be achievable*
IV. Marketing Strategies—Four Ps
V. Advertising Objectives
VI. Advertising Strategies — *Promotion*
VII. Copy Strategy
VIII. Copy Plan — *Interchangeable*
IX. Media Strategy
X. Media Plan
XI. Sales Promotion Strategy
XII. Sales Promotion Plan
XIII. Special Objectives, Strategies, & Plans
XIV. Budget Summary — *Not a % of sales* — *How much does each line cost = Total cost*
XV. Schedule of Activities → *Prevents managers from being caught by surprise*

Sales Forecasting

Research about the Future

- **The process of predicting sales totals over some specific future period in time.**

- **Helps in the planning and control of production, distribution, pricing, and promotion activity.**

- **Provides information for the control function by establishing an evaluation standard.**

Inventory is in excess when you miss forecast
↳ can become obsolete

when you run out of inventory (over forecast)
↳ bad for supplier/retailer because customers could switch

Personality Inventory

Please mark a "1" by the personality trait that pertains to you.

L*ion*	O*tter*	G*olden Retriever*	B*eaver*
LIKES AUTHORITY _1_	ENTHUSIASTIC _1_	SENSITIVE FEELINGS ___	ENJOYS STRUCTURE _1_
TAKES CHARGE _1_	TAKES RISKS _1_	LOYAL _1_	ACCURATE ___
DETERMINED _1_	VISIONARY _1_	CALM—EVEN KEEL ___	CONSISTENT ___
CONFIDENT _1_	MOTIVATED _1_	NONDEMANDING ___	CONTROLLED _1_
FIRM ___	ENERGETIC ___	AVOIDS CONFRONTATION _1_	RESERVED ___
ENTERPRISING _1_	VERY VERBAL ___	ENJOYS ROUTINE _1_	PREDICTABLE ___
COMPETITIVE _1_	PROMOTER ___	DISLIKES CHANGE ___	PRACTICAL _1_
ENJOYS CHALLENGE _1_	FRIENDLY _1_	WARM & RELATIONAL _1_	ORDERLY ___
PROBLEM SOLVING _1_	MIXES EASILY _1_	GIVES IN ___	FACTUAL ___
PRODUCTIVE _1_	ENJOYS POPULARITY _1_	INDECISIVE ___	CONSCIENTIOUS _1_
BOLD _1_	FUN-LOVING _1_	DRY HUMOR _1_	PERFECTIONIST ___
PURPOSEFUL GOALS _1_	LIKES VARIETY _1_	ADAPTABLE _1_	DISCERNING ___
DECISION MAKER _1_	SPONTANEOUS _1_	SYMPATHETIC _1_	DETAILED _1_
ADVENTUROUS _1_	ENJOYS CHANGE _1_	NURTURING ___	ANALYTICAL _1_
INDEPENDENT _1_	CREATIVE—NEW IDEAS _1_	PATIENT _1_	INQUISITIVE _1_
SELF-RELIANT _1_	GROUP ORIENTED _1_	TOLERANT _1_	PRECISE _1_
CONTROLLING ___	INITIATES _1_	GOOD LISTENER _1_	PERSISTENT ___
PERSISTENT ___	INFECTIOUS LAUGH ___	PEACEMAKER _1_	SCHEDULED _1_
ACTION ORIENTED _1_	INSPIRATIONAL _1_	SAYS "LET'S KEEP THINGS THE WAY THEY ARE!!!" ___	SENSITIVE _1_
SAYS: "LET'S DO IT NOW!!!" _1_	SAYS "TRUST ME IT WILL WORK OUT!!!" _1_		SAYS: "HOW WAS IT DONE IN THE PAST?" _1_
17 TOTAL × 2 = **34**	18 TOTAL × 2 = **36**	10 TOTAL × 2 = **20**	11 TOTAL × 2 = **22**

The Marketing Environment

- **Microenvironment**
  - **Objectives and resources**
- **Macroenvironment**
  - **Competitive environment**
  - **Legal/political environment**
  - **Sociocultural environment**
  - **Economic environment**
  - **Technological environment**

Marketing Environment

Key Federal Legislation Affecting Marketers

Sherman Act (1890)	Prohibits combinations, contracts, or conspiracies to restrain trade or monopolize
Clayton Act (1914)	Prohibits price discrimination, exclusive dealer arrangements, and interlocking directories that lessen competition
Federal Trade Commission Act (1914)	Created the FTC and gave it investigatory powers
Robinson-Patman Act (1936)	Expanded the Clayton Act to prohibit sellers from offering different deals to different customers
Wheeler-Lea Act (1938)	Expanded powers of FTC to prevent injuries to competition before they occur.
Celler-Kefauver Act (1950)	Expanded the Clayton Act to prohibit acquisition of physical assets as well as capital stock in another corporation when the effect is to injure competition
Magnuson-Moss Act (1975)	Grants the FTC the power to determine rules concerning warranties and provides the means for class action suits and other forms of redress
Consumer Goods Pricing Act (1975) **Fair Debt Collection Act (1980)**	Repealed "fair-trade" laws and prohibited price maintenance agreements among producers and resellers. Requires creditors to act responsibly in debt collection (e.g., bans false statements) and makes harassment of debtors illegal
FTC Improvement Act (1980)	Provides Congress with the power to veto the FTC industrywide Trade Regulation Rules (TRR); limits the power of the FTC
Federal Antitampering Act (1983)	Prohibits tampering with a product and threats to tamper with a product
American with Disabilities Act (1990)	Prohibits discrimination against consumers with disabilities (e.g., stores and hotels must be accessible to shoppers or guests who use wheelchairs)
North American Free Trade Agreement (1993)	Allows for free trade between the United States, Mexico, and Canada without tariffs and trade restrictions
Nutritional Labeling and Education Act	Requires that certain nutritional facts be printed on food product labels
Labeling Act (1994)	Requires that stickers be placed on all new vehicles stating the percentage of domestic and foreign parts used to make them.

Sample of Specialized Federal Legislation Affecting Business

Legislation	Major Provisions
Federal Hazardous Substances Act (1960)	Requires warning labels on hazardous household chemicals
Kefauver-Harris Drug Amendment (1962)	Requires that manufacturers conduct tests to prove drug effectiveness and safety
Child Protection and Toy Safety Act (1969)	Prevents marketing of products so dangerous that adequate safety warnings cannot be given
Consumer Credit Protection At (1968)	Requires that lenders fully disclose true interest rates and all other charges to credit customers for loans and installment purchases
Public Health Smoking Act (1970)	Prohibits cigarette advertising on TV and radio and revises the health hazard warning on cigarette packages
Poison Prevention Labeling Act (1970)	Requires safety packaging for products that may be harmful to children
Child Protection Act (1990)	Regulates the number of minutes for advertising on children's television
Cable Television Act (1992)	Regulates the price of cable television subscriptions

Competitive Market Structures

- **Pure Competition**
  —No barriers to competition
  —Homogeneous goods
- **Monopolistic Competition**
  —A large number of sellers offering similar products with minor differences
- **Oligopoly**
  —A small number of sellers dominate the market
- **Monopoly**
  —No competition

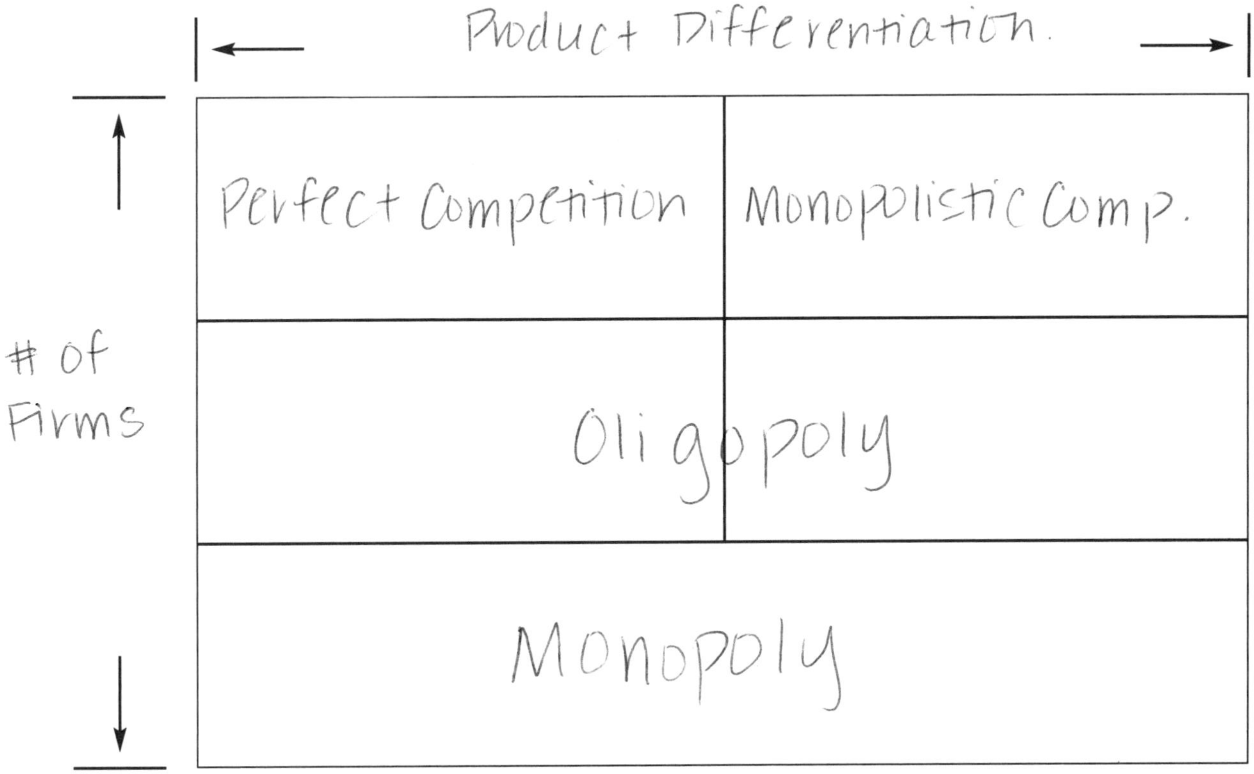
Product Differentiation.
Perfect Competition
Monopolistic Comp.
# of Firms
Oligopoly
Monopoly

Research Process

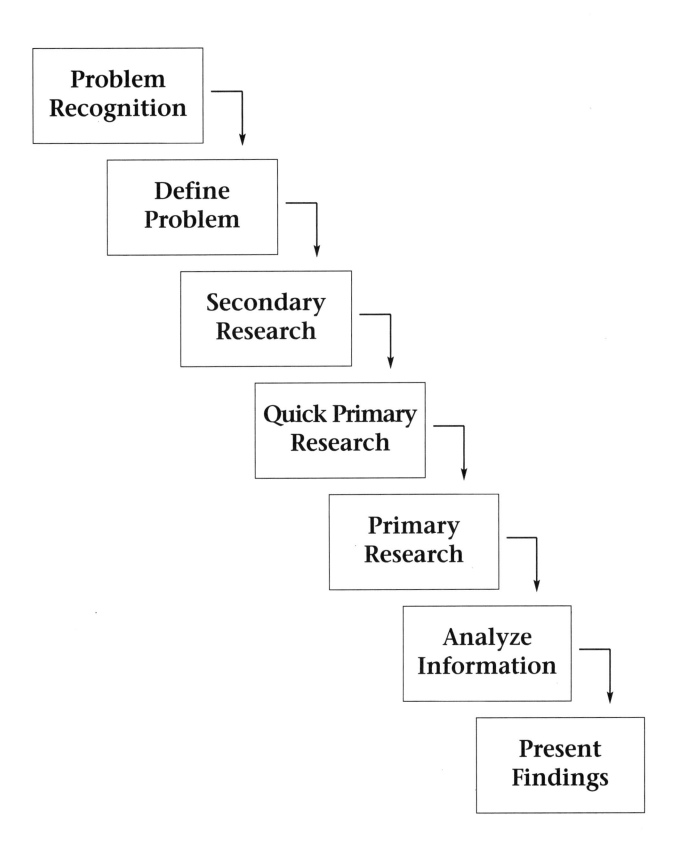

Secondary Data Sources

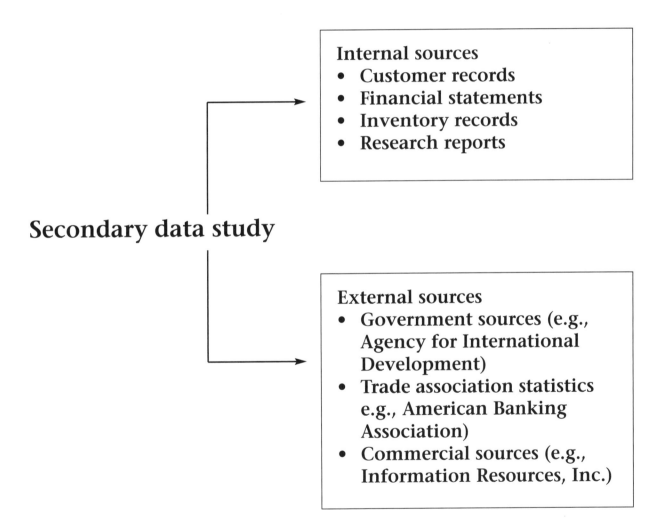

A Consumer Behavior Model of How the Decision-Making Process Works and What Influences It

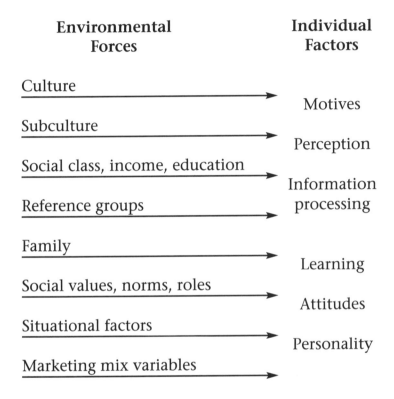

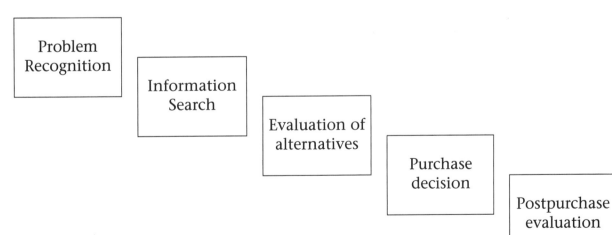

Decision-Making Process

ROUTINE   EXTENSIVE

←——————————————————————————————→

The Types of Risk That Concern Potential Buyers

Type of Risk	Typical Concern
Performance risk	The brand may not perform its function well; it may not work; it may break down.
Financial risk	The buyer may lose money; pay too much; miss buying something else.
Physical risk	The product may be harmful or unhealthy; it may cause injury.
Social risk	Friends, relatives, or significant others may not approve of the purchase.
Time-loss risk	Maintenance time of time required to return the product to the place of purchase may be excessive.

Maslow's Hierarchy of Needs

The Diffusion Process

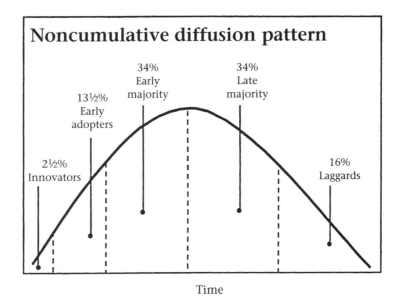

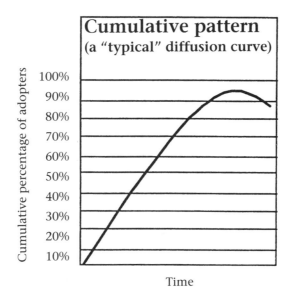

Organizational Buying Situations

- **Straight Rebuy**
  —Continuing or recurring requirement, handled on a routine basis
- **Modified Rebuy**
  —Buying alternatives are known, but they are changed
- **New Task Buying**
  —A requirement or problem that has not arisen before

Organizational Buying Process

- Problem Recognition
- General Description of Need
- Detailed Description of Product Specs
- Supplier Search
- Acquisition and Analysis of Proposals
- Supplier Selection
- Selection of an Order Routine
- Performance Review

- ❏ **A problem that can be solved or opportunity captured by acquiring a specific product**
- ❏ **Triggered by internal or external forces**

What Is Market Segmentation?

- **Market Segmentation**
  - Process of dividing a large market into smaller target markets or customer groups with similar needs and/or desires

Market Segmentation

- Dividing a heterogeneous market into a number of smaller, more homogeneous submarkets.
- Not all buyers are alike.
- Subgroups of people with similar behavior, values, and/or backgrounds may be identified.
- The subgroups will be smaller and more homogeneous than the market as a whole.
- It should be easier to satisfy smaller groups of similar customers than large groups of dissimilar customers.
- A single company is unlikely to pursue all possible market segments.
- Choose one or a few meaningful segments.
- Concentrate efforts on satisfying those segments.
- Targeting

What Is a Market?

❑ **Individuals or organizations who:**
- **Are willing, able, and capable of purchasing a firm's product**
- **Segmentation is critical because demand is often heterogeneous**

Market Criteria

❏ **Segmentable markets are:**
- **Heterogeneous**
- **Measurable**
- **Substantial**
- **Actionable**
  - Companies must be able to respond to preferences with an appropriate marketing mix
- **Accessible**
  - Market must be efficiently reachable

Target Market Selection

- Identify Total Market
- Determine Need for Segmentation
- Determine Bases for Segmentation
- Profile Each Selected Segment
- Assess Potential Profitability of Segment and Select Target Segment
- Select Positioning Strategy
- Develop and Implement Appropriate Marketing Mix
- Monitor, Evaluate, and Control

Undifferentiated

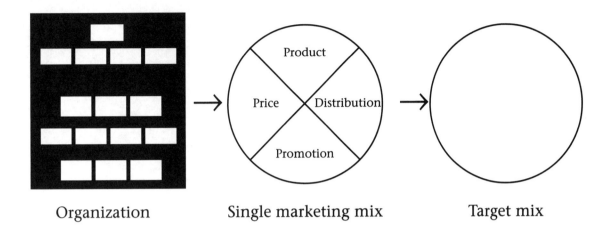

Organization   Single marketing mix   Target mix

Differentiated

MULTISEGMENTED

Companies don't take care of All segments - only the ones they do the best

```
                    ┌─────────────┐
                    │   Product   │
                    │ Price × Distribution │
                    │  Promotion  │
                    └─────────────┘
                    Marketing mix I


  Organization  →   Marketing mix II   →   Target markets
                                            (Segment I / II / III)


                    Marketing mix III
```

Concentration

Organization → Single marketing mix → Market

Typical Bases for Segmentation of Consumer Markets

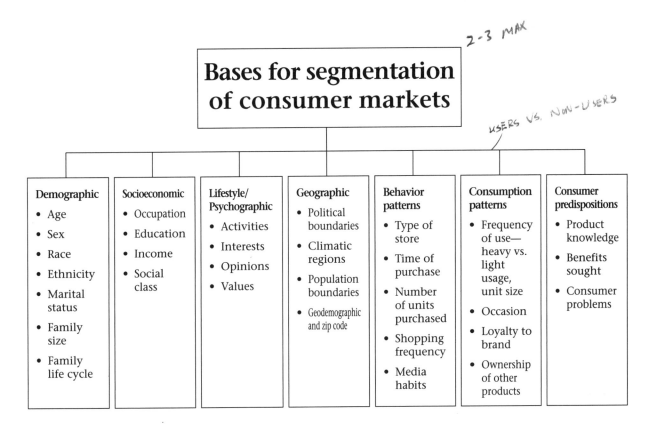

Handwritten annotations: "2-3 MAX" (pointing to Bases for segmentation of consumer markets); "USERS VS. NON-USERS" (pointing to Consumption patterns)

Bases for segmentation of consumer markets

- **Demographic**
  - Age
  - Sex
  - Race
  - Ethnicity
  - Marital status
  - Family size
  - Family life cycle

- **Socioeconomic**
  - Occupation
  - Education
  - Income
  - Social class

- **Lifestyle/ Psychographic**
  - Activities
  - Interests
  - Opinions
  - Values

- **Geographic**
  - Political boundaries
  - Climatic regions
  - Population boundaries
  - Geodemographic and zip code

- **Behavior patterns**
  - Type of store
  - Time of purchase
  - Number of units purchased
  - Shopping frequency
  - Media habits

- **Consumption patterns**
  - Frequency of use—heavy vs. light usage, unit size
  - Occasion
  - Loyalty to brand
  - Ownership of other products

- **Consumer predispositions**
  - Product knowledge
  - Benefits sought
  - Consumer problems

Selected Bases for Segmentation of Business Markets

Bases for segmentation of organizational markets

Geographic
- Political boundaries (cities, states, etc.)
- Domestic/international boundaries

Organizational characteristics
- Industry type
- Organizational size
- Technology used

Purchase behavior and usage patterns
- Order size (heavy vs. light usage)
- Centralized vs. decentralized purchasing
- Type of rebuy (e.g., straight rebuy vs. new task)

Organizational predisposition or policy
- Product knowledge
- Benefits sought
- Organizational problems
- Multiple vs. single-supplier policy

Segmentation Options

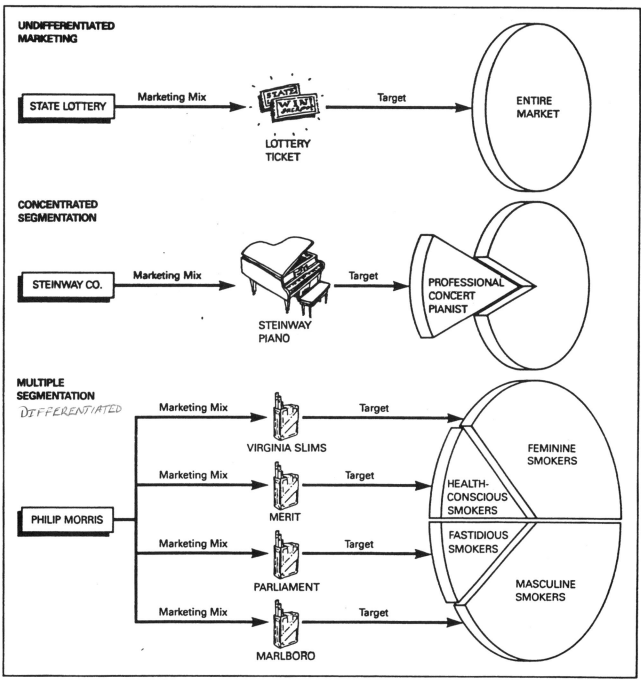

Not all people want same things

Widely Accepted Classifications for Consumer Products

Criteria	Types of Products
Tangibility and durability	Goods
	Durable goods
	Nondurable goods
	Services
Consumer behavior	Convenience products
Willingness to expend effort	Shopping products
	Specialty products

Goods-Services Continuum

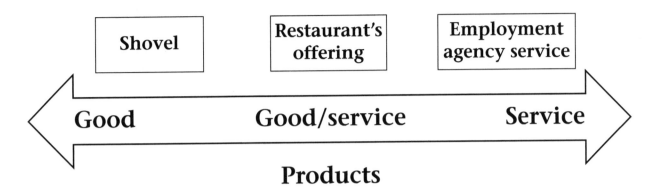

Core, Tangible, and Augmented Product

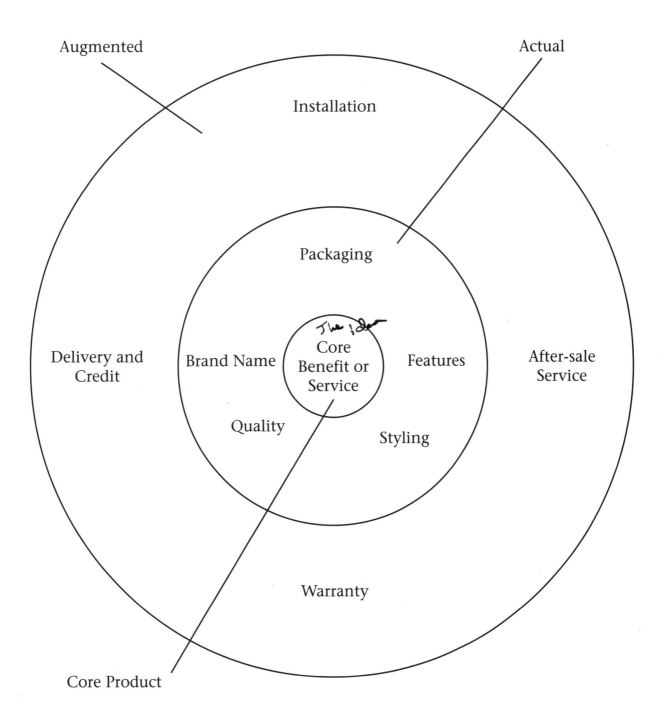

Convenience Products

- **Relatively inexpensive**
- **Purchased on a regular basis**
- **Purchased without a great deal of thought**
- **Minimum of consumer shopping effort**
- **Make the product available in almost every possible location**
- **One brand is easily substituted for another**
- **Personal selling effort by retailers is nonexistent**

Shopping Products

- **Buyers expect to benefit from shopping around**
- **Decisions are not made on the spur of the moment**
- **Generally priced higher than convenience products**
- **Consumers are more involved with the purchases**
- **Homogeneous shopping products**
  - **Similar in quality and features, different in price**
- **Heterogeneous shopping products**
  - **Identifiable product differences**

Specialty Products

- Consumers believe they know exactly what they want
- Seldom-purchased items
- Buyers gather a great amount of information
- Brand insistence can be strong
- Exclusive distribution of the brand

Branding, Packaging, Labeling Decisions

- **Brands—used to simplify choices and reduce purchase risk for consumers**
- **Brand equity—marketplace value of a brand based on reputation and goodwill**

Branding, Packaging, Labeling Decisions

❑ **Brand name, logo, trademark should:**
  - **Attract attention**
  - **Be memorable**
  - **Help communicate the positioning of the product**
  - **Distinguish the product**

Four Service Characteristics

Intangibility
Services cannot be seen, tasted, felt, heard, or smelled before purchase

Inseparability
Services cannot be separated from their providers

Variability
Quality of services depends on who provides them and when, where, and how

Perishability
Services cannot be stored for later sale or use

SERVICES

A Service Model

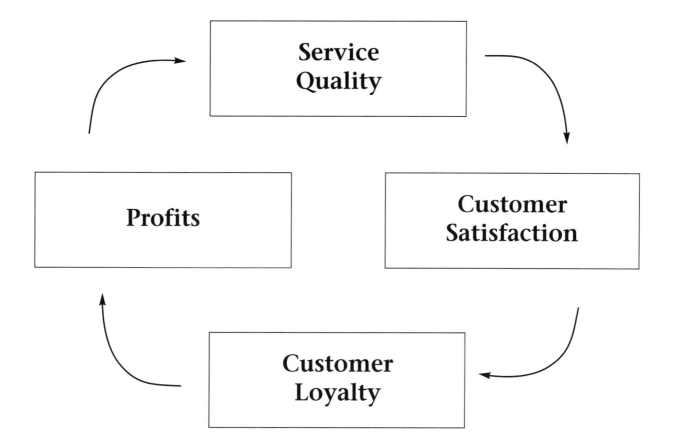

Product Mix Decisions

- **Product mix**—all the products a company markets
- **Product mix width**—the number of product lines a company markets
- **Product mix depth**—the number of brands within each product line

The Product Life Cycle

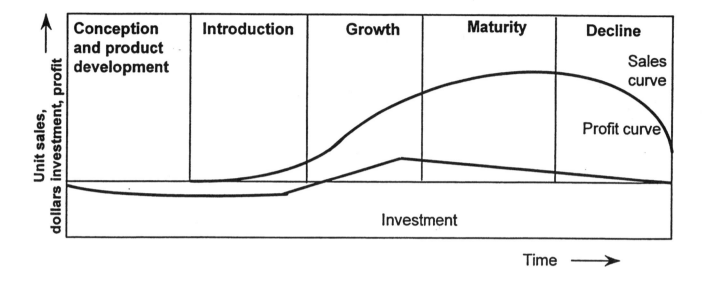

Product Growth Opportunities

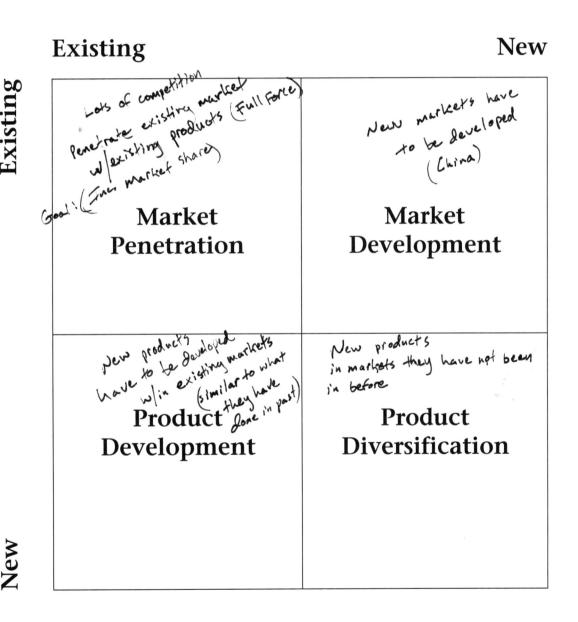

The General Stages in the Development of New Products

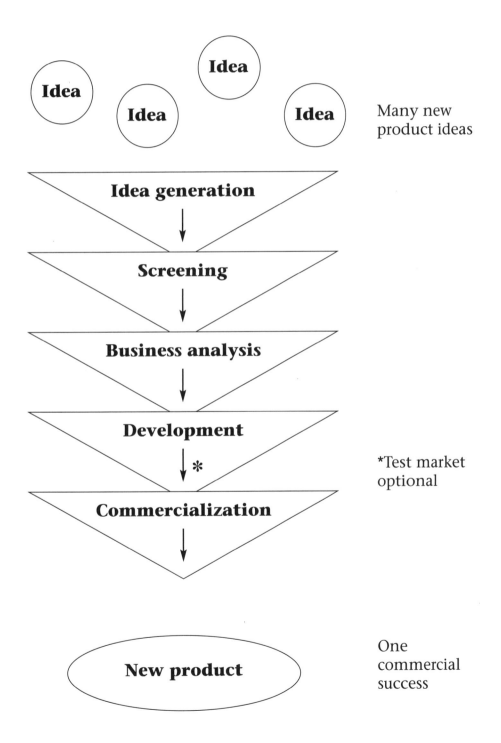

Product Failure

- ❏ **Reasons for product elimination**
  - **Poor sales**
  - **Incompatibility with the organization's strategies**
  - **Poor market outlook**

Product Failure

- **Reasons for product failure**
  - **Bad timing**
  - **Insignificant point of difference**
  - **Poor quality**
  - **Poor marketing execution**
  - **Markets too small or inaccessible**
  - **Lack of top management commitment**

Why Do New Products Fail?

- **Firm Misread Customer Needs**
- **Products are Poorly Positioned**
- **Products Experience Poor Performance**
- **There is Inadequate Marketing Research**
- **There is Inadequate Competitive Analysis**

Industry Profit and the Product Life Cycle

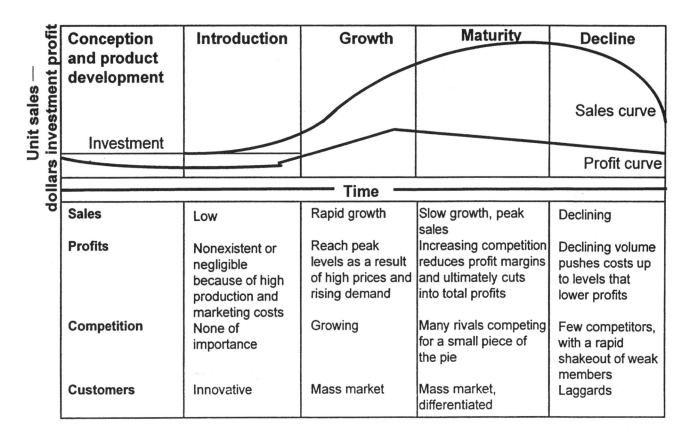

Typical Marketing Strategies during the Product Life Cycle

STAGES OF PRODUCT LIFE CYCLE

	Introduction	Growth	Maturity	Decline
Overall strategy	Market acceptance; product awareness and trial purchase	Market penetration; persuade mass market to prefer the brand; expand users	Defense of brand position; check the inroads of competition and use	Reduction of expenses; preparation for removal; milking the brand dry of all possible benefits
Product	Basic design with competitive advantage	Product improvements; expanding product line	Product differentiation; full product lines	Minimal changes; product line reduced to best sellers
Prices	High, to recover some of the excessive costs of launching	High, to take advantage of heavy demand	What the traffic will bear; need to avoid price wars	Low enough to permit quick liquidation of inventory
Distribution	Selective as distribution is slowly built up	Intensive; employ small trade discounts, because dealers are eager to stock	Intensive; give heavy trade allowances to retain shelf space	Selective; slowly phase out unprofitable outlets
Promotion	Informative, to generate brand awareness	Persuasive, to create brand loyalty and product differentiation	Minimal	Minimal to none

The Diffusion Process

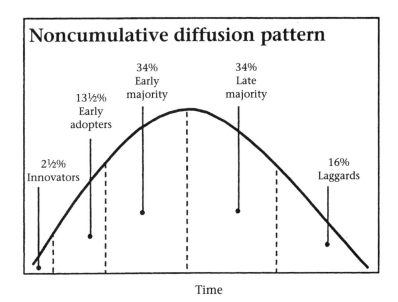

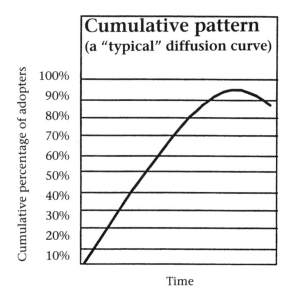

What Is Price?

- **Price is the sacrifice that one party pays another to receive something in exchange**
- **In our case, price is a monetary value charged by an organization for the sales of its products**

Setting Price

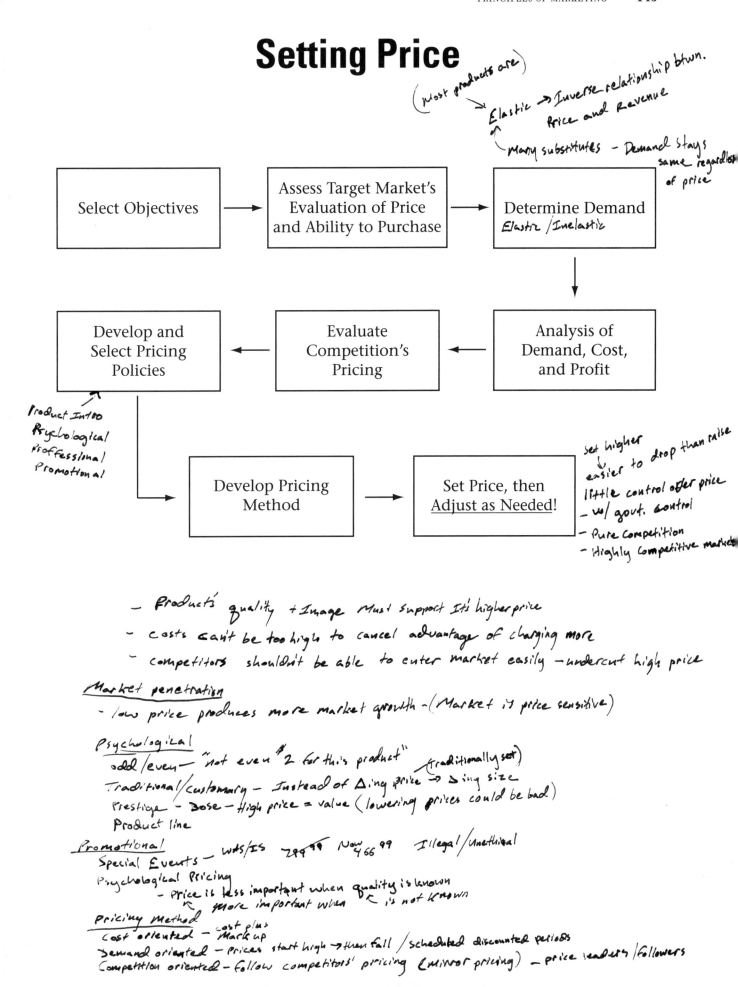

(most products are) → Elastic → Inverse relationship btwn. price and Revenue
↳ Many substitutes - Demand stays same regardless of price

Determine Demand — Elastic/Inelastic

Develop and Select Pricing Policies ← Product Intro / Psychological / Proffessional / Promotional

Set Price, then Adjust as Needed!
- set higher — easier to drop than raise
- little control over price — w/ govt. control
- Pure Competition
- Highly Competitive markets

- Product's quality + Image must support it's higher price
- costs can't be too high to cancel advantage of charging more
- competitors shouldn't be able to enter market easily - undercut high price

Market penetration
- low price produces more market growth - (Market is price sensitive)

Psychological
- odd/even — "not even $2 for this product" (traditionally set)
- Traditional/customary — Instead of Δing price → Δing size
- Prestige — Dose — High price = value (lowering prices could be bad)
- Product line

Promotional
- Special Events — WAS/IS $29.99 Now $66.99 Illegal/Unethical
- Psychological Pricing
  - Price is less important when quality is known
  - more important when it's not known

Pricing Method
- Cost oriented — cost plus / Mark up
- Demand oriented — Prices start high → then fall / scheduled discounted periods
- Competition oriented — follow competitors' pricing (mirror pricing) — price leaders/followers

The Relationship of Pricing Decisions to Company Objectives

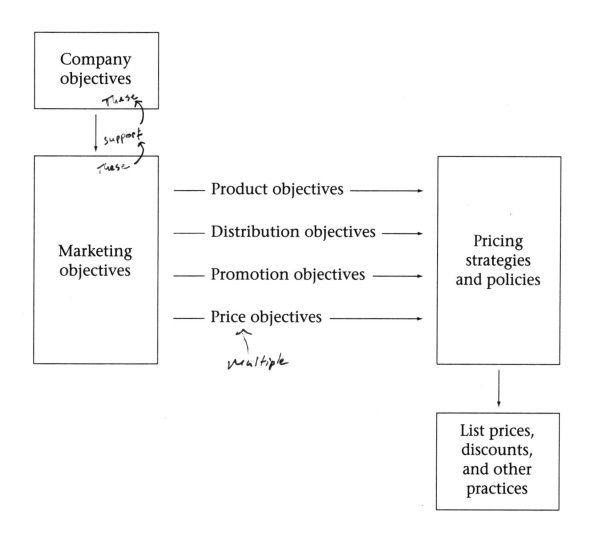

The Relationship of Pricing Decisions to Company Objectives

Costs, Revenues, and the Break-Even (B/E) Point

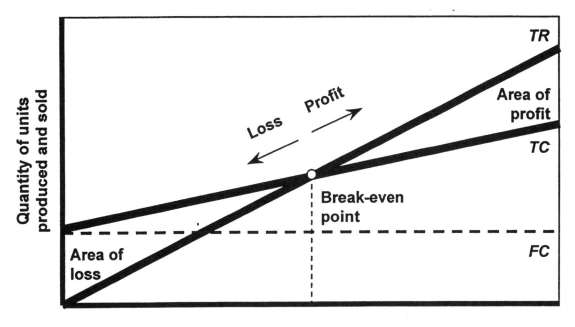

B/E Problems

1. **The Apex Company wishes to use break-even analysis. Its fixed costs for the year are estimated at $100,000; the variable costs are usually about 70% of sales. Sales for the coming year are expected to reach $380,000. What is the break-even point? Expected profit? If sales were forecast at only $200,000, should the Apex Company shut down operations? Why?**

B/E Problems (continued)

2. The XYZ Corporation has fixed costs of $300,000. They are considering selling an item for $10 per unit where variable costs are $7 per unit. Expected sales for the next year are $1,200,000.
   (a) What is the break-even point in units? _____
   (b) What is the break-even point in dollars? _____
   (c) What will the profit (loss) be with sales of $1,200,000? _____
   (d) What will the profit (loss) be with sales of $650,000? _____
   (e) In the short run should the firm close down with these sales (i.e., $650,000)?
   Yes _____ No _____ Why?

B/E Problems (continued)

3. The Flear Company has a maximum production capacity of 210,000 units per year. Normal capacity is regarded as 180,000 units per year. Variable manufacturing costs are $11 per unit. Fixed factory overhead expenses are $360,000 per year. Variable selling expenses are $3 per unit, and fixed selling expenses are $252,000 per year. The unit sales price is $20.

   The operation results for last year were: Sales, 150,000; production, 160,000; beginning inventory, 10,000; ending inventory, 20,000 units.

   Required:
   (a) What is Flear Company's break-even point in *dollar* sales?
   (b) How many *units* must be sold to earn a net income of 10% on *sales* per year?
   (c) How many *units* must be sold to earn $60,000 per year? (ignoring taxes)
   (d) If the total asset of Flear Company for last year was $1,000,000, how many *units* would they have had to sell to earn a 10% ROA?

B/E Problems (continued)

4. The profit and loss statement for June for the XYZ Company is as follows:

	Retailers	Hospitals & Schools	Total
Sales:			
80,000 units at $.70	56,000		56,000
20,000 units at $.60		12,000	12,000
Total	$56,000	$12,000	$68,000
CGS	40,000	10,000	50,000
GM	$16,000	$2,000	$18,000
Expenses:			
Variable	6,000	1,500	7,500
Fixed	5,600	900	6,500
	$11,600	$2,400	$14,000
Profits:	$4,400	$(400)	$4,000

If competitive conditions made price increases impossible and management had already cut costs as much as possible, should XYZ stop selling to hospitals and schools? Why?

What Is a Marketing Channel?

❑ **Marketing channel (a.k.a. distribution channel)—network of organizations that create time, place, and possession utilities for consumers**

Who Is Involved in a Basic Channel of Distribution?

Flow of product or title	Definition	Example
Manufacturer	Producer of a finished product from raw materials or component parts	Coors Beer Company, Golden, Colorado
↓		
Wholesaler	An intermediary who neither produces nor consumes the finished product but sells to retailers, manufacturers, or institutions that use the product for ultimate resale (perhaps in another product form).	Los Angeles Coors Distributor
↓		
Retailer	An intermediary who neither produces nor consumes the finished product but sells to the ultimate consumer.	Safeway Stores
↓		
Consumer	A person who buys or uses the finished product.	You

Organizational Examples

1. IBM ──────────────────────→ User—ASU
2. John Deere ──→ Local Distributor ──→ User—Farmer
3. American ──→ International tours ──→ User—West
   Airlines   Travel Agency   Publishing Co.
4. Escort Cruise ──→ Auto Wholesaler ──→ Cash & Carry ──→ User—Joe's Garage
   Control   Autoparts (Whl'er)
5. Remington ──→ Sales Agent ──→ Byco Equipment ──→ User—Home
   Chain Saw   (Industrial Jobber)   Building Contractor

The Objectives of Physical Distribution

To minimize cost while maximizing customer service!

General Comparison of Attributes of Various Transportation Modes

Low Cost	Speed	Reliability of Delivery	Ability to Deliver to Many Geographical Areas	Reputation for Delivering Undamaged Goods
(1) Pipeline	(1) Air	(1) Pipeline	(1) Motor	(1) Pipeline
(2) Water	(2) Motor	(2) Air	(2) Rail	(2) Water
(3) Rails	(3) Rail	(3) Motor	(3) Air	(3) Air
(4) Motor	(4) Pipeline	(4) Rail	(4) Water	(4) Motor
(5) Air	(5) Water	(5) Water	(5) Pipeline	(5) Rail

NOTE: These comparisons are of a very general nature intended only to show the trade-offs involved when cost of use is compared with other attributes of modes of transportation.

Retail and Wholesale

❏ **Retailers perform the final steps needed to place merchandise in the hands of the consumer**

❏ **Wholesalers provide retailers and other organizational buyers with merchandise but do not sell significant amounts to end consumers**

Definition of Retailing

Retailing consists of all business activities involving the sale of goods and services to ultimate consumers. The government definition includes all institutions that make more than 50% of their sales to ultimate consumers.

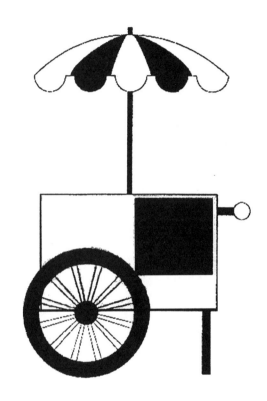

Retailers Classified by Prominent Strategy

Major Group	Retailer Classification	Brief Description
In-store	Specialty store	Narrow variety, deep selection within a product class; personalized service; makes up large bulk of all retailing operations
	Department store	Generally chain operations, wide variety, full range of services
	Supermarket	Wide variety of food and nonfood products, large departmentalized operation featuring self-service aisles and centralized checkouts
	Convenience store	Little variety, shallow selection, fast service
	General merchandiser	General category for stores characterized by wide variety that cuts across product categories, shallow selection of high-turnover products, low prices, few customer services
	Discount department store	General mass merchandiser offering wide variety of merchandise ranging from drug and cosmetic items to appliances and clothing, no-frill atmosphere, low prices
	Catalog showroom	General mass merchandiser using a catalog to promote items
	Warehouse club	General mass merchandiser that requires membership, uses showroom as a storage space
	Specialized mass retailer	General category for high-volume, low-price retailers that carry a product selection that is limited to a product class or a few product categories
	Off-price retailer	Discounter selling a limited line of nationally known brand names
	Category discounter	Retailer offering deep discounts and extensive assortment and depth in a specific product category
Direct Marketing	Mail order/Direct response	Generally low operating costs, emphasis on convenience, computerized lists utilized
	Television home shopping	Direct-response seller with high capital costs for technology, products priced high
	Door-to-door selling	High labor cost, image problems
	Vending machines	High-turnover products, low prices

PRINCIPLES OF MARKETING 173

Communications Flow

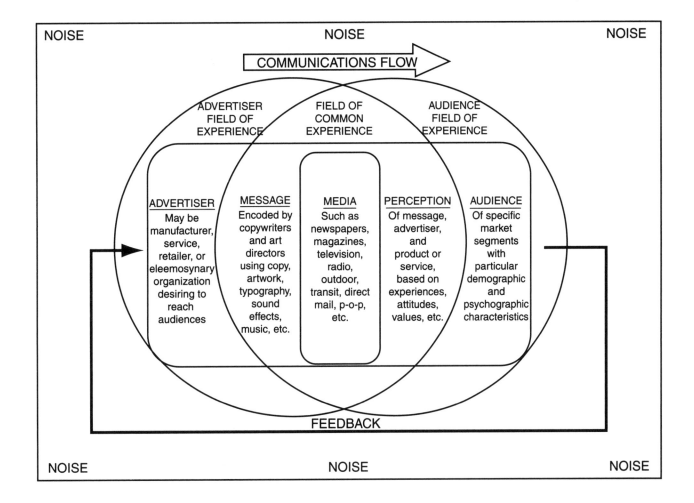

Characteristics of the Four Elements of Promotion

	Personal Selling	Advertising	Publicity*	Sales Promotion
Mode of communication	Direct and personal	Indirect and nonpersonal	Indirect and nonpersonal	Indirect and nonpersonal
Regular and recurrent activity?	Yes	Yes	No—only for newsworthy activity	No—short-term stimulation
Message flexibility	Personalized and tailored to prospect	Uniform and unvarying	Beyond marketer's direct control	Uniform and unvarying
Direct feedback	Yes	No	No	No
Marketer control over message content?	Yes	Yes	No	Yes
Sponsor identified?	Yes	Yes	No	Yes
Cost per contract	High	Low to moderate	No direct costs	Varies

*Public relations firms and departments work to manage publicity. In other words, a primary function of public relations is the management of publicity.

Managing the Communications Process

- Selecting Target Market
- Establishing Objectives
- Setting Budget
- Formulating and Implementing Message and Media Strategies
- Evaluating Program Effectiveness

Sales Promotion

Legalized bribing—to get consumers to try our products

A.   Consumer:

B.   Trade:

Publicity

Greater credibility than advertising techniques:

Types of Media

Mass Media

Broadcast
- Network TV
- Cable TV
- Radio

Print
- Newspaper
- Magazines
- Directory
- Yellow Pages

Outdoor
- Billboard
- Posters

In-Store
- Point-of-purchase
- Displays
- Video presentations

Other
- Movie theater
- Transit

Direct Media

Letters & pamphlets

Catalogs

Bill inserts

Flyers

Phone/Fax
- Computerized calls
- Fax advertisements

Electronic/Computerized
- Commercial services
- Electronic mail

Developing Ad Campaigns

1. **ID and Analyze Target Market**
2. **Define Advertising Objectives**
3. **Create Advertising Platform**
4. **Determine Appropriate/Budgets**
5. **Develop Media Plans**
6. **Create Advertising Messages**
7. **Evaluate Advertising Effectiveness**

Measuring the Effectiveness of Advertising

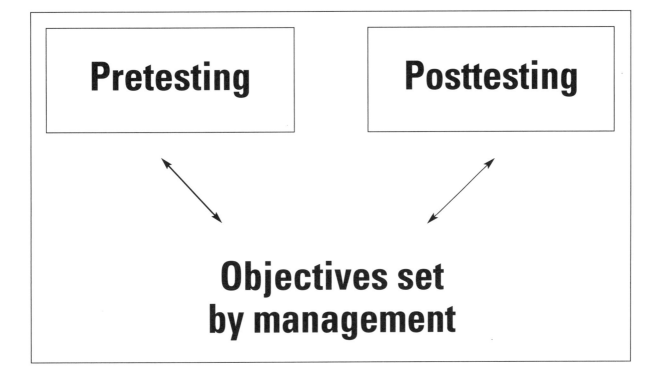

Uses of Advertising

1. **To Promote Products/Organizations**
2. **To Stimulate Demand**
   A. **Primary**
   B. **Selective**
3. **To Offset Competition**
4. **To Make the Sales Staff Effective**
5. **To Increase Uses of Product**
6. **To Remind and Reinforce**
7. **To Reduce Sales Fluctuations**

Measuring the Effectiveness of Advertising (continued)

Measurement Tools:
- **Focus groups**
- **Mall intercepts**
- **In-home projector tests**
- **Trailer tests**
- **Personal interviews**
- **Technical equipment**
- **Recall**
    - —Unaided recall
    - —Aided recall
    - —Related recall
- **Recognition**
    - —Noted
    - —Associated
    - —Read most
- **Attitude change over time**
- **Inquiries, calls, and coupons received**
- **Sales**

Harry's

Est. 1911, Paris

"Sank Roo Doe Noo"

A Space for Thought.

The Creative Selling Process

The true creative professional salesperson must use an adaptive process that begins with the identification of specific potential customers and tailors the sales dialogue and product offering to each prospect's needs. The salesperson sells a solution to the customer's problem.

1. Prospect and evaluate
2. Preparation—preapproach
3. Approach
4. Presentation
5. Overcome objections
6. Close
7. Follow up

Types of Salespeople

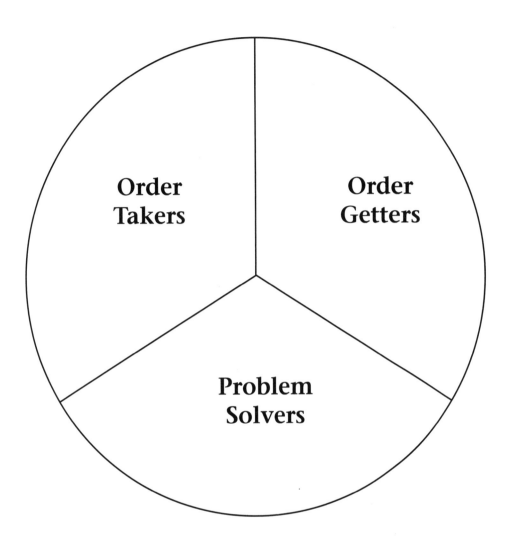

Social Styles

FACT-ORIENTED

ANALYTICAL	DRIVER
AMIABLE	EXPRESSIVE

RISK ADVERSE   *RISK TAKERS*

PEOPLE-ORIENTED

Guidelines for Effective Listening

1. **Do Not Interrupt.**
2. **Do Not Let Your Mind Wander.**
3. **Do Not Fake Attention.**
4. **Listen for the Ideas.**
5. **Be Interested.**
6. **Use Silence.**

Good vs. Bad Listening
1. **Marginal**
2. **Evaluative**
3. **Active**

Sales Management

RECRUITING

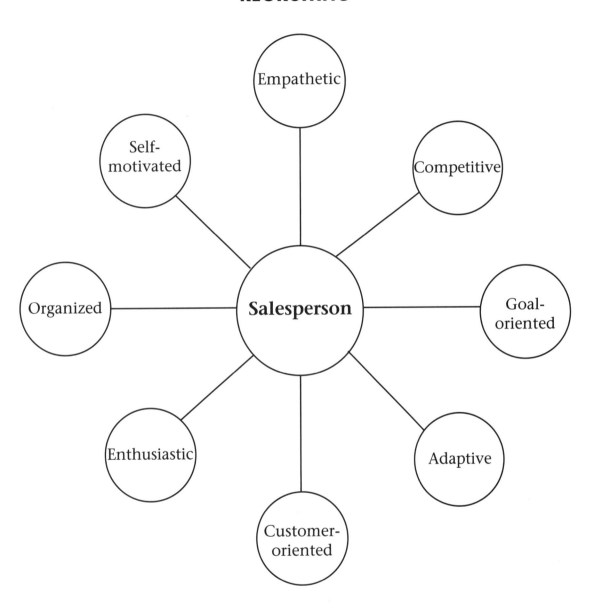

- **Individuals with desirable salespersons traits**
- **Individuals whose values and goals match those of the firm**

Standard Hours

NC = **Number of Customers**	**2500**
FC = **Number of Sales Calls**	**4x's/yr**
LC = **Length of Call & Travel Time**	**2 hrs**
AH = **Available Hours**	**50 wks × 40 hrs × 67%**
NS = **Needed Salespeople**	

$$NS = \frac{NC + FC + LC}{AH}$$

T.O.

NS = Number of Salespeople Needed
S = Annual Sales Forecast = 10,000,000
P = Estimated Sales Productivity = 500,000
T = TO% = 20%

$$NS = \frac{S}{P} \; TO$$

Equalized Work Load

1. **Classify:** Class A (Large)   100 Accts
   Class B (Med.)   180 Accts
   Class C (Small)   220 Accts

2. **Estimate of Time/Visit:**
   A—30 min. × 150 (calls/yr) = 75 hrs
   B—20 min. × 210 (calls/yr) = 70 hrs
   C—15 min. × 160 (calls/yr) = 40 hrs

3. **Total Work Load:**   A—100 × 75 = 7,500
   B—180 × 70 = 12,600
   C—200 × 40 = 8,800
   Total   28,900

4. **Time Available:**
   40 hr/wk × 45 wk = 1800 hrs/yr

5. **Divide by Task:**
   a) Selling   55%   →   990
   b) Non Selling   20%   →   360
   c) Travel   25%   →   450
                              1800 hrs

6. **Work Load ÷ Available Hours:**

$$\frac{28{,}900}{990} = 29.2 \approx 30$$

Direct Marketing

Face-To-Face
Direct Mail
Catalog Sales
Telemarketing
Direct Response TV
Kiosk Marketing

Online/Electronic Marketing

Marketing Conducted through Interactive Online Computer Systems Linking Consumers with Sellers Electronically

    Commercial SCVS . . . AOL & Prodigy

    World Wide Web aka the Web

The Internet Today

- **3 developments were needed to make the Internet an effective marketing tool**
  - **Development of e-commerce (intra- and extranets)**
  - **Server growth and fast connection technology**
  - **Consumer access**

E-Commerce Today

- **Intranet**
  - **Improved security and communication**
  - **59% of companies, 1997**
  - **77% of companies, 1998**
- **Extranet**
  - **Accessible to outsiders**
  - **Require user name and password**
  - **Info exchange for business partners**

E-Commerce Today

- 53% report sales activity
- 80% business-to-business, 2001
- 97% large businesses have website
- 10% small businesses have website

E-Commerce Today

- 30% www sales profitable
- 80% of CEOs believe it will significantly reshape their competition

Benefits of Internet Marketing

- **Benefits of internet marketing**
  - **Increase brand equity**
  - **Develop customer base**
    - Match customer needs to company offerings
  - **Improve customer (self) service**
  - **Information transfer**
  - **Increasing returns**

International Marketing

Casual or accidental exporting	Active exporting	Full-scale international marketing involvement
Occasional, unsolicited foreign orders are received. There is no real commitment to international marketing.	The recognition that foreign markets exist. Attempts are made to cultivate sales across national boundaries. Little effort is made to consider foreign markets in the overall strategy. Minor adjustments may be made for foreign market product acceptance.	Markets across national boundaries are a consideration in the marketing strategy. International marketing activities are an integral part of the overall marketing program. Divisions or subsidiaries may be developed to better serve the foreign target market.

National or domestic orientation ←→ International orientation

Section 2

Articles

The Role of Marketing: Theory, Practice, and Conceptual Conflict

Banton Macchiette & Abhijit Roy

Can you think of a theory, concept, or practice that has not been influenced by the recently revolutionized marketing environment? For example, communications and information technology is causing marketers to rethink the most basic tenets of its traditional institutions. These developments represent major benchmarks for theory relating to the evolution of marketing. The expanded boundaries for reaching consumers with an explosive array of product choices in new and different ways has created questions concerning levels of pervasiveness and ethical issues.

Are age-old practices such as "cold calls" and "prospecting" for customers becoming obsolete? Now the Internet allows interaction with thousands of multilevel marketers in ways that were previously unimaginable. Long-established theories that product positioning requires a singular, focused, unique selling proposition that is sustained through large promotional budgets committed to brand building and repetition are now in a state of flux. Are today's real-time consumers with insatiable demands for immediate satisfaction threatening these traditional marketing concepts?

New technologies are forcing marketers to reinvent how they form lasting consumer relationships, and concepts such as customer retention, customer-delivered value, and augmented services are emerging as dominant themes. The industrial revolution was to manufacturing what the information revolution is to marketing. Traditional models of marketing are being challenged on every front. Questions of ethics and societal influence are also becoming inordinately significant as "e-life" is shaping the marketing environment for the new millennium.

- ❏ Does Marketing Have Appropriate Boundaries?
- ❏ Is the Practice of Multilevel Marketing Legitimate?
- ❏ Has the "Keep It Simple" Concept Become "All Change, All the Time"?
- ❏ Is Relationship Marketing a Tenable Concept?

From *Taking Sides: Marketing*. Copyright © 2000 by The McGraw-Hill Companies, Inc. All rights reserved. Reprinted by permission of McGraw-Hill/Dushkin Publishing.

ISSUE

Does Marketing Have Appropriate Boundaries?

YES: D. Kirk Davidson, from *Selling Sin: The Marketing of Socially Unacceptable Products* (Quorum Books, 1996)

NO: Michael F. Jacobson and Laurie Ann Mazur, from *Marketing Madness: A Survival Guide for a Consumer Society* (Westview Press, 1995)

Issue Summary

YES: D. Kirk Davidson, an assistant professor of marketing, explores the development and ethical dimensions of applying marketing techniques to "sin products," such as tobacco, alcohol, pornography, and gambling. While he does not applaud these marketing efforts, he emphasizes the relevance of freedom of speech and the rights of consumer choice.

NO: Michael F. Jacobson, executive director of the Center for Science in the Public Interest, and Laurie Ann Mazur, a writer and consultant, consider the intrusiveness and pervasiveness of "hybrid advertising," such as the video news release (VNR), advertorial, and product placement in sitcoms and movies and conclude that these messages transcend the perceptual boundaries of traditional advertising.

The origins of the issue of "where should marketing be applied?" can be traced to the mid-1960s with a position paper by the Ohio State University faculty, which viewed marketing as a "social process" while the American Marketing Association (AMA) prior to 1985 considered it to be a set of "business activities." In the July 1969 issue of the *Journal of Marketing*, Philip Kotler and Sidney J. Levy prescribed broadening the concept of marketing to include non-business organizations like churches, police stations, and public schools, since they all had products and customers and implemented the normal tools of the marketing mix. William Lazer supported some of the same views in the same issue of the journal, calling for a broader view of marketing rather than just looking at it as the technology of the firm. David J. Luck (1970), however, disagreed and felt that the field had a broad enough scope by considering *just* organizational business practices that resulted in market transactions.

As we fast forward to the new millennium, four specific categories of marketing boundaries can be delineated. They include matters of deception and taste, where marketing is applied, acceptable methods of marketing, and the pervasiveness of marketing in society.

Matters of deception and taste are perhaps the most common criticisms. Unsubstantiated claims and false statements challenge the dimensions of marketing, while examples of taste relate more to socially acceptable boundaries. The clothing company Bennetton has been criticized

From *Taking Sides: Marketing.* Copyright © 2000 by The McGraw-Hill Companies, Inc. All rights reserved. Reprinted by permission of McGraw-Hill/Dushkin Publishing.

for utilizing an actual photograph of a dying AIDS victim and real mug shots of convicted criminals as a form of "shock advertising." These are contextual issues raising questions of tactics appeal and intent.

The second dimension, applications of marketing, has demonstrated a radical shift in philosophy in the past three decades toward the acceptance and growth of this *broadened concept* of marketing. But are contemporary applications of marketing transcending appropriate boundaries? For example, The Vatican recently opened the first of 400 worldwide theme stores in New York, promoting Pope Paul II china and sheets, replicas of Italian art, and assorted religious artifacts. Frito-Lay was a sponsor for the Pope's last trip to Mexico. The Pope's licensing agent was quoted in *Newsweek* as saying, "There is no better brand name in the world."

D. Kirk Davidson discusses acceptable marketing methods for questionable sin products. He explores the issues unique to marketing applications of sin products, such as gambling, pornography, firearms, and alcohol. All of these industries confront the challenge of a hostile environment—the public and a variety of special interest groups. Davidson examines the importance of establishing the *legitimacy* of marketing's role in these industries. He notes that established traditional tools of marketing, such as targeting new customers and increasing product usage, take on negative dimensions when applied to sin products. Davidson considers the strategies common to marketers in their efforts to legitimize applied marketing in the gray areas of sin products.

The dimensions of pervasiveness and methods of "hybrid" marketing have surfaced with public concerns for privacy and the alleged intrusiveness of direct markets and "Spam," or advertising in the form of unsolicited e-mail. Michael F. Jacobson and Laurie Ann Mazur focus on the negative attributes of hybrid marketing practices such as advertorials, infomercials, product placement, and the video news release (VNR). The VNR, a commercial message that is generated from a company's public relations agency and ostensibly portrayed as actual news, is the quintessential example of "blurred distinctions" in commercial messages. Since it is most often perceived by the audience as actual news, the credibility factor is much higher than that of an advertisement. It is much more cost effective because it is programming rather than commercially bought time. Should consumers be better informed to distinguish VNRs, product placement, and other hybrid marketing techniques? Who should be responsible? Do these methods transcend acceptable boundaries of marketing?

D. Kirk Davidson

YES

Selling Sin

In the long run a company's right to continue in business is granted by society, not by its profitability. If an organization is to maximize its return to its shareholders, it must maximize its contribution to the society in which it operates. This means earning and maintaining the trust of that society—in other words, establishing the firm's legitimacy—and marketers have a critical role to play in this.

The marketing questions we have explored... are extraordinary ones. They are different from the problems discussed in most marketing texts because these deal with the fundamental relationship between business and society. This is an interactive relationship. It is clear that the decisions made by marketers will affect how society accepts the firm and its products. Equally clear is that the extent to which society grants its approval—grants legitimacy—will have a major impact on the firm and especially on its marketing function.

[We have] focused on five specific industries because they are good examples of what happens when an industry begins to lose its legitimacy. In the United States of the mid-1990s, tobacco, alcoholic beverages, firearms, gambling, and pornography all face the challenges of a hostile environment and significant opposition by various groups for a variety of reasons.

In other industries, under other circumstances, similar marketing challenges can arise in regard to specific products even though the company and the industry are given a relatively clean bill of health by society. For example, there is little criticism of the chemical industry in its entirety although specific products, such as certain agricultural chemicals and napalm for military use, have encountered severe opposition. No one finds the athletic shoe industry, qua industry, unacceptable, although there has been sharp criticism of the marketing of very expensive shoes in low-income neighborhoods. There is general acceptance now of biotechnology products used for medical purposes, although genetically engineered bovine growth hormone to stimulate milk production in the dairy industry, and other biotech products used in the food industry, still encounter severe opposition. In other words, problems of legitimacy and social unacceptability can crop up in specific areas of otherwise perfectly respected and accepted product lines, companies, and industries.

Marketers, therefore, across all industries can benefit from studying the lessons, experiences, and challenges described [here]. Of course, there are no universally applicable solutions. More precisely, there are no "solutions" at all. Even among the five industries studied here, there are no tactics or strategies that can be considered applicable across the board. Just as one product's marketing strategy, no matter how successful, cannot be replicated and used with any guarantee of similar success for a different product, or in a different industry, so one company's approach to dealing with problems of social unacceptability cannot be prescribed across product lines or across industries. In marketing, as in all social science fields, there are simply too many variables: too many differences in products, markets, company cultures, and surrounding environments.

The benefits, then, for marketers will come, as with any case analysis work, from the generation of ideas: from seeing what works or doesn't work under a particular set of circumstances, and from using that knowledge to tailor a strategy to the marketer's unique needs and conditions.

What are some of the lessons we as marketers can learn from the material collected [here]?

From *Selling Sin: The Marketing of Socially Unacceptable Products* by D. Kirk Davidson. Copyright © 1996 by D. Kirk Davidson. Reproduced with permission of Greenwood Publishing Group, Inc., Westport, CT.

Expansion of Market

Perhaps the first lesson to be learned is that the most basic objectives of marketing—to expand the business, to attract new customers, to increase usage of the product—must be reconsidered if the product category or the industry faces questions of social acceptability. Critics may tolerate continued consumption or usage of the product by current customers, but the degree of opposition will increase dramatically when manufacturers are perceived as going after new markets, recruiting new customers, or trying to increase usage. To encourage people to gamble more, to drink more alcoholic beverages, or certainly to smoke more would be totally unacceptable and would be like pouring fuel on the opposition's fire. Giving the appearance of encouraging nongamblers to begin buying lottery tickets (as with the slogan "You can't win if you don't play") or encouraging nonsmokers to take up the habit (you can be cool like Joe Camel or rugged and individualistic like the Marlboro Man) is a dangerous message in terms of inflaming the critics. Even the tobacco companies, in their public relations utterances if not in their actions, eschew recruiting new smokers. After forty years of mounting evidence about the health problems associated with smoking, the firms now acknowledge some risks but counter that many products, even Twinkies, present risks, and insist that adults should make their own individual choices.

The firearms industry presents a definite exception to this rule. To the extent that the National Rifle Association (NRA) represents the views and furthers the strategy of the industry's member firms, the message that they project is that more and more people who do not now own guns should acquire them! In spite of a high level of social protest, in spite of very active and very vocal advocacy groups working to limit the spread of guns, especially handguns, the NRA and the industry are not backing down or softening in any way their marketing efforts to increase the size of the market by recruiting new customers.

The marketers of cigarettes and beer, on the other hand, claim that all of their formidable marketing budgets and efforts are aimed only at current customers. They claim not to be trying to attract new customers, only to defend, or better yet to increase, their current market share. In other words, they say they are not trying to increase the size of the pie, only to get a larger slice of the present pie. [W]e have shown that these claims are widely disputed by the industries' opponents.

This battle of words—of claims and counterclaims—can never be won. Inevitably, consumer advertising that a manufacturer insists is meant to defend or increase its brand's market share will be perceived by critics as meant to entice new users. Circumstantial evidence can be gathered—for example, that 75 percent of underage smokers smoke the three most heavily advertised brands—yet the cigarette companies will insist that the intent of their ads is not to attract new, young smokers. By extension, all consumer advertising for socially unacceptable industries or products becomes suspect because it would seem to legitimate the use of that product in our society.

Under these conditions an argument can be advanced that a manufacturer should emphasize a "push" strategy rather than a "pull" strategy. Promotion budget dollars should be shifted away from consumer advertising and consumer-oriented sales promotion tactics, which are the most visible elements of the entire marketing mix and the most subject to public scrutiny, into increased marketing efforts directed at the trade channels that are less obvious and less likely to incite the product's critics. Larger and more active sales organizations making more calls on retailers and increased dealer incentives should result in increased sales and market share without triggering the level of opposition that consumer advertising is certain to initiate.

It would be naive to suppose that in a mature industry such as cigarettes or beer, dominated a few large, powerful competitors, that any one company could unilaterally reduce its consumer advertising dramatically. Even though the benefits of advertising are notoriously difficult to measure, very few marketing executives are daring enough to cut back on advertising their brands and risk losing some market share that would be very expensive to regain. The threat is simply too great. What is suggested here is that in the planning of an overall marketing strategy and in the budget allocation process, the avoidance of social criticism is an additional factor to consider in weighing the relative merits of consumer advertising versus trade promotions.

The Woes of Targeting: Pricing and Distribution Issues

As important as precise, careful targeting is in the marketing of most products, it is almost certain to backfire in the marketing of socially unacceptable goods. As we have seen, targeting is meant to identify segments of the market with some common characteristics so that a specific marketing strategy can be developed that will be especially effective with that defined group. Critics of the product can readily paint this as a picture of exploitation: a large, billion-dollar corporation zeroing in on a small segment of society, employing all of its marketing muscle and persuasive powers to increase the sales of its product. When the product carries some risk or danger, as do all socially unacceptable products, and when the targeted segment is perceived as being vulnerable in any way, this creates an exploitative situation that is intolerable in our society.

Problems can surface as a result of targeting a wide variety of groups: women, racial or ethnic minorities, the elderly, or lower-income groups. But no targeted group arouses more sympathy and protection than children do.... [T]he five product categories studied [here] have been defined by our society as adult products, and so there is a natural inclination for young people, especially teens, to be attracted to them as a way of assuming adulthood. When cigarette manufacturers or brewers or pornography merchants are perceived as targeting children, therefore, a strong backlash of social pressure and criticism is unleashed. Many possible measures have been suggested to constrain the marketing of tobacco products, including higher excise taxes and the disallowance of advertising as a tax-deductible expense, but the tobacco control program brought forward by the Food and Drug Administration (FDA) in 1995 was all about protecting children because the Clinton administration recognized this would have the widest popular appeal. In a similar vein, it is the protection of children from the pornography found in popular music lyrics, in 900 telephone messages, and in cyberspace that engenders the most widespread attention and support.

The lesson or message to marketers, then, is obvious. If your product is socially unacceptable to some degree, choose targets with the greatest of caution. Targeting almost any group other than well-to-do white males will be criticized. And by all means, avoid even the perception of targeting children.

Just as with targeting, pricing decisions must be made with an eye to how they will be perceived by the market, especially by the product's critics. With mainstream products, low prices are not only accepted but welcomed as an introductory tactic or as a way to move potential customers to the trial or adoption stage of the product adoption process. Not so with socially unacceptable products. Special prices on cigarettes or alcoholic beverages to attract new consumers or encourage present customers to consume more would ignite a storm of protest.

The price lining of the major brewers—Anheuser-Busch's Michelob in the superpremium category, Budweiser at the premium level, and Busch at popular prices, for example—must be administered as simply catering to the needs of beer drinkers in different income brackets. So, too, with the premium, value, and generic or private label cigarette brands. Philip Morris' fateful price cut on Marlboro and its other premium brands in 1993 had to be explained as a desperate measure to regain market share from the generics and private labels, which it indeed was. Handgun control advocates are especially critical of cheap Saturday night specials because they are purposely priced low to encourage increased sales.

Casinos have an advantage in that they can disguise their price promotions. Traditionally they have offered their hotel rooms and meals—and sometimes their Hollywood extravaganza shows—at quite reasonable prices, not to mention free drinks for those gambling at the tables or machines. A thin disguise, perhaps, but the low prices are associated with the rooms, food, and drinks rather than directly with the gambling.

Distribution strategies used by producers of socially unacceptable products have received less attention than targeting, pricing, promotion, and product line management decisions. If a product, such as any one of our five, is subject to a significant degree of social criticism, it would seem to make sense to shorten, to whatever extent possible, the channel of distribution. The longer the product is in the stream of commerce and the more hands it passes through, the more public exposure it receives and the more likely it is to be criticized.

From the producer's viewpoint, the ideal form of distribution is direct to the consumer. This entails the least amount of public exposure. For convenience goods such as beer and cigarettes, which in theory and in practice require the longest channels and the widest distribution, this would be impossible. However, it is widely accepted that the major cigarette manufacturers are building enormous databases of their customers, in the hopes of being able to turn this information into a direct marketing program at some point. Pornographic conversations through 900 telephone numbers are a form of direct distribution, as are the various pornography sites on the World Wide Web.

Public policy interests point in the opposite direction. Whether the product is guns, alcoholic beverages, cigarettes, lottery tickets, or slot machine bets, whatever social and regulatory controls are to be exercised—and whatever taxes are to be collected—require that these products be distributed through a totally open and transparent system. There are already prohibitions against distributing guns and alcoholic beverages through the mail. Cigarette companies have been stymied so far in selling by mail by the problem of verifying minimum age requirements. But there are plenty of proposals being floated for at-home betting on horse races, lotteries, or even casinos in cyberspace, and the prospect of 500 channels being available for television viewing raises the prospects of direct access to more X-rated movies or perhaps entire channels devoted to pornography.

Addressing the Issues

There comes a time for every firm facing social pressures, criticism, and disapproval when the issues on which those difficulties are based must be addressed. How will the firm defend itself, its products, and its right to continue in business? Making adjustments in the firm's marketing strategy—promotion mix, product line management, pricing decision, choice of targets, and so on—while necessary and helpful, does not deal with the underlying problem. Can the criticism at least be blunted, if not silenced? Can the critics be isolated and industry supporters be organized and energized? Can some degree of legitimacy be restored?

Accomplishing these tasks goes well beyond the normal duties of the firm's public relations department and beyond the traditional scope of marketing strategy. But we have considered them [here] because they are in fact public relations issues, they must be coordinated carefully with the everyday marketing activities of the firm, and they are absolutely crucial to the success of the firm over the long run.

In reviewing the five industries we have studied [here], several common themes emerge.

Deflect the Criticism

Perhaps the most common ploy in attempting to deal with social criticism is to deflect the criticism away from the firm's core products. The alcoholic beverage and gambling industries have been rather successful in doing this; the National Rifle Association, as a stand-in for the firearms industry, has used this tactic with somewhat less success.

Alcoholic beverages are not the problem, insist the industry representatives, certainly not as they are normally used and as they should be used. The problems are excessive drinking, underage drinking, and drunk driving. The industry strives to focus social attention on these limited issues and works with its critics on developing and financing programs to deal with them. The hope, of course, is that this will leave the industry relatively free to produce and market wine, beer, and spirits with a minimum of controversy.

"Guns don't commit murders; people do" is the message from the NRA. Firearms themselves are simply tools: essential for various sports and personal protection. It is the criminal use or careless use of guns that must be curbed. To this end the NRA and the industry sponsor training classes in the proper use of guns and safe shooting for both children and adults.

The gambling industry has followed the same course. Gambling per se is not the problem; it is excessive gambling that society must prevent, and the industry demonstrates its concerns by providing money and initiative to ameliorate the problem. Changing the word "gambling" to "gaming" also is a tactic to deflect criticism, as is the transformation of a casino into a family entertainment complex. How can anyone criticize games and family fun?

The tobacco industry has stumbled badly in its inability to deflect criticism from its core products and now confronts an intractable problem. Scientific studies have confirmed that any level of smoking is harmful to one's health—and to the health of those around the smoker. For sixty years the tobacco firms have known about these health concerns and have attempted to hide them. Even since the 1950s and 1960s, when the smoking and health problems first came to the public's attention, the firms have reduced the tar and nicotine content in many of their cigarettes but have been unwilling to remove all of it—to develop a "safe" cigarette—because smokers prefer the taste and the "lift" that the tars and nicotine provide. The long-run viability and legitimacy of the industry was sacrificed to meet quarterly and annual sales and profit goals.

Cure Is Worse Than the Disease

An alternative to the deflection strategy is to try to show that whatever social concerns are raised by the industry's products, they are less serious than the critics' proposed solutions. Marketers of pornography answer their critics by waving the First Amendment banner. Censorship, they proclaim, and the loss of freedom of speech are a far more serious threat to our society than pornographic magazines and videos that people, after all, can either buy or ignore, as they choose.

The NRA also uses this approach, but its rallying cry is the Second Amendment. Whatever social ills gun critics complain about, whatever the level of violence in our society, however many deaths are the result of guns and their proliferation, as serious as these problems may be, they are not as serious as the threat to Americans of whittling away at the freedoms guaranteed by the Bill of Rights. When gun control advocates warn of violence and death resulting from handguns and assault weapons, the NRA and allied organizations warn of midnight searches of homes and property by "jackbooted" federal agents.

This is also the thrust of the 1994–1995 institutional ad campaigns sponsored by Philip Morris and Reynolds Tobacco. In response to the FDA's proposals for limiting the sale of cigarettes to minors, Reynolds ran full-page newspaper ads showing a smirking, corpulent, generally unattractive man asking whether a parent or some government bureaucrat is better able to guide and care for children. The ads called for a rational debate and urged that the industry and its critics work out public policy issues together. Here again the message is perfectly clear. As Reynolds framed the debate, whatever social problems are associated with tobacco, they are not nearly so dangerous as the proposed solution, which would mean more regulation (i.e., more bureaucracy) and less freedom of individual choice.

The Economics Card

If there is one thing that the five industries represented [here] have in common, it is that each of them, when confronted with criticism based on social concerns or moral values, responds with a justification based on economics. This fundamental struggle between personal, material well-being and moral principles is as old as Adam and Eve's fateful decision to taste the forbidden apple.

Every proposal for a new gambling enterprise—a riverboat for Indiana, a casino for Baltimore, a racetrack for Tennessee—promises more jobs and more tax revenues for the state. Never does the proposal try to convince us that gambling is a virtuous and healthy form of entertainment; the argument is that the economic benefits outweigh the social costs. How does a state government rationalize being in the business of owning and operating a gambling enterprise (i.e., a lottery)? Only by citing the economic necessities of the state and assuring the electorate that the social consequences will not be so bad.

What is the tobacco industry's response when the federal government proposes a stiff hike in the excise tax on cigarettes? The benefits to society would seem unassailable: reduced consumption, especially among teenagers, and the resulting improvements in public health. Inevitably, the response comes in the form of warnings of economic chaos. Hundreds of thousands of jobs would be lost just in the convenience store industry. End U.S. government intervention that ensures advertising of American cigarettes in foreign countries? This would have a terrible effect on our balance of payments. Restrict cigarette advertising in any of a dozen ways? The entire advertising industry joins the chorus warning of lost jobs and economic disruption.

Even in the business of pornography, adult videos are defended by explaining just how important they are to the profitable operation of most video rental stores.

And so the debate is framed. With the exception of the firearms industry, or more specifically the NRA, the marketers of these socially unacceptable products do not try to convince us that the character of their products has been unfairly impugned. Alcoholic beverage and gambling proponents readily admit that their products are sometimes used to excess and, as noted, join with their critics in looking for solutions. Purveyors of pornography recognize that their product should be purchased only by adults and are willing to join in the effort to keep it away from children. Even cigarette marketers now reluctantly admit that there are health risks associated with their product. For all of these industry representatives, however, the economic justification is sufficient: jobs for workers and managers, taxes for governments, contracts for suppliers, and profits for shareholders.

Cynics may assume that economics will always win out over morality, but such is not the case. Questions of heath and safety, and especially the protection of children, often are enough to tip the balance in favor of social and moral values. Tobacco products are still with us, but because of the now unassailable health concerns, significant restrictions have been imposed on how they are marketed. Economic pressures, along with social preferences, may have rescued the alcoholic beverage industries from Prohibition, but when Mothers Against Drunk Driving framed the issue as the safety of our children, society was willing to get tough on the problem of underage drinking. And the setbacks for gambling in the 1994 elections show that in some states and under some circumstances, the electorate will give social and moral values the priority over economic arguments.

Legitimacy: Lost, Maintained, Regained?

Finally, a review of these five industries and their marketing strategies must offer some insights regarding the question of legitimacy: for individual companies or for entire industries. Legitimacy itself is difficult to define, because it is dependent on the shifting sands of public opinion and social mores; it is all the more difficult to try to measure the legitimacy of a firm or an industry or to determine whether that legitimacy is waxing or waning.

Over the years a number of scholars have developed approaches and models that can help in this effort, even if they do not provide definitive or precise answers. For example, Charles Summer suggested that when firms find themselves in the "conflict stage" of their life cycle—and all of our five industries are in such a conflict situation—the question becomes whether the "zone of opposition" or the "zone of approval" will expand at the expense of the other. In these terms we can conclude that for the tobacco companies, their zone of opposition has without question been growing at the expense of their zone of approval. The gambling firms are experiencing just the opposite.

Ed Epstein and Dow Votaw have suggested three strategies by which firms can deal with challenges to their legitimacy: adapt to society's values, change society's values, or associate with other organizations that enjoy legitimacy. The major brewers have taken some steps along the first of these paths, the tobacco firms and the NRA have chosen the second, and the gambling companies, to the extent they have allied themselves with the hospitality industry, have opted for the third.

Christine Oliver has created a framework . . . for classifying companies' responses to societal pressures. The tobacco and firearms industries have been pursuing the manipulation and defiance strategies, alcoholic beverages and gambling have chosen avoidance and sometimes compromise, while pornography lies in between, choosing defiance on some occasions and avoidance on others.

Accommodation or Opposition

More is at stake here than simply marketing a product. We are discussing the marketing of the firm, or perhaps the entire industry: how that firm or industry will relate to and respond to the society in which it is operating. But the different levels of marketing are inescapably linked. The decision of Reynolds Tobacco to continue the Joe Camel ad campaign for a year or more, even after strong protests from critics, is a part of the firm's, and the industry's, broader decision to choose a defiant stance against its detractors. The brewers' willingness to promote responsible drinking and similar messages are part of their choice of "compromise" and "pacify" as their corporate and industry marketing strategies.

Ultimately, the marketing of socially unacceptable products comes down to a choice of accommodation or opposition between a firm and the society in which it is embedded. Can the firm find a way to adapt its product and the way it promotes and distributes it, perhaps even shift its choice of markets, to fit more comfortably within society's constraints? Or will it choose opposition and continue to fight a rearguard, minimize-our-losses kind of action?

The tobacco firms have operated very profitably under the latter strategy for several decades, so one cannot dismiss that choice. It is carried out, however, at great cost to the firms and to society, and there is scant hope for anything but a continuously deteriorating situation. For any kind of healthy, long-term relationship—if there is to be any hope for legitimacy—there must be a congruence between the operating decisions of the firm and the expectations of society. Achieving this relationships falls on the shoulders of the firm's manager's and especially its marketers; it will depend on the decisions they make, the tactics they choose, and the strategies they develop.

NO
Michael F. Jacobson and Laurie Ann Mazur

Blurring the Distinctions: Infomercials, Advertorials, and More

Late-breaking news bulletin: To announce the introduction of its new Almond Kiss, Hershey Foods drops a 500-pound replica of the candy from a building in Times Square. Cut to commercial. Good Morning America *host Joan Lunden sits behind an anchor desk, reporting authoritatively on a breakthrough in "skin science"—the discovery that Vaseline Intensive Care lotion helps dry skin.*

Frequently, news items bear an uncanny resemblance to commercials, and commercials masquerade as news. Who can tell the difference? Often we can't, and that's the point. Knowing that consumers view ads with skepticism, marketers sneak through our defenses by blurring the lines between advertising, news, and entertainment.

Newsfakers: The Video News Release

One of the most sinister line-blurring innovations is the video news release (VNR). Descendants of the printed press release, VNRs are supplied to news broadcasters on tape or by satellite. VNR providers include corporations, public relations firms, government, advocacy groups—virtually anyone with a product to plug or a spin to doctor. A VNR may contain background footage on a particular issue or a complete, ready-to-roll canned news story. It usually offers a news "hook," however manufactured or self-serving, and features compelling visuals. "A good VNR should be indistinguishable from a news story," says producer Larry Pintak. "The key is to look like, sound like, and have the elements of a news story."

VNRs blend seamlessly into news programs. In June 1991, for example, 17 million Americans watched a "news" story on the fiftieth anniversary of Cheerios cereal. The feel-good report included a tour of the Cheerios factory and some footage of a giant Cheerio made specially for the occasion. Few viewers suspected—and were not told by newscasters—that the segment was conceived, filmed, and produced by Cheerios manufacturer General Mills, then beamed via satellite to local television stations across the country. Similarly, when *Good Morning America* ran a lighthearted human-interest story about a Maine farmer's cow with spots shaped like Mickey Mouse's head, few guessed that the tape had been supplied by a thoughtful Disney World.

Why, you may ask, do newscasters air these obvious promotional pieces? In a word, desperation. Competition from cable and other factors has forced deep budget and staff cutbacks at many stations. At the same time, programmers have allotted more time for news shows, which are less expensive to produce than entertainment programs. As a result, news departments have lots of airtime to fill, but they must do so cheaply. VNRs, which offer high-quality, prepackaged "news" for free, are an irresistible temptation. According to Nielsen Media Research, 80 percent of the nation's news directors say they use VNR material at least several times every month. A 1993 Nielsen study found that every one of the ninety-two stations surveyed used VNRs, and another study

From *Marketing Madness* by Michael Jacobson. Copyright © 1995 by The Center for the Study of Commercialism. Reprinted by permission of Westview Press, a member of Perseus Books, L.L.C.

found that less than 50 percent of the VNR segments identified their source. Medialink, a company that distributes VNRs, says that 5,000 VNRs were sent to newscasters in 1991, up from 700 in 1986.

For marketers, VNRs are an inexpensive way to reach a huge audience. It costs between $15,000 and $80,000 to produce and distribute a VNR nationwide; in comparison, a thirty-second commercial can run to $250,000. There is no guarantee that stations will air VNR footage, but many have achieved astonishingly high visibility. McDonald's VNR on the introduction of its McLean Deluxe hamburger was seen by approximately 22 million Americans, and Coors reached 27 million with news of a court victory in a battle over its ads.

Disturbingly, some corporations use VNRs to circumvent restrictions—or bans—on advertising their products. For instance, in 1987 the James B. Beam Distilling Company issued a VNR congratulating itself for using only American grains in the manufacture of Jim Beam bourbon. The video was seen by TV viewers in forty cities, although network and industry guidelines expressly forbid television advertising of distilled spirits.

Drug companies have also used this ruse. Advertising claims about pharmaceutical products are strictly regulated by the Food and Drug Administration (FDA), but for many years the FDA did not screen VNRs sent out by drug companies. Not surprisingly, drug-company VNRs touted new products as miracle cures and neglected to mention side effects or contraindications. In one case, a VNR was used to hype a drug that proved deadly. In 1982, Eli Lilly and Company sent out a video extolling the virtues of Oraflex, its new arthritis drug. Within a few months, Oraflex had been blamed for twenty-six deaths in the United States, and the drug was discontinued. Lilly was later found guilty of suppressing information about severe adverse reactions, including deaths, during Oraflex trials overseas. Newscasters contributed to this tragedy by uncritically airing Lilly's video as though it were an unbiased source of news. In response to criticism, the FDA has begun to review pharmaceutical VNRs before they are sent to stations.

But drug companies plant news stories in other media as well. *Consumer Reports* magazine raised the issue, stating, "So much of what we are told about health and disease now comes in some way from the people in business to sell drugs." *Consumer Reports* interviewed several freelance health writers, who reported that drug companies had offered them money to write stories about their products and pitch them to national magazines without revealing the financial arrangement to the editors of those magazines.

VNR producers say they offer a valuable public service. The videos, they say, provide broadcasters with free footage that might otherwise be costly or impossible to obtain. Moreover, they argue, a VNR is just a high-tech version of the press release, which has long been considered a legitimate news source for reporters. But VNRs and other planted news stories give corporations an unparalleled opportunity to define and interpret current events. Would a news organization run a story about the anniversary of a breakfast cereal—*unless* it were ready-made with a catchy visual? Corporate propaganda also fills airtime that might otherwise be devoted to real news. Faced with a choice between running a prepackaged bit of commercial fluff or sending out a news crew to do some investigative reporting, many news directors choose the former. Furthermore, when corporate videos are the *only* source of information on a given topic—as is often the case in stories on medical or technical subjects—how can we know the information they provide is objective?

Press releases, too, have been subject to abuse; reporters have been known to write entire articles straight from releases. But good reporters always attribute information drawn from press releases; most VNR broadcasts go unacknowledged. Eugene Secunda, a professor of marketing at Baruch College, believes that news directors fear disclosure would hurt their image of objectivity. "If you are a news director," he says, "why would you do anything that might in any way compromise the believability of your program?"

Clearly, the biggest problem with VNRs is that viewers usually don't know they're watching them. For marketers, this is the whole point. A commercial is immediately identifiable as corporate propaganda, but a VNR masks propaganda as fact, borrowing the objective aura of the newsroom. "That's the great thing about VNRs," said Susan Fleming, an account executive at a company that produces VNRs. "Everybody sees them, but nobody realizes it. You have a corporate message to get across, and there's television news anchor saying it to millions of the people. It's one of the most legitimate ways to get your message to the public."

Many marketers conduct slick publicity campaigns to promote "new" or "improved" products, and the media obligingly present them as news. For instance, when Polaroid introduced its new min-instant camera, *USA Today* ran a half-page editorial spread, complete with sample photos and customers' praise. Suzanne Somers showed up in various gossip columns endorsing the sequel to her Thighmaster fitness gadget.

Public relations experts are eager to win over traditional advertisers to such free—and quality—publicity. Writing in the *Advertiser*, Thomas Mosser of Burson-Marsteller Public Relations urged companies to work the news media into their ad campaigns. "The implied editorial endorsement created by national publicity efforts can give a brand promotion added impact," said Mosser. "Just think how much more credible the advertising for McDonald's McLean sandwich was after the *New York Times* ran a Sunday front-page about how good the sandwich tasted."

It's a Program . . . It's an Ad . . . It's an Infomercial!

When they're not sneaking into the evening news, commercials are posing as regular TV shows. "Infomercials" or "program-length commercials," as these impostors are known, mimic the format of talk shows, newscasts, sitcoms, or investigative news programs. These half-hour-long superblurbs have many of the trappings of regular programs: theme music, production credits, listings in the television-guide sections of newspapers, and a "studio audience" of regular-looking folks who have been paid $50 or $75 apiece to feign enthusiasm. They even have "commercial breaks"—for the same product that has been advertised throughout the "show," of course.

Typical of the genre is "Morgan Brittany on Beauty," an infomercial that appeared to be a late-night talk show hosted by the former *Dallas* star. Brittany first introduced the actor George Hamilton, promising, "Today, for the first time ever, he's going to reveal his very own personal method for looking so good." His secret turned out to be the George Hamilton Skin Care System, which viewers were urged to purchase for $39.95 by calling a toll-free number. Alert viewers may have noticed a few departures from talk-show convention. For example, Hamilton was the only guest, and the conversation did seem peculiarly limited to the subject of skin care. But the talk-show illusion was carefully maintained: Brittany welcomed "my guest today" as though she were hosting an ongoing program that had other days, other guests. And at another point, Brittany said to Hamilton, "When I heard you were going to be on the show . . ." as if he were not the show's sole reason for being.

The infomercial concept is not new; for decades marketers have tried to get their commercials to blend in with the shows they interrupt. In the 1970s, "Great Moments in Music" and "100 Paintings" were mail-order ads in the guise of cultural programs. But these early infomercials were forced off the air by limits on commercial length and other regulations. It was not until 1984, when Reagan's FCC lifted restrictions on broadcast ads, that infomercials truly began to flourish. (Appropriately enough, Reagan's deregulation paved the way for his son, Michael, to appear in a 1990 infomercial for the Euro Trym Diet Patch, a bogus weight-loss aid. Euro Trym's manufacturer was nabbed by the FTC and forced to refund money to its many disgruntled customers.)

Deregulation, along with the availability of cheap airtime that accompanied the soaring popularity of cable TV, brought forth a deluge of infomercials. By 1993, some 175 products vied for infomercial spots, and according to *Advertising Age*, 90 percent of all U.S. television stations broadcast infomercials. Cable was the first to exploit the infomercial genre and continues to support it heavily: Lifetime airs about forty-three hours of infomercials per week and the Family Channel averages twenty-eight hours a week. Regular broadcasters are also waking up to the $400 million spent on infomercial airtime per year; noncable stations now make 60 percent of infomercial sales.

Initially confined to off-peak time slots, infomercials can now be seen at all hours of the day and night, with nearly 15 percent shown during prime time, according to a 1993 industry survey. Cable executives are developing many infomercial-based channels as part of their interactive TV ventures. In 1994, CBS announced plans to run on the stations it owns prime-time promotions of late-night infomercials, urging early-to-bed audiences to *videotape* the infomercials for later viewing.

In addition to the usual dice-o-matics and costume jewelry, infomercials increasingly feature mainstream companies such as General Motors' Saturn division, McDonald's, Volvo, and Philips Electronics. In fact, one ABC affiliate in Miami preempted the popular *Wheel of Fortune* to air the Philips CD video player infomercial in prime time. Meanwhile, *Wheel*'s hostess, Vanna White, stars in her own infomercial for Perfect Smile tooth whitener.

Although most infomercials feature bouncy, entertaining formats, some companies are going after the skeptical, upscale audience with a softer sell. For instance, McDonald's produces "The Mac Report," which masquerades as a sophisticated business newsmagazine—but only about McDonald's. As infomercials earn broader acceptance, they are also attracting a higher order of celebrity hosts: Ted Danson, Cher, and Jane Fonda have appeared in recent infomercials.

Infomercials are likely to continue thriving with the expected boom in new cable channels. Tele-Communications Inc. (TCI) is creating as many as twenty-five single-subject channels, primarily to showcase the products of sponsors. William Airy, a TCI executive overseeing the marketing of new cable ventures, prophesized, "The future . . . includes special-interest channels that will provide opportunities for infomercial advertisers that are able to target by lifestyle, target demographically, psychographically." The only channels to survive, according to Craig Evans, author of *Marketing Channels: Infomercials and the Future of Televised Marketing*, "will be the advertiser-supported channels that in some way, shape, or form promote product brands or images."

The success of infomercials leads inescapably to the conclusion that *people must be watching them*. Infomercials sold between $750 million and $900 million worth of products in 1993 alone. "What people seem to want from the infomercial is an experience that is wholly and brainlessly affirmative," said Mark Crispin Miller, professor of media studies at Johns Hopkins University. And as Rick Marin concludes in a *New York Times* article, "In a decade with much talk about dysfunction, the world of the infomercial is mesmerizingly functional, even multifunctional. Everything works, or seems to. And if it doesn't? There's always the money-back guarantee."

So what's wrong with infomercials? First, despite the proliferation of infomercials for better-quality products, many of the goods sold this way are ripoffs: weight-loss plans, get-rich-quick schemes, "cures" for baldness, aging, and impotence. And like the home-shopping channels, infomercials owe their success to impulse buying based on limited, biased information. Moreover, infomercials further convert the news and information medium of television into a sales device and add to the chorus of voices urging us to *consume*.

Proliferating infomercials are also forcing conventional shows off the programming schedule. That arrangement suits both advertisers and broadcasters: Infomercial time is cheaper for advertisers than the equivalent in traditional advertising, and television stations can make more money on one thirty-minute block than on a series of thirty-second ads within a regular broadcast. "It's schlock TV," admitted one broadcasting executive at a major station. "But it's a lot of money. If your competitors do that business and you don't, then you lose." Jayne Adair, program director at Pittsburgh's KDKA-TV, is equally positive. "[Infomercials] are the fastest-growing program segment in terms of production values and the quantity of programs being produced," she said. "They are a legitimate form of programming."

But perhaps the biggest problem with infomercials is the element of deception. Infomercials invariably seek to make viewers forget that they are watching a commercial and believe that the advertised product is really the subject of a talk show or news report. Most infomercials provide only cursory notice of their true commercial nature at the beginning or end and at the "commercial" breaks. In an age of remote-controlled electronic "grazing" among channels, many viewers are likely to miss these disclaimers entirely. According to Rader Hayes, a professor of consumer science at Marquette University, there has been no research to determine whether a "reasonable consumer" could distinguish infomercials from regular programming. Hayes, who has studied infomercials since 1985, says they can escape detection even by a trained eye. "Even after all my years of watching," she says, "I was fooled by one this spring." More troubling still are infomercials aimed at kids, who have even fewer skills to make the call.. . .

In their defense, marketers argue that infomercials offer an opportunity to provide in-depth product information. "What better mass vehicle to inform, educate, convince, motivate and sell is there than thirty minutes of TV time?" asked Gene Silverman, vice president of marketing at Hawthorne Communications, in a letter to *Advertising Age*. That is a defensible proposition as long as viewers *know* they are watching a commercial. Broadcasters could, for example, superimpose an easily recognized icon—say, the word "AD" in a circle—in a corner of the TV screen during infomercials. (A similar icon could be used to identify VNR tapes on newscasts.) This simple remedy has been suggested by media critics and consumer advocates but has been rejected by marketers and broadcasters.

The New Hybrid Breed

Marketers continue to experiment with new hybrid formats that merge news, entertainment, and advertising. Bell Atlantic, for example, has produced a "sit-commercial" ad that poses as a situation comedy. "The Ringers," as the show is called, follows the adventures of a suburban family that gets out of typical sitcom dilemmas with the help of call waiting, speed dialing, and other telephone services. The *Wall Street Journal* observes that the sitcommercial's "jokes aren't any worse than any network sitcom" (a depressing commentary on current network fare). The ads' creators believe that by drawing in viewers with a story line, they'll improve sales. "If people actually enjoy watching it and get interested in the characters, they will respond more positively," says Richard Alston, vice president of marketing at Bell Atlantic. In the same spirit, Sominex sleeping pills were the focus of "The Good Night Show," a skit-filled infomercial from the fictional Cable Snooze Network. To its credit, the Sominex infomercial did contain many on-screen disclaimers.

Ads also impersonate documentary films. For example, SmithKline Beecham USA produced a half-hour "documercial" on the importance of calcium in women's diets. SmithKline Beecham makes TUMS antacid, which has been promoted as a source of calcium. Here, the company is trying to fool not only viewers but television stations as well. "When we go to stations and try to get them to run this, we don't want them to think this is a commercial," said Pat McGrath, president of the ad agency Jordan, McGrath, Case and Taylor, which is credited for developing both the sit-commercial and the documercial.

Ads have even been disguised as TV movies. In 1994, NBC sold Mirage Resorts an hour of prime time to broadcast a mini-movie promoting Mirage's new Las Vegas casino, Treasure Island. "Anyone can do a thirty-second commercial," said Mirage spokesman Alan Feldman. "This is much more fun." And much more effective, if viewers get swept away in the adventure-saga formula. NBC tried to keep viewers blissfully unaware that they were viewing a commercial; NBC spokeswoman Mary Neagoy said they were calling it "an entertainment show, an extravaganza." Neither the TV listings nor the network promotions made reference to the show's sponsor.

Another recent innovation that blurs the line between advertising and entertainment is the use of celebrity endorsers who play their TV-character roles in television commercials. Advertisers have always used celebrities to pitch their products; the new wrinkle is that the celebrities appear not as themselves but as the characters they play on TV. For example, Tim Allen, star of *Home Improvement*, played the quirky do-it-yourselfer in a commercial for Kmart's Builders Square. Craig T. Nelson and Shelley Fabares star in a commercial for Kraft Healthy Favorites that could pass for a scene from their popular serial *Coach*. Jerry Seinfeld jokes his way through a commercial for

American Express, Sinbad performs his characteristic antics in a Polaroid commercial, and Bart Simpson and family advertise Butterfingers in their trademark dysfunctional style.

Similarly, talk shows have revived the practice of live endorsements, whereby the show's host personally plugs a sponsor's product. When Jay Leno announced that he would endorse products on the *Tonight Show*, the *Wall Street Journal* reported that advertisers "applauded Mr. Leno's move, since they believe viewers are less likely to zap a commercial if it's performed as part of the show." In one episode, Leno held up a giant Intel Inside logo and welcomed the chip manufacturer as a new sponsor on the air. (Late-night rival David Letterman refuses to endorse sponsors on his show.)

Particularly disturbing is the use of former or current newscasters in ads to create an impression of objectivity. For instance, former *CBS This Morning* host Kathleen Sullivan appeared in an ad for the Collagen Corporation. In what looked like a scientific news show, Sullivan presented collagen injection as a safe, effective treatment of skin problems—despite intense debate within the medical community over its safety. Mary Alice Williams also used her credibility as an Emmy Award-winning newsanchor to flack for NYNEX, a telecommunications company. "My job is to stay on top of what they're doing and keep you posted," she said in a TV ad.

One of marketers' newest gambits appeared in September 1994 in the form of a hybrid TV show called *Main Floor*. The half-hour show includes brief features about fashion and beauty. The catch is that some of the features are paid commercials, while others are not; viewers may not be told which are which until the credits at the end. For a fee of about $25,000 (much cheaper than a typical thirty-second commercial), Lee jeans, Chanel cosmetics, and other sponsors can buy two- to three-minute spots to feature their products in the show.

Walt Disney Co. has sponsored what is perhaps the most egregious example of hidden advertising. The company bought time in local newscasts for its "Movie News" spots. The ads, which include an anchorman who sits behind a desk and clips from *The Lion King* and other . . . movies, are designed to look exactly like the entertainment segment of a newscast, but they are pure hype for the movies. Only an easy-to-miss notice at the end of the minute-long spots indicates they are "Paid for by Buena Vista," Disney's distribution company.

Blurring the Lines on Radio

Radio, too, is breaking down the barriers between ads and programming. In Washington, D.C., WPGC-AM runs several talk shows on financial topics that are actually program-length ads for their sponsors' products. Ron Petersen hosts a show about investments, which serves to drum up business for his brokerage firm; Jerome Wenger's talk show is really an ad for his financial newsletter. A single sentence at the beginning of each program informs viewers that the show is "furnished," "sponsored," or "brought to you" by its hosts. However, most listeners miss the implications of the disclaimer. The shows are effective marketing tools precisely because most people do not identify them as ads. According to Arnold Sanow, a small-business marketing consultant who once hosted a weekly busienss show on WPGC, "Having *you* on the radio, nobody realizes that you've paid to be the host of that show. They don't think of that."

Moreover, having one's own radio show provides instant respectability. Carolann Brown, who uses her WPGC program *The Money Manager* to promote her book of the same name, says, "It does give you a lot of credibility.. . . Somehow [people] think that if you're on TV or on the radio that you're already credible." Such deceptions are particularly disturbing when used to sell financial services, where life savings are invested on the strength of perceived reputation and objectivity.

Imitation Editorial

In 1988, Ann Landers received a letter from a reader wanting more information on a miraculous diet pill that dissolves fat while you sleep, based on what appeared to be a legitimate news story. Landers replied, horrified, "What you read wasn't a news story but an advertisement.... How these charlatans get away with this stuff is beyond me."

Landers and her reader had stumbled upon the print media's version of the infomercial—the "advertorial," or advertising disguised as editorial copy. Advertorials—and consumer complaints about their deceptive nature—have been around for decades. They evolved from "reading notices" of the late 1800s, in which advertisers paid newspapers—or promised them future business—to publish news stories lauding their product or service. Although a 1912 provision to the Newspaper Publicity Act banned advertising disguised as news copy, advertisers and publishers today continue to push the legal limits.

In 1967 the FTC ruled that advertorials must carry the word "advertisement" at the top of the page. Still, it's easy to get fooled. An advertorial spread in the August 1993 issue of *Mademoiselle* titled "What's Next" plugs a variety of products: clothes, makeup, shampoo. The ad's copy style, layout, and photos all mimic the magazine's regular features. A quiz prepared by Centrum titled "How healthy is your diet?" is placed next to an ad for Centrum vitamins. An advertorial in *Travel and Leisure* for Stouffer's Vinoy Resort includes an engaging essay by George Plimpton about a friend with writer's block who checks into the hotel to finish a novel. Again, the ad's title, byline, and typography closely match the magazine's editorial articles.

Advertorials are proliferating madly. According to *Advertising Age*, the recession of the early 1990s gave advertisers more power, which they are using to demand advertorials as part of their contract deals with publishers. In 1992, advertorials filled 6,998 pages in the magazines tracked by the Publisher's Information Bureau. This number was down slightly from the previous year, but up 51 percent from 1986. Even industry organ *Advertising Age* worries about the ethical implications of advertorials. Reporter Scott Donaton writes that "there's a danger that it becomes more difficult for readers to make the distinction between regular editorial matter and special advertising sections."

But fooling the reader is what advertorials are all about. As Ruth Whitney, editor in chief of *Glamour*, told Donaton, "The only thing that's bad about [advertorials] is the effort to deceive the reader, which was really their purpose in the beginning, to convince the reader that this was editorial material. It's imitation editorial."

Now, marketers are taking the advertorial one step further by producing entire magazines to flaunt their products and advertising. Called magalogs, these custom publications sell at newsstands, contain articles and regular ads—but, unlike real magazines, they are published expressly to promote the sponsor's products. For instance, Mary Kay cosmetics publishes *Beauty* magazine, which could be easily mistaken for any other women's magazine. General Motors puts out *Know How*, which covers car matters for women. (*Know How's* premiere issue was even reviewed in *USA Today*.) Pepsi publishes *Pop Life*, which claims to be a "magazine for today's teens." The publication—full of Pepsi ads—includes interviews with Cindy Crawford and Pepsi's other celebrity spokes-people. Although magalog publishers claim to offer a legitimate information source, the contents are biased by definition; single-sponsor magazines will not include any information that could threaten the profits of their backers.

What People Have Done

VNRs, infomercials, and advertorials all disguise their advertising content in order to fly beneath consumers' commercial-detecting radar. The only way to make these "stealth ads" less deceptive is to require a clear indication of their commercial nature. For example, radio infomercials would be punctuated with clear announcements every several minutes, and TV infomercials would include a constant on-screen notice identifying the broadcast as an advertisement. In 1991, the Center for the Study of Commercialism (CSC), together with other consumer-advocacy groups, petitioned the Federal Communications Commission (FCC) to require better identification of infomercials (the FCC had not acted by October 1994). In 1993 the FCC also invited comments on whether to impose commercial time limits on broadcasters; CSC recommended a daily or weekly maximum of commercial content, which would restrict the amount of commercially blurred material allowed on the public airwaves.

POSTSCRIPT

Does Marketing Have Appropriate Boundaries?

Jacobson and Mazur emphasize the horrific consequences of commercialism, which "engulf everything from schools to professional sports to scientific research." Examples of "stealth marketing" (like the stealth bomber—unforeseen attacks camouflaged to an unsuspecting target) practices are more apparent every day. For example, a recent article in *Business Week* (February 28, 2000) critiques the use of promotional deals between hospitals and TV stations, whereby consumers are fed paid "news reports" instead of unbiased medical information. The editorial integrity of the *Los Angeles Times* was recently questioned when the editors aggressively publicized the "Staples Center" while simultaneously sharing ad revenues with the company.

There is little question that commercialism has grown by leaps and bounds in newer arenas, and marketers may be culpable for "crossing the line" in many cases. But shouldn't we also consider *demand side* factors, such as audience taste and our tolerance for such lowest common denominator forms of entertainment and programming? "Shock jock" Howard Stern and talk show host Jerry Springer are on TV because there is a sizable and lucrative audience that continues to tune in. As critics consider the degradation of popular culture, are irresponsible marketers culpable for this decline, or are they merely reacting to the demands of the marketplace?

Suggested Readings

Bart Macchiette and Abhijit Roy, "Social Issues and Sensitive Groups: Are You Marketing Correct?" *Journal of Consumer Marketing* (vol. 11, no. 4, 1994)

Richard Ohmann, ed., *Making and Selling Culture* (Wesleyan University Press, 1996)

Paul Raeburn, "The Corruption of TV Health News," *Business Week* (February 28, 2000)

Leigh Eric Schmidt, *Consumer Rites: The Buying and Selling of American Holidays* (Princeton University Press, 1995)

Barry Schwartz, *The Costs of Living: How Market Freedom Erodes the Best Things in Life* (W. W. Norton, 1994)

R. George Wright, *Selling Words: Free Speech in a Commercial Culture* (New York University Press, 1997)

From *Taking Sides: Marketing*. Copyright © 2000 by The McGraw-Hill Companies, Inc. All rights reserved. Reprinted by permission of McGraw-Hill/Dushkin Publishing.

ISSUE 2

Is the Practice of Multilevel Marketing Legitimate?

YES: Dale D. Buss, from "A Direct Route to Customers," *Nation's Business* (September 1997)

NO: Stephen Barrett, from "The Mirage of Multilevel Marketing," *Quackwatch*, <http://www.quackwatch.com/01QuackeryRelatedTopics/mlm.html> (August 26, 1999)

Issue Summary

YES: Writer Dale D. Buss depicts the booming growth of multilevel marketing (MLM) in various arenas. He outlines the techniques of one-to-one selling as well as the home party method. Buss also notes how the legitimate companies in the MLM industry take special care to distance themselves from phony operations.

NO: Retired psychiatrist Stephen Barrett argues that people who join in the later stages of an MLM operation will likely not do well. He discusses the example of health-related food supplements, where claims are subject to government intervention and public scrutiny as to their effectiveness. Barrett also examines questionable claims and people's motivations and methods of selling.

Multilevel marketing (MLM) is used by a wide range of companies to distribute their goods in the marketplace without significant promotional cost. According to Dale D. Buss, there are over 1,000 companies employing more than 7 million people involved in this industry. A diverse range of products and services are sold extensively using this strategy, such as personal care products, home and family care products, vitamins, long distance telephone plans, books, and educational leisure products and services.

MLM can be practiced in two distinct ways—through one-to-one selling or the home party method. Two-thirds of the companies use individual, one-to-one selling either at home, in the workplace, at public events such as fairs, or over the phone. The rest (primarily women) try to sell in a social gathering by offering products "whose sales are enhanced by the strong marketing context" provided by the occasion. What distinguishes a legal MLM company from a pyramid scheme is that by law it limits the maximum number of over-rides on distributors generating new distributors. Conversely, pyramid schemes truly afford continuing payoffs for its top originators as the pyramid grows exponentially. Such schemes allow the top numbers to accumulate great wealth at the expense of later entrants to the system.

MLM firms have largely shed their spurious image, and today there are numerous independent distributors selling products to neighbors, friends, and relatives. Many individuals have achieved great success in recruiting others and building a "downline" from which they receive commissions. Buss notes that the legitimate MLM industry is very careful to maintain its clean image.

From *Taking Sides: Marketing*. Copyright © 2000 by The McGraw-Hill Companies, Inc. All rights reserved. Reprinted by permission of McGraw-Hill/Dushkin Publishing.

Some major MLM companies have gone public in recent years with several stocks listed on both the New York Stock Exchange (NYSE) and NASDAQ. Amway, Avon, Tupperware, and Shaklee are examples of companies that have established legitimacy and distanced themselves from the fear of deceptive practices. However, skepticism still exists, states Stephen Barrett. He warns people not to be surprised if a friend or acquaintance tries to sell them vitamins, herbs, homeopathic remedies, weight loss powders, or other health-related products. Barrett sees the attraction as being in tune with the trend toward out-of-home businesses, whereby for a few hundred dollars, working part-time holds the promise of a successful entrepreneurial venture. He comments that many of the pyramid-type MLM companies still exist and seem more prevalent in health care and cosmetic industries. They often prey upon the faith of unsuspecting distributors that the products will provide the results they promise.

Barrett also portrays the attraction of MLM as a derivation of aging baby boomers, who are vulnerable to sales pitches, often from relatives and friends, that promise a healthier and more youthful lifestyle. Such sales pitches also promise monetary rewards devoid of a truthful depiction of the time and effort the undertaking really requires for success. The distributors most frequently are not trained in health and nutrition but simply pass on to their customers the promotional information provided by the company. They can easily become victims of their own hype when they listen to company-made tapes, telephone conference calls, and propaganda at company rallies.

MLM offers the benefits of short-cutting retail distribution, reducing costs, selling new customers in a personal way, and initiating a cult of followers equally committed to making the venture a success. However, the actual hours of commitment and market development are often underplayed by MLM providers. Once initiated, the new MLM recruits sell to everyone and anyone to whom they have access, which is usually a circle of friends, family, and business colleagues. Frequently, after purchasing the "minimal inventory" or sample kits, they are stuck with excessive product.

While thousands of MLM endorsers have profited from their efforts, just as many have struggled in their support without achieving the riches of their sponsors. Although major MLM participants, such as Amway, claim over 10,000 distributors, many of these are people who like and endorse the product but become distributors only to secure access to discounted prices of the product for themselves and a close circle of friends.

Dale D. Buss   **YES**

A Direct Route to Customers

If she's done it once, she's done it 458 times—literally. But on a sunny June evening in the flower-splashed back yard of a home in Menomonee Falls, Wis., Mary Adashek is using all her enthusiasm to demonstrate the patented peeler-corer-slicer marketed by the company she represents, Pampered Chef.

Over a card table, Adashek uses the gee-whiz tool to prepare fresh apple rings, to spiral-slice fillings for pie, to ready apples for the dehydrator—even to peel potatoes and create curly fries.

"I wish I'd had this all the years I've been making apple pies," says one convinced customer among the half-dozen women who have accepted homeowner Laurie Barker's invitation to see Pampered Chef products and to socialize.

By the time Adashek is done for the evening and leaves for her home in nearby Cedarburg, she has sold about $400 worth of gizmos, including the apple tool, clay "baking stones," and measuring cups with a plunger so butter won't stick to the inside. Add that amount to the more than $250,000 in Pampered Chef sales she has rung up the past four years.

Adashek's earnings from the evening are about $100, below her average of about $125. But by arranging with hostesses to appear at about 10 such parties a month and by reaping commissions from other "sales consultants" she has helped establish, Adashek netted more than $17,500 last year—"enough to pay the mortgage," she says. And that doesn't count the free trips she gets: all-expense-paid sales-reward junkets that Adashek and her husband, a property manager, have taken to London, San Diego, Disney World, and Alaska. Hawaii beckons next year.

"The more people I share this with, the more benefits there are for myself, yes," says the 33-year-old Adashek, a former cardiovascular technician who likes to be able to stay home during the day with her 4-year-old daughter, Sarah. "But we also offer people a way to make life in the kitchen easier and more enjoyable.... And people love these products!"

Indeed, as Adashek climbs the ladder of success, she actually is doing a lot more than selling kitchen implements and enlarging the family budget: She's building her own micro-enterprise while promoting a business opportunity for other women. She is one of the more than 7 million Americans who work, mostly part time, as sales representatives for companies—such as Pampered Chef Inc., based in Addison, Ill.—that rely on multilevel marketing.

Such marketing—also known as MLM, direct selling, or network marketing—is being used by a growing number of companies to get their goods into the marketplace without the expenses of advertising or staffing a sales department.

Each MLM sales representative is, in effect, a business owner working as an independent contractor for a company that may have few "real" employees. Reps earn commissions on their own sales. They also share commissions with the "upliners" who recruited them and manage them. And, in turn, they recruit and supervise salespeople, called "downliners," who learn from and share commissions with them. Low overhead, work-time flexibility, and lots of potential are all part of the allure.

Cosmetics to Cookware

MLM is booming, with sales reaching an estimated $18 billion in 1995, the latest year for which figures are available. That's up from about $13 billion in 1991, according to the Direct Selling Association, a trade group in Washington, D.C.

Reprinted by permission, *Nation's Business*, September 1997. Copyright 1997, U.S. Chamber of Commerce.

To be sure, MLM has a highly notorious side. Some companies create a cultlike environment, motivating sales reps to lean on friends and family to join them. Dozens of firms have been pursued by law-enforcement authorities amid allegations that the companies are using pyramid schemes—illegal scams in which large numbers of people at the bottom of the pyramid pay money that flows to a few people at the top. The illegal operations typically focus on recruiting downliners and sweeping in their signup fees rather than on selling products.

The legitimate MLM industry takes great pains to distance itself from these seamy pretenders.

More than 1,000 companies now use MLM as their primary distribution method, compared with fewer than 700 five years ago, the association says. Personal-care products such as cosmetics and jewelry accounted for about 39 percent of revenues in the direct-selling industry in 1995; home and family-care products, including cleaning solutions and cookware, made up 34 percent; services such as telephone long-distance plans accounted for 10 percent; vitamins, weightloss products, and other health formulas, 9 percent; and books and educational and leisure products or services, 8 percent.

Home is the primary venue of operation, and personal relationships are the main vehicle. About 59 percent of MLM sales occur in homes, according to the Association; an additional 16 percent are made over the phone; 15 percent in the workplace; 5 percent at public events such as fairs; and 5 percent elsewhere.

Two Approaches

In-person salesmanship is the common denominator, but MLM methodology falls into two basic camps: Two-thirds of the companies use individual, one-to-one selling, the association says, while one-third use the home-party method.

Many MLM companies strive to duplicate the accomplishments of renowned direct marketers such as Tupperware, the consumer-products company, Mary Kay, the cosmetics enterprise, and Amway, the home-care-products giant.

One company that takes the one-on-one sales approach developed so successfully by Amway is Excel Communications Inc. Founded by Kenny Troutt in 1989, the Dallas-based provider of long-distance phone service grew from a $20 million company [in the early 1990s] to $14 billion in revenues [in 1996] with its army of 979,000 independent sales reps. The company buys huge blocks of long distance time from the big providers and resells it to consumers at very competitive prices. In May 1996, Excel went public as one of the New York Stock Exchange's youngest new listings ever.

A decade ago, when Troutt got into the business of reselling long-distance capacity—after holding jobs selling life insurance and working in the construction and oil industries—he chose MLM without hesitation. Most Americans obviously knew how to use their phones, he reasoned, but "nobody really understood their rates, nobody really cared what company they were with."

As long as the price is right, he deduced, many phone customers would rather let a relative or friend pocket sales commissions from their purchase if it's a purchase virtually everyone is going to make anyway.

Troutt also correctly concluded that sales reps prefer not having to manage an inventory.

A Way That Works

Robert Montgomery has built Reliv International Inc. into a huge organization in less than 10 years via one-to-one selling of the firm's line of about 25 nutritional supplements and weightloss products, such as Cellebrate. It is a powder that is mixed with water to make a drink, and Reliv says it has been designed to "burn and block fat, curb appetite, and reduce food intake . . . without side effects." The company has more than 50,000 distributors worldwide.

Montgomery says he considered offering Reliv's line through pharmacies, health-food stores, even gyms and health clubs, but he chose MLM because of the effectiveness of personal salesmanship.

"We believe that our products could be put in a health-food store or a grocery store and just sit there and really not do anything but gather dust unless people can demonstrate them, and talk to someone about what's in the product, and tell them why they should be taking the product," says Montgomery, who is president, chairman, and CEO of the Chesterfield, Mo.-based company.

Such "value-added" selling allows most MLM companies to price their goods higher than they could at retail, says Greg Martin, CEO of ShapeRite Concepts Ltd., another marketer of nutritional products. ShapeRite, based in Sandy, Utah, has more than 70,000 sales reps.

"You need a fairly adequate or hefty margin to be able to pay your distributors fairly for their efforts," says Martin, who founded the company in 1989 with an imported dietary supplement. Compensation for ShapeRite's reps amounts to 54 percent of sales revenue.

Selling in a Social Gathering

Home-party companies, the other MLM camp, typically offer products whose sales are enhanced by the strong marketing context provided by a social gathering of women.

Rhonda Anderson, a Montana homemaker, already knew from demonstrations she had given that her hobby of producing heirloom-quality albums for family photos was party-friendly and that it struck a strong emotional chord in her mostly female audiences. So when she and a friend, Minneapolis business woman Cheryl Lightle, decided to form a business, Creative Memories Inc., home parties seemed the right way to go.

Creative Memories mushroomed from six consultants and $20,000 in sales in 1988 to more than 15,000 reps and $40 million in sales last year. The company just completed a 30,000-square-foot headquarters building in St. Cloud, Minn.

The reason for this exponential growth is a "passion that is common in the consultants who stay with us," says Susan Iida-Pederson, vice president of promotion and communications. "You're not just selling [customers] a product or teaching them a skill, you're really contributing to a tradition they're starting, and it feels good."

"Unit managers"—those with several downliners—earn about $25,000 to $40,000 a year, Iida-Pederson says; a small number of managers earn $60,000 to $80,000; and the rare superstars break $125,000. Some upliners do so well that they quit pitching at parties and spend all their time managing their corps of reps.

Longaberger Co., a Dresden, Ohio, manufacturer of baskets, ceramics, and other goods for the home, also benefits from the warm feelings that home parties generate. Last year its 38,000 reps across the country generated sales of more than $500 million.

Getting Out of the House

As a regional sales manager for Longaberger, Heidi Proefrock is a certifiable MLM star and another weaver of the social fabric in homey Cedarburg, a Milwaukee suburb of 10,000 people. Proefrock has steadily built her business from $8,000 in annual revenues with just six downliners 11 years ago, when she was a part-time water-aerobics instructor, to $40,000 to $50,000 a year net and nearly 60 downliners in nine states.

The operation has grown so big that she is moving it out of the basket-bedecked restored farm home where she and her husband, Steve, a real-estate agent, live. She is relocating her business to an old schoolhouse nearby that she refurbished as an office.

"When I got started with this, I wasn't thinking of making a business out of it at all," says the 38-year-old mother of four. "Like most people, I was just looking to get out of the house a little bit and make some extra grocery money."

In fact, the hallmark of some of the most successful MLM companies is that the business aspect, at least initially, seems secondary to the participants' convictions about the good that they're doing.

Twenty years ago, for example, Lane Nemeth wanted to open a store to demonstrate educational toys. But because parents were her target, her husband suggested the Tupperware-party method. Someone else suggested that she reward people for recruiting. Now Discovery Toys, based in Martinez., Calif., has more than 30,000 reps, and it reached $85 million in sales last year in the United States alone.

"It was all sort of learn-as-you-go," says Nemeth, a former teacher. "What I did have was this enormous, driving mission to get parents to understand that the right kinds of products, the right kinds of stimulation . . . produce a significantly different child. I was not going into business for the sake of the business." That kind of passion for a quality product or service—a commitment that is easily embraced by others—is the biggest predictor of success for an MLM company, practitioners say.

Successful and reputable MLM companies share a number of other attributes. Among them:

- They make it easy to get in.
- Low barriers to entry are crucial to getting a strong flow of new reps. MLM companies rarely set education or experience requirements.
- There's no commitment by the contractor to a specific tenure, and part-time work is the norm.

The average initial investment required of MLM consultants is only about $100, according to the Direct Selling Association, and its members pledge to buy back at 90 cents on the dollar any resalable goods held by reps who want to exit the business. If a company requires more than an initial small amount for a kit of product samples and other materials, the association says, it could be trying to boost its revenues by making contractors pay in advance for vast supplies of goods regardless of whether they have customers' orders for the products.

The required initial order for a new rep of Biogime International Inc., a Houston-based company that sells skin-care products via MLM, is just $40.

And instead of asking new reps to place orders for a large inventory of skin creams that would have to be stored in a garage or basement, Biogime set up a toll-free telephone line for reps or their customers to call in their orders. The company then credits the rep with the amount of the sale and ships the goods directly to customers, who are billed directly.

"This way doesn't prevent distributors from having a good ongoing relationship with customers, but it stops them from having to invest in inventory and spend unnecessary time delivering products, which really is downtime," says Julie Martin, CEO and co-owner of Biogime. "You don't want people to regret their investment in your program."

They make it attractive to stay on.

Most sales reps leave just as easily as they arrive. Turnover for some MLM companies is 100 percent a year.

Commissions, of course, greatly affect each company's turnover rate because they're the only form of compensation offered by nearly all MLM companies. While commission formulas range widely in the industry, consumables such as nutritional supplements generally carry lower percentage commissions than big-ticket items such as vacuum cleaners. The commissions that sales reps receive from downliners also vary greatly and can have a big impact on contractors' incomes. To help stem departures and to build their reps into successful sellers, good MLM companies produce a wide stream of information for reps on the company's new products and services, sales techniques, and other topics.

The companies also offer regular and continual training sessions that are held one-on-one or at local, regional, or national gatherings.

Longaberger, for example, starts a new consultant with a kit containing printed, video, and audio information, including sample scripts for recruiting hostesses. The company sends out a monthly newsletter as well as a separate monthly publication that suggests product uses, and it hosts a three-day annual national convention, including a full day of training on sales and recruiting.

The company aggressively discourages hyped claims about products and services.

As independent and largely unsupervised agents with strong incentives to attract downliners, MLM reps can be tempted to make unsubstantiated or even outlandish claims about their products, services, and incomes.

Companies such as ShapeRite and Reliv have to be especially vigilant in educating their distributors to ensure that they do not run afoul of recent federal regulations regarding health claims. These companies' training materials and newsletters make clear what distributors should not say when pitching products.

The enterprise avoids fast-buck opportunists.

Because business opportunities can ebb and flow, some reps become what the industry calls "junkies" or "poster boys" who move from company to company trying to get in, and out, at the right times—often taking hundreds or even thousands of downliners with them.

"They're not for long-term companies." says Biogime's Martin. "They're a flash in the pan. It's a big problem in this industry."

The company jealously protects its niche.

The most successful MLM companies quickly attract imitation products, often in conventional retail settings. Consequently, continued innovation in products and services is essential. It prompted Longaberger, for example, to add the ceramic bowls, wallpaper designs, and other housewares to its original focus on baskets.

And Creative Memories has acted assertively to protect its coattails, urging reps not to subscribe to, distribute, or promote a magazine produced by a firm that could become a competitor.

The firm understands the awkwardness of working for an MLM company.

The biggest obstacle for sales reps—and, therefore, for MLM companies—is the fact that reps need to rely on family members and friends for sales, at least initially. Awkwardness often prevails in these social and personal interactions, and the best MLM companies help reps work through that problem—and refrain from pressuring them into feeling like they must turn everyone they know into a customer or a downliner.

"It requires that you commercialize noncommercial relationships," says Robert L. Fitzpatrick, an industry critic and author of a new book, *False Profits: Seeking Financial and Spiritual Deliverance in Multi-Level Marketing and Pyramid Schemes* (Herald Press, $12.95). "It means that you will approach your son-in-law, your girlfriend, your wife, your brother-in-law, your next-door neighbor, your customers—you will invite people who perhaps you have a very different kind of relationship with based on trust, based on family, blood, love, nationalities, something—and you're going to convert that into a business relationship."

The best way for MLM companies to avoid the appearance of exploitation is to market a highly desirable, thoroughly genuine product or service with the utmost integrity—and to let it do its own "talking."

We really are out there as a mission company which happens to have a wonderful learning opportunity," says Nemeth of Discovery Toys. "You'd never come to a Discovery Toys opportunity event and hear all about the people who got rich. You hear about all the parents who got helped."

No

Stephen Barrett

The Mirage of Multilevel Marketing

Don't be surprised if a friend or acquaintance tries to sell you vitamins, herbs, homeopathic remedies, weight-loss powders, or other health-related products. Millions of Americans have signed up as distributors for multilevel companies that market such products from person to person. Often they have tried the products, concluded that they work, and become suppliers to support their habit.

Multilevel marketing (also called network marketing) is a form of direct sales in which independent distributors sell products, usually in their customers' home or by telephone. In theory, distributors can make money not only from their own sales but also from those of the people they recruit.

Becoming an MLM distributor is simple and requires no real knowledge of health or nutrition. Many people do so initially in order to buy their own products at a discount. For a small sum of money—usually between $35 and $100—these companies sell a distributor kit that includes product literature, sales aids (such as a videotape or audiotape), price lists, order forms, and a detailed instructional manual. Most MLM companies publish a magazine or newsletter containing company news, philosophical essays, product information, success stories, and photographs of top salespeople. The application form is usually a single page that asks only for identifying information. Millions of Americans have signed up, including many physicians attracted by the idea that selling MLM products can offset losses attributable to managed care.

Questionable Financial Opportunity

Distributors can buy products "wholesale," sell them "retail," and recruit other distributors who can do the same. When enough distributors have been enrolled, the recruiter is eligible to collect a percentage of their sales. Companies suggest that this process provides a great money-making opportunity. However, it is unlikely that people who don't join during the first few months of operation or become one of the early distributors in their community can build enough of a sales pyramid to do well. And many who stock up on products to meet sales goals get stuck with unsold products that cost thousands of dollars. Some companies permit direct ordering of their products, which avoids this problem. In July 1999, the National Association of Attorneys General announced that complaints about multilevel marketing and pyramid schemes were tenth on their list of consumer complaints.

An Amway Corporation report indicates that the vast majority of its distributors make very little money. Amway's 1998 "Business Review" tabulates figures gathered from April 1994 through March 1995, from distributors who attempted to make a retail sale, presented the Sales and Marketing Plan, received bonus money, or attended a company or distributor meeting in the month surveyed. The average "gross income" for these "active distributors" was $88 per month. The report defines "gross income" as the amount received from retail sales minus cost of products, plus any bonus. It does not take any business expenses into account. If this figure includes purchases for personal use, the potential profit would, of course, be less. The report also notes that "approximately 41% of all distributors of record were found to be active."

"The Mirage of Multilevel Marketing" by Stephen Barrett, www.Quackwatch.org with permission.

Dubious Health Claims

More than a hundred multilevel companies are marketing health-related products. Most claim that their products are effective for preventing or treating disease. A few companies merely suggest that people will feel better, look better, or have more energy if they supplement their diet with extra nutrients. When clear-cut therapeutic claims are made in product literature, the company is an easy target for government enforcement action. Some companies run this risk, hoping that the government won't take action until their customer base is well established. Other companies make no claims in their literature but rely on testimonials, encouraging people to try their products and credit them for any improvement that occurs.

Most multilevel companies tell distributors not to make claims for the products except for those found in company literature. (That way the company can deny responsibility for what distributors do.) However, many companies hold sales meetings at which people are encouraged to tell their story to the others in attendance. Some companies sponsor telephone conference calls during which leading distributors describe their financial success, give sales tips, and describe their personal experiences with the products. Testimonials also may be published in company magazines, audiotapes or videotapes. Testimonial claims can trigger enforcement action, but since it is time-consuming to collect evidence of their use, government agencies seldom bother to do so.

Government enforcement action against multilevel companies has not been vigorous. These companies are usually left alone unless their promotions become so conspicuous and their sales volume so great that an agency feels compelled to intervene. Even then, few interventions have substantial impact once a company is well established.

Recent Promotions

During the past 15 years, I have collected information on more than 100 multilevel companies marketing health products. Here are some examples of improper marketing activities:

- Body Wise International, of Carlsbad, California, markets "fitness" products and weight-management products. In 1995 the FTC [Federal Trade Commission] charged the company with making unsubstantiated claims that *Cardio Wise* was "designed to give an extra margin of insurance against heart disease" and that its weight-management products would foster weight loss without dieting. The company signed an FTC consent agreement prohibiting it from making unsubstantiated health-related claims in the future.

- Mary Kay, well known for its cosmetic products, is now marketing a $29.50-per-month daily supplement packet alleged "to help bridge the gap between what a healthy diet provides and what a woman needs for optimum health and beauty." *Tufts University Diet & Nutrition Letter* has observed: (1) the supplements contain huge amounts of thiamin, riboflavin, vitamin B6, and vitamin B12, which almost all Americans get from their food; (2) they lack iron, which might benefit some women of childbearing age; and (3) more rationally formulated multivitamin/mineral preparations are available elsewhere for one tenth the cost.

- In 1993, Melaleuca Inc., of Idaho Falls, Idaho, began offering a "wellness assessment" by a company that provided in-home testing. The procedure included a questionnaire, a blood cholesterol test, a blood-pressure reading, and an estimate of the percentage of body fat. The resultant report evaluated personal risk factors and recommends modifications in diet, exercise habits, and lifestyle. The recommendations include taking a "balanced vitamin/mineral supplement every day" and "working closely with a 'Vitality for Life counselor' " (a Melaleuca distributor) to implement the suggested changes. Prospects were then encouraged to purchase a "Vitality Pack" of "55 different vitamins, minerals, and other nutrients, all in the proper amounts and proper proportions," which wholesales for $263.40 for an annual supply. Although the health-risk appraisal could provide useful information, the Vitality Pack is a waste of money. People who wish to take a multivitamin/multimineral formula can obtain equivalent nutrients at a drugstore for less than $50 per year. The company also marketed a patented "fat conversion activity bar," an expensive candy bar whose ingredients are claimed to make exercise easier by "inhibiting the body's ability to hold on to fat."

- Matol Botanical International, a Canadian firm, markets *Km*, a foul-tasting extract of 14 common herbs. *Km* was originally marketed as *Matol*, which was claimed to be effective for ailments ranging from arthritis to cancer, as well as for rejuvenation. Canada's Health Protection Branch took action that resulted in an order for the company to advertise only the product name, price, and contents. In 1988 the FDA [Food and Drug Administration] attempted to block importation of *Matol* into the United States. However, the company evaded the ban by adding an ingredient and changing the product's name. The product literature acknowledges that *Km* has never been tested for effectiveness against any disease and states that distributors should not diagnose or recommend its products for any specific disease. However, many distributors do so.

- Nature's Sunshine Products, of Spanish Fork, Utah, markets herbs, vitamins, other nutritional supplements, homeopathic remedies, skin and hair-care products, water treatment systems, cooking utensils, and a weight-loss plan. Its more than 400 products include many that are claimed to "nourish" or "support" various body organs. Its salespeople, dubbed "Natural Health Counselors," are taught to use iridology (a bogus diagnostic procedure in which the eyes are examined), applied kinesiology (a bogus muscle-testing procedure), and other dubious methods to convince people that they need the products.

- Nu Skin International, Inc., of Provo, Utah, sells body-care products and dietary supplements. Nu Skin's Interior Design division markets expensive antioxidant, phytochemical, and "active enzyme" products. The enzyme products are said to be important because "the majority of cooked or processed foods we eat lack an ideal level of enzyme activity" needed for digestion. This statement is nonsense because the enzymes needed for digestion are made by the body's digestive organs. In 1993, the company and three of its distributors agreed to pay a total of $1,225,000 to settle FTC charges that they made unsubstantiated claims for *Nutriol Hair Fitness Preparation* and two skin-care products. In 1997, the company agreed to pay $1.5 million to settle charges that it had made unsubstantiated claims for five more of its products. The products, which contained chromium picolinate and L-carnitine, were falsely claimed to reduce fat, increase metabolism, and preserve or build muscle.

- Sunrider Corporation, of Torrance, California, claims that its herbal concoctions can help "regenerate" the body. Although some ingredients can exert pharmacologic effects on the body, there is little evidence they can cure major diseases or that Sunrider distributors are qualified to advise people about how to use them properly. During the mid-1980s the FDA ordered Sunrider to stop making health claims for several of its products. In 1989 the company signed a consent agreement to pay $175,000 to the state of California and to stop representing that its products have any effect on disease or medical conditions. The company toned down its literature but continued to make therapeutic claims in testimonial tapes included in its distributor kits. In 1992 a jury in Phoenix, Arizona, concluded that Sunrider had violated Arizona's racketeering laws and awarded $650,000 to a woman who claimed she had been misled by company representations and had become ill after using some of its products. On January 7, 1997, *The Wall Street Journal* reported that Sunrider's president Tei-Fu Chen and his wife Oi-Lin Chen were indicted for conspiracy, tax evasion, and smuggling. The article stated that they had (1) underreported their 1987–90 income by more than $125 million, (2) used foreign companies they controlled to overcharge Sunrider for ingredients so the company could understate its profits, (3) wired millions of dollars to pay the inflated charges, but "recycled" the money to purchase U.S. real estate and Chinese antiques, and (4) filed falsely low customs declarations to reduce the import duty on dozens of art works. In September 1997, the Chens and the company pled guilty to tax and customs frauds. Mr. Chen was sentenced to two years in federal prison, to be followed by two years of supervised release including six months of home detention. Mrs. Chen was sentenced to two years probation, including six months of home detention. The financial penalties totaled $99.8 million. The Corporation was fined $500,000 for filing a false tax return for 1989. Mr. Chen agreed to pay the Customs Service $4 million to avoid forfeiting antique items that had been seized. In related actions, the Chens had paid the Internal Revenue Service $93 million in back taxes, interest, and penalties, and paid the Customs Service $2.3 million in additional duties. In 1998, the FDA issued a warning letter citing manufacturing violations and stating that it was illegal for the company to market "spray vitamins" as dietary supplements.

Motivation: Powerful but Misguided

The "success" of network marketing lies in the enthusiasm of its participants. Most people who think they have been helped by an unorthodox method enjoy sharing their success stories with their friends. People who give such testimonials are usually motivated by a sincere wish to help their fellow humans. Since people tend to believe what others tell them about personal experiences, testimonials can be powerful persuaders.

Perhaps the trickiest misconception about quackery is that personal experience is the best way to tell whether something works. When someone feels better after having used a product or procedure, it is natural to give credit to whatever was done. However, this is unwise. Most ailments are self-limiting, and even incurable conditions can have sufficient day-to-day variation to enable bogus methods to gain large followings. In addition, taking action often produces temporary relief of symptoms (a placebo effect). For these reasons, scientific experimentation is almost always necessary to establish whether health methods are really effective. Instead of testing their products, multilevel companies urge customers to try them and credit them if they feel better. Some products are popular because they contain caffeine, ephedrine (a stimulant), valerian (a tranquilizer), or other substances that produce mood-altering effects.

Another factor in gaining devotees is the emotional impact of group activities. Imagine, for example, that you have been feeling lonely, bored, depressed or tired. One day a friend tells you that "improving your nutrition" can help you feel better. After selling you some products, the friend inquires regularly to find out how you are doing. You seem to feel somewhat better. From time to time you are invited to interesting lectures where you meet people like yourself. Then you are asked to become a distributor. This keep you busy, raises your income, and provides an easy way to approach old friends and make new ones—all in an atmosphere of enthusiasm. Some of your customers express gratitude, giving you a feeling of accomplishment. People who increase their income, their social horizons, or their self-esteem can get a psychological boost that not only can improve their mood but also may alleviate emotionally-based symptoms.

Multilevel companies refer to this process as "sharing" and suggest that everyone involved is a "winner." That simply isn't true. The entire process is built on a foundation of deception. The main winners are the company's owners and the small percentage of distributors who become sales leaders. The losers are millions of Americans who waste money and absorb the misinformation.

Do you think multilevel participants are qualified to judge whether prospective customers need supplements—or medical care? Even though curative claims are forbidden by the written policies of each company, the sales process encourages customers to experiment with self-treatment. It may also promote distrust of legitimate health professionals and their treatment methods.

Some people would argue that the apparent benefits of "believing" in the products outweigh the risks involved. Do you think that people need false beliefs in order to feel healthy or succeed in life? Would you like to believe that something can help you when in fact it is worthless? Should our society support an industry that is trying to mislead us? Can't Americans do something better with the billion or more dollars being wasted each year on multilevel "health" products?

Physician Involvement

During the past few years, many physicians have begun selling health-related multilevel products to patients in their offices. The companies most involved appear to be Amway, Body Wise, Nu Skin (Interior Design), and Rexall. Doctors are typically recruited with promises that the extra income will replace income lost to managed care. In June 1999, the AMA House of Delegates approved ethical guidelines emphasizing that physicians should not coerce patients to purchase health-related products or recruit them to participate in marketing programs in which the physician personally benefits, financially or otherwise, from the efforts of their patients. The guidelines clearly frown on doctors profiting from the sale of health-related nonprescription products such as dietary supplements.

Recommendations

Consumers would be wise to avoid health-related multilevel products altogether. Those that have nutritional value (such as vitamins and low-cholesterol foods) are invariably overpriced and may be unnecessary as well. Those promoted as remedies are either unproven, bogus, or intended for conditions that are unsuitable for self-medication.

Government agencies should police the multilevel marketplace aggressively, using undercover investigators and filing criminal charges when wrongdoing is detected. People who feel they have been defrauded by MLM companies should file complaints with their state attorney general and with local FDA and FTC offices. A letter detailing the events may be sufficient to trigger an investigation; and the more complaints received, the more likely that corrective action will be taken.

POSTSCRIPT

Is the Practice of Multilevel Marketing Legitimate?

While many perceptual concerns of MLM exist, and legal public scrutiny is certain to endure, the simple reality is that this marketing practice is here to stay, and it has become embedded in America's controversial marketing culture. Financial success portends the growth of more sophisticated versions of MLM augmented by the growth of the Internet, affinity marketing, and the quest for building relationships. As we face the new millennium, many factors are collectively creating a fertile environment of MLM. Baby boomers' desire to "cocoon" (i.e., work out of the home), computer technology, and the quest for independence are alluring for a large percentage of many demographic segments seeking autonomy and financial success.

The method of multilevel marketing has made millions of dollars for distributors of Amway products, Mary Kay Cosmetics, and thousands of companies embracing the benefits of utilizing friendships, contacts, and person-to-person selling with the motive of having one's own distributorship. Given its uniqueness, how should this form of distribution be evaluated?

Despite the illegality of pyramid schemes, action from the government in enforcing regulations against such companies has not been forthcoming. Unless their promotions become so conspicuous and sales so extreme that an agency feels compelled to intervene, there will likely be less than vigorous law enforcement. The burden of the decision will remain with the consumer.

The direct sales appeal has not been without criticism, because of the negative connotation inherent in "pyramid selling." Enhanced by e-commerce, chat lines, and databases, multilevel marketing is experiencing unprecedented growth with its unique advantages and alleged savings to all parties involved.

Suggested Readings

Norm Brodsky, "Multilevel Mischief," *Inc.* (June 1998)

Cheryl Coward, "How to Spot a Pyramid Scheme," *Black Enterprise* (February 1998)

Richard Eisenberg, "The Mess Called Multilevel Marketing," *Money* (June 1987)

Constance Gustke, "Multi-level Investing: Some of the Hottest Stocks Around Are Issued by Network Companies. Here's How to Analyze and Invest in Them," *Success* (September 1998)

Rob Laymon, "Multi-Level Marketing Proves a Hit on 'Net," *Philadelphia Business Journal* (August 20, 1999)

Jim Salter, "Multi-Level Marketing Goes Mainstream," *Marketing News* (September 1997)

Kristine Zwica, "ABCD . . . MLM," *Success* (May 1999)

"What's Wrong With Multi-Level Marketing?" http://www.vandruff.com/mlm.html

Spree.com. http://www.spree.com

From *Taking Sides: Marketing.* Copyright © 2000 by The McGraw-Hill Companies, Inc. All rights reserved. Reprinted by permission of McGraw-Hill/Dushkin Publishing.

ISSUE 3

Has the "Keep It Simple" Concept Become "All Change, All the Time"?

YES: Regis McKenna, from *Real Time: Preparing for the Age of the Never Satisfied Customer* (Harvard Business School Press, 1997)

NO: Jack Trout with Steve Rivkin, from *The Power of Simplicity: A Management Guide to Cutting Through the Nonsense and Doing Things Right* (McGraw-Hill, 1999)

Issue Summary

YES: Regis McKenna, chairperson of the McKenna Group, proclaims that the era of "adaptive" marketing has arrived—now driven by new technologies of communications and information. Keeping in close touch with ever-changing consumer needs is now the only constant for marketing managers, he concludes.

NO: Jack Trout, president of the marketing firm Trout & Partners, and Steve Rivkin, a faculty member of the Department of Economics at Amherst College, see an overcommunicated culture of clutter. They argue that simplicity and the "focused benefit" must be encoded into one integrated singular message and emphasize the importance of a consistent "value proposition" packaged into a simple message, which is memorably positioned in the minds of consumers and prospects in a creative way.

Two distinct schools of thought have emerged as contemporary marketing orientations. Recent developments in information technology have tended to galvanize these perspectives. The first can be summarized by the following illustration: How many times have you been to a friend's or relative's house and seen the time on their VCR perpetually blink "12:00"? It is not a very difficult task to set the time correctly, but many lack the motivation to try and figure out how to do it. This is why many companies follow the KISS (Keep it simple, stupid!) policy. The origins of this theme can be traced to the early theory of Rosser Reeves, who introduced the concept of the Unique Selling Proposition (USP). He emphasized identifying and focusing on one differentiating attribute that can be "hammered" into the minds of consumers. Advertising mogul David Ogilvy then refined the concept by stressing the importance of developing a clear product personality, or the complex symbol known as the *brand image*. The need for clarity, simplicity, and consistency are essential in each advertising campaign, which is creating an "investment" in building the brand.

Product positioning emerged as the strategic mantra of the late 1970s and remains the core concept for Jack Trout and Steve Rivkin. Their quest is for a clear value proposition binding the essence of consumer benefit to the market offering. For example, in the automotive industry,

From *Taking Sides: Marketing.* Copyright © 2000 by The McGraw-Hill Companies, Inc. All rights reserved. Reprinted by permission of McGraw-Hill/Dushkin Publishing.

Volvo has established the safety position, Mercedes prides itself upon engineering quality, while Porsche touts itself as being the best sports car. It is necessary to provide customers with a salient reason to patronize one company's brand over the competitive offering. A simple positioning platform must carry a clearly construed core message and provide a meaningful idea for differentiation. The rationale for returning to simplicity and clarity is also at the heart of the integrated marketing communication (IMC) concept, which is defined by the American Association of Advertising Agencies (AAAA) as "a concept of marketing communications planning that recognizes the added value of a comprehensive plan that evaluates the strategic roles of a variety of communications disciplines—for example, general advertising, direct response, sales promotion and public relations—and combines these disciplines to provide clarity, consistency and maximum communications' impact through the seamless integration of discrete messages."

In other words, instead of a heavy reliance on any one promotional tool, several tools are blended to deliver a consistent and coherent brand image, which is presented to the customer at every brand contact.

The common thread for all these developments is what might be termed the *complexity avoidance syndrome*. Consumers seek to avoid confusion, hassles, and clutter. Bombarded by thousands of stimuli, they are loathsome of intrusive telemarketers and the onslaught of the thousands of "me, too" products found in the supermarket.

The opposing perspective focuses on the necessity for "real-time marketing" or "adaptive marketing." This assumes that consumers are constantly driven by their wants and needs, possessed by instant gratification, and empowered with product information. Regis McKenna argues that the advancements in communications technology and interactive advantages of the Internet can devastate loyalty to the company, as customers can eliminate geographic constraints and literally "shop the world." He believes that the need for extraordinary flexibility and instant reaction time has become crucial in offering consumers both choice and access.

Experts say that the themes of *speed* and *innovation* should replace the outmoded notion of celebrating consistency. This is a logical extension of *turbomarketing*, whereby companies are trying to establish a competitive advantage by responding faster to the fickle and ever-changing demands of the marketplace. Other sources suggest that adaptations, customization, and rapid response to smaller-niche markets are the themes for marketing in the new millennium.

YES

Regis McKenna

Real Time

The Real Time Message

Society and technology are in a continual dance, each moving and swaying in response to unanticipated moves by the other. Real time technology swiftly embeds itself in everything, everywhere, profoundly affecting the marketplace and every business participating in it. To discover how best to use the new technological tools to cross traditional market or geographic boundaries, adapt their modus operandi, and still keep their customers happy, managers must first get acquainted with the dimensions of the new technological power and its incipient social effects.

The Never Satisfied Customer

Right here. Right now. Tailored for me. Served up the way I like it. If the new consumer's expectations were spelled out on a billboard, that is how they would read. Top managers monotonously repeat, as if intoning mantras, that this is the age of customer service or the age of the consumer. Yet few of these managers realize what they must do for that customer to earn his or her complete approval. Consumer criteria for absolute satisfaction from supplier organizations, whether a company or a branch of government, have become so stringent as to seem unreal by the standards of the past.

Still, some of the most unlikely institutions have gotten parts of the message ahead of the rest: they have understood the need for extraordinary flexibility and have adapted accordingly, offering consumers both choice and access. One of these is a public agency upending government's reputation for sloth and rigidity. The Department of Motor Vehicles (DMV), seeking to maximize public cooperation with the enforcement of driving laws, offers some traffic offenders—as an alternative to steep fines and a hike in their auto insurance rates—a staggering array of choices for remedial instruction, known as traffic school. These are among the options available in several states to a driver who has earned, say, one too many speeding tickets: seven hours of daytime instruction on any day of the week, including Saturday and Sunday, or three and a half hours each on two consecutive weekday evenings. In California, the reforming speeder can attend any of 3,000 classrooms scattered across the state, run by certified, independent instructors (not government employees). The class offerings include those run by comedians who sugarcoat the predictable lessons with unpredictable wit and those held in pizzerias where students also get their dinner. There are the "Escuela Latina De Trafico-Espanol," an "Armenian-Persian-Spanish Classes" outfit, variations on "Finally a Gay Traffic School," budget-conscious operations such as the "Ultimate Discount and Fun Safety Traffic School," and the catchall establishment that advertises itself as "Laffs & Comedy—Low Cost—AM/PM—7 Days."

Traffic offenders of the near future can, of course, be expected to take their punishment over the Internet, from on-line schools. But the DMV had a glimmer of consumer attitudes to come way back in 1986, when it handed over the job of remedial teaching to outside contractors who, being in competition with each other, have every incentive to be accommodating.

From *Real Time: Preparing for the Age of the Never Satisfied Customer* by Regis McKenna, 1997 Harvard Business Publishing. Copyright © 1997 the President and Fellows of Harvard College. All rights reserved. Used with permission.

The Conditioning of the Consumer

Choice gives the customer power. An empowered customer becomes a loyal customer by virtue of being offered products and services finely calibrated to his or her needs. That amounts to a reversal of the pattern of the past, in which consumers or users of things had to arrange their lives according to the product or service desired. People had to shop during relatively limited store hours, to buy an automobile from one of the Big Three, to make phone calls from fixed locations, to treat the office computer room like a temple, approaching it only through intermediary MIS [mass information systems] priests.

The personal computer [PC] remains the most stunning marker for the transition, putting personal information and network access into the hands of consumers and reinforcing consumers' growing sense of autonomy by giving them access to ever more finely tuned information on which to base buying decisions. Personal computers surpassed television set sales in revenues in 1994, outpaced VCR unit sales in 1996, and are expected to outpace TV unit sales in 1997. At the time of the PC's invention in the 1970s, the idea of buying a low-cost computer for use by one person from a specialty retail store like Circuit City (www.circuitcity.com) seemed about as plausible as purchasing a personal aircraft or personal train from Sears Roebuck (www.sears.com) or JCPenney (www.jcpenney.com).

Yet the conditioning of the new empowered consumer, expecting more or less instant gratification, took place at a steady pace over many decades. Most middle-aged adults probably have some equivalent of my first glimpse of the possibilities of real time. One summer in the early 1950s, I remember racing with my friends down to the new dry cleaner in town, in whose window flashed a big red neon sign announcing, "One Hour Shirt Cleaning." Amazed at the efficiency, we stuck our noses against the glass to watch the astonishing maneuvers of the automatic shirt-pressing machine.

Like every other technology-toned consumer, I have in the intervening years come to take for granted other marvels of compressed time: direct-dial telephone and fax services for communicating almost anywhere in the world; packages delivered overnight, with the bonus of being able to discover, at almost any time of day, the whereabouts of a parcel in transition with an 800 call to a customer service representative or with track-it-yourself software. Other time-compressed, mind-altering technologies include instantaneous, worldwide news from CNN, pagers, cellular phones, mobile and wireless computing, video conferencing, and instant credit card verification with the swipe of a plastic card through a machine.

The expanding expectations of choice characteristic of the new consumer are one effect of growing time pressure. To the time-conscious shopper, the most generous possible menu of purchase options offering several different price-points cuts down on time spent driving around hunting and comparison shopping. Category-killing, price-sensitive retail chains like Wal-Mart (www.wal-mart.com) and "warehouse clubs" like Price-Costco (www.wal-pricecostco.com) and Sam's Club (www.samsclub.com) serve the needs of discount-minded and low-income shoppers who want to pile up the largest number of bargains with the smallest outlay of time and effort. Pier 1 Imports (www.pier1.com) actually urges shoppers to take home a piece of rattan furniture or a dhurrie rug and try it out. It wants to encourage would-be buyers put off by not having the time to make the perfect selection and afraid of making a costly mistake. The no-questions-asked, hassle-free policies for exchanging or returning goods pioneered by stores like Nordstrom in the early 1980s are similarly motivated.

Yet even these leaders in serving the new consumer's needs have little cause to relax into smug self-congratulation. Today's consumers are made more aware by modern communications, they have more choice, they are more diverse and mobile; yet the pace of life has also made them more discontented. As a result, the American consumer's demands on the supplier appear, for all the world, to be increasing exponentially.

The New Consumer Is Never a Satisfied Consumer

A 1995 report in *Fortune* (http://pathfinder.com/fortune) set out the results of a customer satisfaction survey by the University of Michigan Business School (www.bus.umich.edu) and the American Society for Quality Control (www.asqc.org). Not even Federal Express—"a service star"—earned a rating above 85 on a scale of 0 to 100. (Although Dole Foods, purveyor of pineapple rings and other packaged consumables, did earn a top score of 90. See www.dole5aday.com.) According to the report:

> "(I Can't Get No) Satisfaction" is the theme song of consumers who clearly believe the nation's companies are doing a lousy job of meeting their needs.... Many of the losers on the list are champs in both size and reputation. Citicorp [www.citicorp.com] has the most advanced ATM system in the world and a global strategy as ambitious as Coca-Cola's [www.cocacola.com]. But consumers find banking there anything but refreshing.... Nordstrom [www.nordstrom.com], famous for taking shoppers by the hand, is not the crowd pleaser you might think, either: The department store barely broke 80.

Companies with the clearest view of the new consumer's time-conscious mental landscape that are willing to adapt their modus operandi to its features will have the edge over their competition.

New consumers expect from organizations if not obeisance then, at the very least, the respect accorded an equal. Traditional business language reveals a different attitude on the part of managers, who have unthinkingly referred to marketing "targets" slotted into market "segments" of people with wants and needs assumed to be virtually identical. Consumers have been thought of in terms of classification statistics—"30–40 age bracket, $70,000–$100,000 income range, 2.5 children, 2.5 cars"—or categories—such as DINKS (dual income, no kids)—to be manipulated into desiring the goods or services a company has to purvey. The general idea has been that if you could name it, classify it, and put it in a database, you had half the marketing problem solved. These practices are symptomatic of an obsession with measurement in the interests of control (over the partitioned groups).

The other half of the misguided marketing equation has dictated that dealing with individual consumers is a waste of time. And time is money. Therefore, the argument goes, it is necessary to classify consumers into large monolithic groups and address them as if they all think and act alike. While this approach may have been expedient in the age of mass marketing, it is unlikely to survive the reign of the new consumer.

A New Model to Fit the New Consumer

The new marketing model reflects a shift from monologue to dialogue in dealings with customers. The result is a reversal of traditional consumer and producer roles, with the consumer dictating exactly how he or she would like to be served. New consumers expect to be asked about their individual preferences and treated—to the most extreme degree possible—as if these preferences are being respected.

A pioneering example of the consultative approach in action is the way Philips Electronics N.V. (www.philips.com), the Dutch multinational giant, developed an on-line product for children in the early 1990s. Philips dispatched industrial designers, cognitive psychologists, anthropologists, and sociologists in mobile vans to communities in Italy, France, and the Netherlands. The researchers invited adults and children to brainstorm ideas for new electronics products. Instead of conducting a survey of these volunteer product designers, Philips arranged discussions in which specialists and customers imagined new possibilities. After examining all the propositions the dialogues produced, Philips reduced them to a short list, then chose one new interactive product. In the next stage, the researchers revisited the communities and tested the new product idea on the same children whose aid had been enlisted.

The gains to be had from consulting consumers in this fashion are also demonstrated by a progressive Parisian designer of women's clothes, Emanuel Ungaro, which licenses a line of garments to Gruppo GFT, which in turn distributes them in America. The "relaxed career wear" bearing the Emanuel label has been one of the few upscale collections in the business to thrive in a shrinking market, the result of an apparent decline in women's interest in high-fashion clothing. Analyzing Emanuel's success in a report on the garment industry, the *New York Times* said in 1996:

> In fashion, manufacturers usually rely on intuition and on feedback from retailers. Instead, Emanuel executives went right to customers, in suburbs as well as cities. "We're doing a lot more analysis today than we did in the past because now the customer wants to tell the designer what she wants," said Maura de Vischier, chief executive of Emanuel.

TQM [total quality management] supplies the model. Enlightened companies invite customers to sit on advisory boards, work as partners in the refinement of specifications and testing, share benchmark data, and fine-tune the balance of supply and demand. Customers have an equal say in such areas as design and inventory management. Customers—like vendors—are treated like partners.

Caution: Slow-Moving Vehicles Ahead

In addition to such exemplary exercises in paying attention to market feedback as displayed by Philips and Emanuel, recent history supplies cautionary tales about companies taking the opposite tack. German automaker Porsche (www.porsche.be), for instance, lost 80 percent of its share of the American luxury car market to Japanese rivals in just five years in the late 1980s and early 1990s. Until the company ran into trouble, it refused to lower its prices—even over a period in which the dollar lost more than half its value against the mark.

Both Porsche and Mercedes (www.daimler-benz.com) mistakenly believed that the appeal of brand exclusivity—and in the case of Mercedes, outstanding engineering—gave them license to price as they pleased. In 1990 I attended a J. D. Power conference at which the keynote address was delivered by the director of marketing for Mercedes America. He boasted that while other automakers were lowering prices and so devaluing their brands, Mercedes would soon announce even more expensive models. Only a few months later, Lexus appeared on the scene, forcing Mercedes to modify its pricing and change many of its other entrenched marketing practices. But a great deal of damage had been done. Daimler-Benz lost almost $4 billion in 1995.

In Porsche's case, large portions of its potential market, in which baby boomers were heavily represented, were starting families and rapidly switching from deluxe cars to minivans or buying the smart new Lexus. In addition, the government slapped on new luxury sales and gas taxes, and the economy was in a recession. Finally, with Porsche in the red and its unit sales dropping steeply, the company, like Mercedes, was sufficiently humbled to introduce new cars with more modest tags. The result was a dramatic increase in sales by 1997. Porsche's slow response was almost catastrophic and its market share growth much slower. Brand name was no protection.

Companies poorly oriented to the technology-toned consumer's changing behavioral terrain often describe their preferences in clever-sounding terms derived from interpretations of research rather than interactive information. But the properly oriented company will set itself the goal of understanding the consumer through dialogue. It knows that customers bombarded with sales propositions that do not reflect responsiveness to their needs will increasingly react with Procrustean fury or, worse, fatal indifference.

Real time marketing permits the constant updating of information about consumers' likes and dislikes; communications and computer technologies are now closely meshed for a constant exchange of information between distributors, retailers, and customers. Networks of this sort already exist and register rapidly changing consumer wishes. Computer-based design and manufacturing technologies are allowing companies to go even further, actually responding to those wishes with fiercely compressed product cycles and processes that incorporate more options and variety.

Virtual Customization Through Service

The fact is, now that the technological means for enormous flexibility exist, what customers expect is customization or personalization of some kind. The costs of customizing manufactured goods are falling steadily as technical refinements and managerial innovations allow flexible production plants with short runs to get closer to the low unit costs of long mass production runs. Undifferentiated manufactured goods are a steadily diminishing proportion of the output of advanced economies.

Manufacturers like Levi Strauss (www.levi.com) have been lighting the way to the future: since 1995, Levi's sales clerks have taken the measurements of women shopping for jeans and entered the numbers into computers that calculate fit. The customized jeans are sewn at a Levi's factory from a computer-generated pattern. A shoe-store chain, the Custom Foot, (www.thecustomfoot.com) lets women design their own shoes, using a three-dimensional foot scanner. Variety, when it is broad enough, can amount to virtual customization—whether in the form of products actually sitting on retail shelves or capable of being ordered directly from the factory in a quantity of one.

From the consumer's viewpoint, individual attention also amounts to virtual customization. For instance, though doctors and lawyers usually draw on the same database of knowledge—a combination of their training and experience—to serve patients or clients, they apply that knowledge to specific clients in specific ways, tailored to individual needs. Every ulcer patient may be prescribed the same drug and dietary regimen, but feels as if he or she has received customized attention.

Unfortunately, health care today is being driven by health care maintenance organizations (HMOs), which are degrading patient care to a one-prescription-fits-all commodity business. Consumers are becoming increasingly dissatisfied with the severe constraints on choice of physicians; cumbersome procedures for treatment approval, endless paperwork, and red tape associated with their health insurance. This approach to service will eventually fail because it violates the basic tenets of good service: interaction, a willingness to listen on the part of the service provider, customized responsiveness, and real time.

Real time technology holds the potential for restoring substance and meaning to the care in health care. I have been a diabetic for more than forty years. In that span of time, I have been able to take advantage of specialized new products and medical technologies—everything from a huge and growing range of sugar-free foods to pen-size, thirty-second test glucose monitors to a miniature pump that acts as an electronic pancreas supplying insulin twenty-four hours a day whenever and wherever I need it. I frequently correspond via e-mail with my doctor, Joe Prendergast. A practicing diabetologist for more than twenty-five years, he runs the Endocrine Metabolic Medical Centre (EMMC) in Atherton, California (www.diabeteswell.com).

EMMC is a model of futuristic responsiveness in health care. Its operation is guided by the findings of the Diabetic Control and Complications Trial, released in 1993. This study showed that any improvement in blood glucose control reduced the risk of the various complications associated with the disease. EMMC has been conducting an experiment with Caresoft, a Silicon Valley startup (www.caresite.com), to help a subset of its patients who are having trouble maintaining their blood glucose levels within desired ranges and happen to be connected to the Internet. Caresoft has developed "condition management" software that enables clinic staff to assist such patients, directly and proactively, over the Internet in a secure environment. "Data are the key to control," says Dr. Prendergast. Hence diabetics upload data from their digital glucose monitoring devices and transmit these to the care givers, and in return they get recommendations and reminders from the system, and instant feedback on actions to take from the care giver.

While the number of patients in this pilot project is small, preliminary results show a marked improvement in their ability to control their ailment. "Patient empowerment," Dr. Prendergast believes, is "probably the most philosophically exciting idea to emerge in medicine in recent years." He is trying to extend many of his findings about the effectiveness of patient power to a wider public through an organization he founded, the Pacific Medical Research Foundation. Empowerment is inextricably linked to customization.

Technology-toned consumers do not merely want a customized end product. They also require some sign that a company acknowledges their individuality in almost all of its dealings with them. Personalized greetings at a hotel—"Welcome back, Mr. McKenna, thanks for staying with us. Your favorite room is available for you"—are not the half of it. I didn't realize what heights my own expectations had reached until a remark I made to a shirt salesman earned a look of horror from my wife. "We sell lots of these," he said, pressing one selection on me. "Now why would I want to wear a shirt that everyone else is wearing?" I snapped at him reflexively.

A similarly harsh and thoroughly contemporary attitude is expressed in the *New York Times* report on the garment industry, mentioned above:

> Walk through the Macy's in Herald Square and experience the world of a lab mouse. Go to the contemporary department, home to shiny sheath dresses and polyester hip huggers, and realize that a coat to wear over them means a trip to another floor. Like that suit and want a nice scarf to wear with it? Trek downstairs to accessories. Over at coats, an indifferent sales clerk, punching sales tags into the computer with all the enthusiasm of a child being immunized, should not be asked to recommend a nice pair of matching boots. They will be nowhere nearby.

New customers want to feel that they have the ear of employees with the authority to make swift decisions and, increasingly, that they can reach someone who can take action. The most progressive companies allow customers access to huge corporate product-related and service databases. Today an 800 number is even printed on a package of M&M's (1-800-627-7852) and a bar of Hershey's chocolate (1-800-468-1714). Some companies have already taken the step of printing the address of their Web site on their products (Pepsi is an example: www.pepsi.com), thereby providing the consumer with a gateway to galaxies of information. Information provided at a hypothetical M&M's site, for instance, could range from a graphical demonstration or video of how the candy is manufactured to research information about the profiles of people who prefer eating green M&M's to red ones. Some day a customer with a malfunctioning electric toaster will be able to download diagrams demonstrating troubleshooting procedures—unless she decides to return or exchange the appliance and is instructed as to how to go about this painlessly over the Internet or by fax.

Making Choice Transparent

Above all, what the new consumers want is control, which chiefly means choice, even if they are not sufficiently conscious of that desire for control (or choice) to be capable of expressing it in a focus group. They want not only the widest array of choices but a choice among choice-making routes.

One route, for instance, would spare people the burden of choosing at all. Someone wanting this option might share the opinion of Natan Sharansky, a member of the Israeli Knesset, who after nine years in Soviet prisons and labor camps complained of feeling lost in the West. Forced to make "thousands of mundane choices [about] all these kinds of orange juice and cereals," he said, "[y]ou lose your life in all these things. Your life becomes very shallow." Precisely that sentiment is echoed at the start of the 1996 film *Trainspotting*, adapted from the novel of the same name, about young, heroin-addicted Scottish dropouts. A voiceover conveys the disgust the main character, Mark Renton, feels over the commercial rituals of modern society:

> Choose life. Choose a job.... Choose a ... big television, choose washing machines, cars, compact disc players and electrical tin openers.... Choose fixed-interest mortgage repayments. Choose a starter home.... Choose leisurewear and matching luggage. Choose a three-piece suit ... in a range of ... fabrics.... Choose your future. Choose life.

For Renton, the burden of choice is overwhelming, but there are constructive new alternatives to his drug-induced oblivion. In 1996, Rates Technology of Long Island patented a telecommunications device that can automatically select the cheapest carrier—among all carriers nationwide, a total of 867 at the time—for every long-distance call placed. As soon as a phone number is punched in, the computerized processor scans all the rates of all the carriers before it makes its selection.

Choice ultimately becomes transparent to the user, by virtue of either an easy-to-use interface or simple familiarity. Transparency means never having to say, "Damnit!" When information is available at the touch of a fingertip, you have transparency. Software developed by the Colorado start-up Netdelivery enables publishers of catalogs, newspapers, newsletters, and any sort of material that requires constant updating to be placed on a subscriber's computer automatically without the user phoning, searching, clicking, or downloading. Transparency! Using such software delivers your daily financial newsletter or Lands' End catalog to the desktop—always current, prices, pictures, and all (www.netdelivery.com). The most successful transparent human interface is the simple, twelve-button alphanumeric telephone keypad, which offers an almost infinite choice of communication links—not just to other owners of telephones but to information services and directories—with the user exerting little thought or effort.

For the majority who actually enjoy being offered a choice, the options provided by real time technology will be unprecedented. The person buying a car, probably long before he or she visits a showroom to kick actual tires and take a test drive, will have done these things "virtually," in some sense, through on-line services. The potential buyer will have browsed through comparative data and the Web site of, say, *Consumer Reports* (www.consumer.org); J. D. Power & Associates (www.JDPower.com), the organization that monitors automobile trends and performance; or the Consumer Information Center at www.pueblo.gsa.gov. Nationally distributed car magazines have Web sites, as do brokers stocked with vast reservoirs of data about the relative costs and benefits of purchasing and leasing. There are Internet bulletin boards linking de facto communities of owners of different makes and models of cars, through which additional help and advice can be sought.

A friend of mine recently purchased a new minivan after using the Internet to gather data and a fax machine to send out requests for bids to dealers. She said it was the "best and most efficient experience I have ever had of buying a car." The automobile business is being reshaped from the bottom up by the discovery of exactly this sort of potential. "The consumer-driven marketplace is changing the heart and soul of this industry," Dave Power, J. D. Power & Associates founder, told me. "The franchise retail system is a hundred years old! Things have to change. The whole system is broken."

Today's leaders—embryonic real time organizations—are already putting in place the managerial and technical infrastructure to give consumers more information and assistance, making choice as easy as possible. They understand the edge this gives them with customers pressured on all fronts: putting in longer work days to stay ahead of the competition or to assuage fears of downsizing; straining to find time to spend with children and equally harassed mates; longing for increasingly scarce leisure time or the time to simply get chores done.

All Information Superhighways Lead to Service

Companies have long competed largely through building brand names—sowing desirable associations in the minds of potential customers with advertising slogans, discounts, and promotions. Customers have been treated like clay to be molded into loyal brand buyers. Today's enlightened company understands that lasting brand loyalty is won only one way: by dynamically *serving* customers. Here *dynamic* means constant interaction and dialogue based on real time information systems.

Real time service is the key to winning the hearts and minds of new consumers, with their seemingly reset circadian clocks. It means being in touch all the time, creating an experience, adding information that addresses individual needs and circumstances, responding without delay, and gaining valuable feedback for new and improved offerings.

Internet enthusiasts eagerly await access to devices that will allow them to be on-line without interruption—or, in the telling phrase they use, "turned on" twenty-four hours a day. Rising businesses aiming to excel in the real time arena have as their goal ubiquitous, nonstop, and transparent service.

The new consumers hate to be kept waiting and are being conditioned, in all spheres of life, to become ever more impatient. "The advances of technology contradict theories of human satisfaction expounded by . . . psychoanalysis," Nobel Prize-winning novelist Nadine Gordimer observes. "Apart from its purely sexual application, Sigmund Freud's deferred pleasure as a refinement of emotional experience does not compare with the immediate joy of hearing a lover's voice, or getting a friend's reply to a letter at once by e-mail."

As I have noted elsewhere, what customers want most from a product is often qualitative and intangible: it is the benefit and service that is integral to the product. Service is not an event; it is the process of creating a customer environment of information, assurance, and comfort. Technology has made it possible to establish such an environment with unprecedented finesse. Many companies are using call centers, kiosks, 800 numbers, expert software, and online services to meld marketing and technology, creating a feedback loop that binds their best interests to those of their customers. This circuit has immensely enhanced sensitivity to customers' requirements and to many of their preoccupations with information and service, most of which have a time-related component.

From its earliest days, the world's leading microprocessor company, Intel, discussed plans for future models of microchips with designer-engineers at customer companies, such as computer makers. As Dave House, a former senior vice president at Intel, explained to me, by blending marketing and engineering, the company has been able to achieve a faster return on investment in new products. Working closely with key customers on specifications—balancing prototype products' technical capabilities against customers' receptivity to new features and requirements—Intel has developed a remarkable relationship with those customers, who are then primed to use the products they helped design. As with Philips and the children who participated in its brainstorming meetings, or the customers of the fashion design firm Emanuel, the consultees not only help to make salable products but become potential buyers of them.

This sort of intimate dialogue between a company and its customers creates a brand loyalty immeasurably deeper than catchy jingles riding on advertising blitzes ever could. It creates a quasi-symbiotic tie. The new interactive technologies collapse the space between consumer and producer. The extraordinary attentiveness to customers' desires by companies using these tools leads their customers to expect a similar response from other companies.

The galloping expectations of the technology-toned consumer can be expected to gain velocity as an electronic infrastructure allowing intensifying interactivity between producers and customers spreads wider. This is the infrastructure composed of the communication revolution's profusion of linked media. Collectively, these media represent a critical watershed. For businesses and branches of government serving the public, the important media of the past were channels for broadcast. The vital new media, by contrast, are channels of access.

Access media hold the key to satisfying the consumer's runaway demands for real time results. This is because access media help organizations serve customers better by making it possible for customers to serve *themselves*. Without any sense of effort, customers are satisfied by means of sophisticated, hidden, or "transparent" technologies about whose workings they need know nothing.

The Real Time Message

New consumers are never satisfied consumers. Managers hoping to serve them must work to eliminate time and space constraints on service. They must push the technological bandwidth with interactive dialogue systems—equipped with advanced software interfaces—in the interest of forging more intimate ties with these consumers. Managers must exploit every available means to obtain their end: building self-satisfaction capabilities into services and products and providing customers with access anytime, anywhere.

Jack Trout with Steve Rivkin

NO

The Power of Simplicity

Simplicity

Why People Fear It So Much

> Simple Simon met a pieman going to the fair.
> Said Simple Simon to the pieman,
> Let me see your ware.
> Says the pieman to Simple Simon,
> Show me first your penny.
> Says Simple Simon to the pieman,
> Indeed, I have not any.
>
> —Mother Goose

Through the years, being called "simple" was never a plus. And being called "simpleminded" or a "simpleton" was downright negative. It meant you were stupid, gullible, or feebleminded. It's no wonder that people fear being simple.

We call it the curse of "Simple Simon."

When psychologists are asked about this fear, they get a little more complex. (Not surprising.) Psychologist John Collard of the Institute of Human Relations at Yale University described seven kinds of common fears. (All of us have some of them.)

1. Fear of failure
2. Fear of sex
3. Fear of self-defense
4. Fear of trusting others
5. Fear of thinking
6. Fear of speaking
7. Fear of being alone

It would appear that not being simple—or not seeking simple solutions—stems from number 5, "fear of thinking."

The problem is that instead of thinking things through for ourselves, we rely on the thinking of others. (This is why the worldwide management consulting business is expected to grow to about $114 billion by the year 2000.)

Says Dr. Collard: "Not only is it hard work to think, but many people fear the activity itself. They are docile and obedient and easily follow suggestions put forward by others, because it saves them the labor of thinking for themselves. They become dependent on others for headwork, and fly to a protector when in difficulty."

From *The Power of Simplicity: A Management Guide to Cutting Through the Nonsense and Doing Things Right* by Jack Trout with Steve Rivkin. Copyright © 1999 by McGraw-Hill Companies. Reprinted with permission of The McGraw-Hill Companies.

This fear of thinking is having a profound impact in the business of news. Some even wonder whether it has much of a future.

Columnist Richard Reeves suggests that "the end of news" may be near. The avalanche of news about the rapid changes of modern life is turning people off. Audiences "do not want complicated and emotionally complex stories that remind them of their own frustrations and powerlessness."

Reeves is probably right about the growing avoidance of complexity. People don't want to think.

That's why simplicity has such power. By oversimplifying a complex issue, you are making it easy for people to make a decision without too much thought. Consider the complex trial of O. J. Simpson and how Johnnie Cochran put the essence of his argument into one memorable line: "If the glove doesn't fit, you must acquit."

"Make your scandals complex and you can beat the rap everytime," says speechwriter Peggy Noonan referring to Whitewater, which, unlike Watergate, lacked the easily grasped story line that people want.

But psychologist Dr. Carol Moog comes at the problem from another vantage point. She states that in our culture there's a "paranoia of omission." There's a sense that you have to cover all your options because you could be attacked at any moment. You can't miss anything or it could be fatal to your career.

In other words, if you have only one idea and that idea fails, you have no safety net. And because we are so success-driven, it magnifies the number one fear, "fear of failure."

You feel naked with a simple idea. A variety of ideas enables a person to hedge his or her bets.

Our general education and most management training teach us to deal with every variable, seek out every option, and analyze every angle. This leads to maddening complexity. And the most clever among us produce the most complex proposals and recommendations.

Unfortunately, when you start spinning out all kinds of different solutions, you're on the road to chaos. You end up with contradictory ideas and people running in different directions. Simplicity requires that you narrow the options and return to a single path.

Dr. Moog also had some interesting observations about buzzwords. To her, a management buzzword is like a movie star with whom we fall in love.

The buzzword comes with a beautiful book jacket and a dynamic speaker that has what we all love, charisma. Whether or not I understand this starlet isn't important, because I'm in love. And besides, people are afraid to question somebody who's a big shot or to challenge what they think is a big idea. (That's "fear of speaking.")

The best way to deal with these natural fears is to focus on the problem. It's analogous to how a ballet dancer avoids getting dizzy when doing a pirouette. The trick is to focus on one object in the audience every time your head comes around.

Needless to say, you have to recognize the right problem on which to focus.

If you're Volvo, the problem on which to focus is how to maintain your leadership in the concept of "safety" as others tries to jump on your idea.

That's pretty obvious.

But there are times when the problem isn't so obvious. Such was the case in recent years for Procter & Gamble, the world's preeminent marketer. You might assume that its problem was to find ways to sell more stuff.

The new management recognized the real problem. Does the world need 31 varieties of Head & Shoulders shampoo? Or 52 versions of Crest? As P&G's president, Durk Jager, said in *Business Week* magazine, "It's mind-boggling how difficult we've made it for consumers over the years."

As the article put it, he and CEO John Pepper realized that after decades of spinning out new-and-improved this, lemon-freshened that, and extra-jumbo-size the other thing, P&G decided it sells too many different kinds of stuff.

This solution to that problem was simple, though implementing it was a complex process. The company standardized product formulas and reduced complex deals and coupons. Gone are

27 types of promotions, including bonus packs and outlandish tactics such as goldfish giveaways to buyers of Spic & Span. (Many froze to death during midwinter shipping.) P&G also got rid of marginal brands, cut product lines, and trimmed new product launches.

So with less to sell, sales went down, right? Wrong. In hair care alone, by slashing the number of items in half, the company increased its share by 5 points.

Our friends at P&G certainly weren't afraid of simplicity. Over the past five years they've used it to increase their business by a third.

That's the power of simplicity.

Common Sense

It Can Make Things Simple

You must draw on language, logic and simple common sense to determine essential issues and establish a concrete course of action.

— Abraham Lincoln

The real antidote for fear of simplicity is common sense. Unfortunately, people often leave their common sense out in the parking lot when they come to work.

As Henry Mintzberg, professor of management at McGill University, said, "Management is a curious phenomenon. It is generously paid, enormously influential and significantly devoid of common sense."

Common sense is wisdom that is shared by all. It's something that registers as an obvious truth to a community.

Simple ideas tend to be obvious ideas because they have a ring of truth about them. But people distrust their instincts. They feel there must be a hidden, more complex answer. Wrong. What's obvious to you is obvious to many. That's why an obvious answer usually works so well in the marketplace.

One of the secrets of the buzzword gurus is to start with a simple, obvious idea and make it complex. A *Time* magazine commentary on a Stephen Covey book captured this phenomenon:

> His genius is for complicating the obvious, and as a result his books are graphically chaotic. Charts and diagrams bulge from the page. Sidebars and boxes chop the chapters into bitesize morsels. The prose buzzes with the cant phrases—empower, modeling, bonding, agent of change—without which his books would deflate like a blown tire. He uses more exclamation points than Gidget.

If you look up the dictionary definition of "common sense," you discover that it is native good judgment that is free from emotional bias or intellectual subtlety. It's also not dependent on special technical knowledge.

In other words, you are seeing things as they really are. You are following the dictates of cold logic, eliminating both sentiment and self-interest from your decision. Nothing could be simpler.

. . . [T]he new management at Procter & Gamble clearly saw the world of the supermarket as it really was: confusing. And that clarity of vision led management to the simple, commonsense strategy of simplifying things.

Consider this scenario. If you were to ask 10 people at random how well a Cadillac would sell if it looked like a Chevrolet, just about all they would say is, "Not very well."

These people are using nothing but common sense in their judgment. They have no data or research to support their conclusion. They also have no technical knowledge or intellectual subtlety. To them a Cadillac is a big expensive car and a Chevrolet is a smaller inexpensive car. They are seeing things as they really are.

But at General Motors, rather than seeing the world as it is, those in charge would rather see it as they want it to be. Common sense is ignored and the Cimarron is born. Not surprisingly, it didn't sell very well. (And we're being kind.)

Was this a lesson learned? It does not appear to be so. GM is now back with the Catera, another Cadillac that looks like a Chevrolet. Like its predecessor, it probably won't sell very well because it makes no sense. You know it and I know it. GM doesn't want to know it.

Leonardo da Vinci saw the human mind as a laboratory for gathering material from the eyes, ears, and other organs of perception—material that was then channeled through the organ of common sense. In other words, common sense is a sort of supersense that rides herd over our other senses. It's supersense that many in business refuse to trust.

Maybe we should correct that. You don't have to just be in business to ignore simple common sense. Consider the complex world of economists, a group that works hard at outwitting simple common sense.

There is nothing economists enjoy more than telling the uninitiated that plain evidence of the senses is wrong. They tend to ignore the human condition and declare that people are "maximizers of utility." In econo-talk we become "calculators of self-interest." To economists, if we all have enough information we will make rational decisions.

Anyone who's hung around the marketing world for a while realizes that people are quite irrational at times. Right now, we're overrun by four-wheel-drive vehicles designed to travel off the road. Does anybody ever leave the road? Less than 10 percent. Do people need these vehicles? Not really. Why do they buy them? Because everyone else is buying them. How's that for "rational"?

The world cannot be put into mathematical formulas. It's too irrational. It's the way it is.

Now some words about intellectual subtlety.

A company often goes wrong when it is conned with subtle research and arguments about where the world is headed. (Nobody really knows, but many make believe they know.) These views are carefully crafted and usually mixed in with some false assumptions disguised as facts.

For example, many years ago Xerox was led to believe that in the office of the future everything—phones, computers, and copiers—would be an integrated system. (Bad prediction.) To play in this world, you needed to offer everything. Thus Xerox needed to buy or build computers and other noncopier equipment to offer in this on-rushing automated world.

Xerox was told it could do this because people saw the company as a skilled, high-technology company. (This was a false assumption. People saw it as a copier company.)

Twenty years and several billion dollars later, Xerox realized that the office of the future is still out in the future. And any Xerox machine that can't make a copy is in trouble. It was a painful lesson in technical knowledge and intellectual subtlety overwhelming good judgment.

Finally, some thoughts about a business school education, which seems to submerge common sense.

By the time students finish their first year, they already have an excellent command of the words and phrases that identify them as MBA wanna-bes. They have become comfortably familiar with jargon like "risk/reward ratio", "discounted cash flow", "pushing numbers", "expected value", and so forth.

After a while, all this uncommon language overwhelms critical thought and common sense. You get the appearance of deliberation where none may exist.

Ross Perot, in a visit to the Harvard Business School, observed, "The trouble with you people is that what you call environmental scanning, I call looking out the window."

To think in simple, commonsense terms you must begin to follow these guidelines:

1. **Get your ego out of the situation**. Good judgment is based on reality. The more you screen things through your ego, the farther you get from reality.

2. **You've got to avoid wishful thinking**. We all want things to go a certain way. But how things go are often out of our control. Good common sense tends to be in tune with the way things are going.

3. **You've got to be better at listening**. Common sense by definition is based on what others think. It's thinking that is common to many. People who don't have their ears to the ground lose access to important common sense.
4. **You've got to be a little cynical**. Things are sometimes the opposite of the way they really are. That's often the case because someone is pursuing their own agenda. Good common sense is based on the experiences of many, not the wishful thinking of some.. . .

Marketing

It's Turning Simple Ideas Into Strategy

Marketing, in the fullest sense, is the name of the game. So it better be handled by the boss and his line. Not staff hecklers.

— Robert Townsend *Up the Organization*

If a CEO conducts the symphony, it's marketing that oversees the arrangement of the music.

Academics have written tomes about the complexity of marketing and all its functions. Ad agencies and consultants have constructed convoluted systems for building brands. One of our favorite pieces of complexity comes from a U.K. consulting firm that claims a brand has nine positioning elements in a customer's mind: functional needs, objective effects, functional roles, attributes, core evaluators, psychological drives, psychological roles, subjective character, and psychological needs. Then the consultants turn all this into a "bridge matrix" [see Figure 1].

(Help, I'm trapped on a bridge to nowhere.)

Another piece of complexity is [what] some agency is pushing [see Figure 2].

(Help, I'm trapped in a marketing labyrinth.)

We'll give you the essence of marketing in two sentences: First, it's marketing's responsibility to see that everyone is playing the same tune in unison. Second, it's marketing's assignment to turn that tune or differentiating idea into what we call a coherent marketing direction.

The notion of a differentiating idea requires some thought. What kind of idea? Where do you find one? These are the initial questions that must be answered.

Figure 1

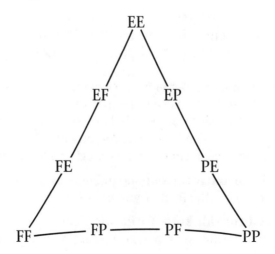

Figure 2

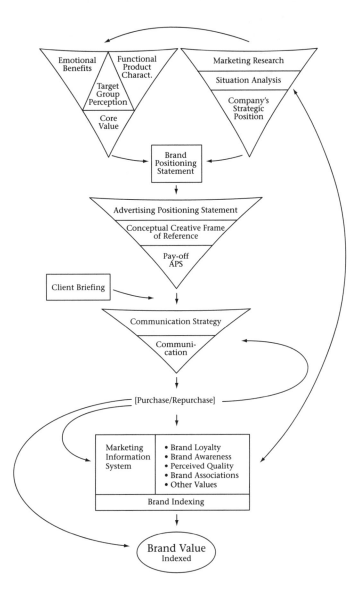

In order to help you answer these questions, we propose using the following specific definition. A differentiating idea is a *competitive mental angle*.

This kind of idea must have a *competitive* angle in order to have a chance for success. This does not necessarily mean a better product or service, but rather there must be an element of differentness. It could be smaller, bigger, lighter, heavier, cheaper, or more expensive. It could be a different distribution system.

Furthermore, the idea must be competitive in the total marketing arena, not just competitive in relation to one or two other products or services. For example, Volkswagen's decision in the late fifties to introduce the "first" small car was an excellent competitive idea. At the time General Motors was manufacturing nothing but big, heavily chromed patrol boats. The Beetle was a runaway success.

The VW Beetle was not the first small car on the market, of course. But it was the first car to occupy the "small" position in the mind. It made a virtue out of its size, while the others apologized for their small size by talking about "roominess."

"Think small," said the Volkswagen ads.

An example of a new bad idea is Volvo's sporty coupe and convertible. We see no competitive angle against BMW, Mercedes, and Audi (just to name a few).

Second, a differentiating idea must have a competitive *mental* angle. In other words, the battle takes place in the mind of the prospect.

Competitors that do not exist in the mind can be ignored. There were plenty of pizza places with home delivery operations when John Schnatter launched Papa John's. But nobody owned the "better ingredients" position in the mind.

On the other hand, there are competitors who enjoy strong perceptions that do not agree with reality. It's the perception that must be considered in the selection of an idea, not the reality.

A competitive mental *angle* is the point in the mind that allows your marketing program to work effectively. That's the point you must leverage to achieve results.

But an idea is not enough. To complete the process, you need to turn the idea into a strategy. (If the idea is a nail, the strategy is the hammer.) You need both to establish a position in the mind.

What's a strategy? A strategy is not a goal. Like life itself, a strategy ought to focus on the journey, not the goal. Top-down thinkers are goal-oriented. They first determine what it is they want to achieve, and then they try to devise ways and means to achieve their goals....

But most goals are simply not achievable. Goal setting tends to be an exercise in frustration. Marketing, like politics, is the art of the possible.

When Roger Smith took over General Motors in 1981, he predicted that GM would eventually own 70 percent of the traditional Big Three domestic car market, up from about 66 percent in 1979. To prepare for this awesome responsibility, GM began a $50 billion modernization program. Boy, was Roger wrong.

Currently, General Motors' share of the Big Three domestic market is 30 percent and falling. His goal was simply not achievable because it was not based on a sound idea.

In our definition, a strategy is not a goal. It's a *coherent marketing direction*. A strategy is *coherent* in the sense that it is focused on the idea that has been selected. Volkswagen had a big tactical success with the small car, but it failed to elevate this idea to a coherent strategy. It forgot about "small" and instead elected to bring into the U.S. market a family of big, fast, and expensive Volkswagens. But other car manufacturers had already preempted these automotive ideas. This opened the way for the Japanese to take over the small car idea.

Second, a strategy encompasses coherent *marketing* activities. Product, pricing distribution, advertising—all the activities that make up the marketing mix must be coherently focused on the idea. (Think of a differentiating idea as a particular wavelength of light and the strategy as a laser tuned to that wavelength. You need both to penetrate the mind of the prospect.)

Finally, a strategy is a coherent marketing *direction*. Once the strategy is established, the direction shouldn't be changed.

The purpose of the strategy is to mobilize your resources to preempt the differentiating idea. By committing all your resources to one strategic direction you maximize the exploitation of the idea without the limitation that the existence of a goal implies.

What are you looking for? You are looking for an angle—a fact, an idea, a concept, an opinion on the part of the prospect that conflicts with the positions held by your competitors.

Take laundry detergents, for example. What does detergent advertising suggest that customers are looking for? Cleanliness. That's why Tide gets clothes "white." Cheer gets clothes "whiter than white." And Bold goes all the way to "bright."

Did you ever watch a person take clothes out of a dryer? If you read the ads, you might think he or she puts on sunglasses so the glare won't ruin the eyes.

In fact, most people hardly look at the clothes at all. But they almost always smell them to see if they smell "fresh." This observation led Unilever to introduce Surf, a detergent whose sole distinguishing characteristic is that it contains twice as much perfume as the competition. *Result*: Surf came in and grabbed a respectable piece of the $3.5 billion U.S. detergent market.

Did you ever watch a commuter buy a cup of coffee to carry on a train or bus? The commuter will often carefully rip a drinking hole in the lid so the coffee won't spill while he or she is drinking it during the trip.

Someone at the Handi-Kup Division of Dixie Products noticed. Handi-Kup introduced a plastic lid with the drinking hole built in.

Some angles are hard to spot because customers express them in the negative. The Adolph Coors Company invented light beer. (Even today there are fewer calories in regular Coors than in Michelob Light.) Yet Coors ignored its own invention until Miller introduced Lite beer.

It was hard to ignore. Before Lite saw the light of day, any Denver bartender could have told you how their customers ordered a Coors. "Give me a Colorado Kool-Aid."

Coors could have preempted the light category with a major advertising program. It didn't. Miller did. So Miller Lite became the first successful light beer.

Most angles are hard to spot because they almost never look like big winners in advance. (If they did, others would already be using them.) Marketing bombshells burst very quickly.

"Great ideas," said Albert Camus, "come into the world as gently as doves. Perhaps then, if we listen attentively, we shall hear amid the uproar of empires and nations a faint flutter of wings, the gentle stirring of life and hope." . . .

When you saw your first bottle of Lite beer, did you say, "This brand is going to become one of the biggest-selling beers in America"? Or did you say, "Here's another Gablinger's"? (The first low calorie beer.)

When you saw the first Toys "R" Us store, did you say, "This is going to be a $10 billion business selling one-fourth of all the toys in America"? Or did you say to yourself, "Why did they make the letter R backward?"

Did you buy a McDonald's franchise in 1955 when it would have cost you all of $950? Or did you wait in line saying to yourself, "How can they make money selling hamburgers for 15 cents?"

Did you buy Xerox stock in 1958? Andy Warhol soup cans in 1968? A condo in Manhattan in 1979?

Did you save your baseball cards? Your Superman comic books?

Opportunities are hard to spot because they don't look like opportunities. They look like angles—a lighter beer, a more expensive car, a cheaper hamburger, a store that sells only toys. Marketing's responsibility is to take that angle or idea and build it into a strategy so as to unleash its power.

Market leader Pizza Hut could have neutralized one or two Papa John's "better ingredients" delivery units. With the strategy of expanding into a nationwide chain of better ingredient delivery units, Papa John's effectively drove a powerful wedge into the competition. It is first into the mind with this idea.

The idea dictates the strategy. Then the strategy drives the idea. To say that one is more important than the other is to miss the essence of the process. It's the relationship between the two that is the crucial aspect of marketing success.

What's more important in aircraft design: the engine or the wing? Neither. It's the relationship between the two that determines whether your design will get off the runway.

The idea differentiates your business from your competitor's. Strategy gives wing to the idea that can make your business soar.

POSTSCRIPT

Has the "Keep It Simple" Concept Become "All Change, All the Time"?

In 1996 Proctor & Gamble (P&G) went through a drastic simplification program, recognizing that 31 varieties of Head and Shoulders shampoo and 52 varieties of Crest toothpaste were overwhelming to the average consumer. Wal-Mart has consistently used an "every day low prices" (EDLP) pricing policy to their advantage. In advertising, some of the more enduring slogans are simple and short: "Just Do It" (Nike), "Diamonds Are Forever" (DeBeers), and "Compassionate Conservative" (George W. Bush). As far as consumer behavior is concerned, a 1999 *Time* magazine cover story examined how most of us are opting for simpler celebrations in life.

We live in an era of "sound bites," and research has shown that simpler and shorter slogans are easier to process cognitively. The argument can be traced back to Claude C. Hopkins (considered the father of advertising), who, in his book *Scientific Advertising* (Chicago, 1923), advised keeping the message as simple as possible. Both David Ogilvy and Hopkins believed in caution with the use of humor in advertising, since it may overwhelm the central message differentiating the product. Conversely, Wendy's "Where's the Beef?" campaign was a humorous means of driving home the simple product advantage of the "beef-to-bun ratio."

Basically, positioning theory and, more recently, integrated marketing communications propose that the proliferation of media and exposure of consumers to exponential increases in marketing stimuli (noise) have created an overcommunicated society and a confused, oversaturated consumer. In an effort to break through this promotional jungle, the need for a single, cohesive, seamless marketing communication is the fundamental common denominator and mandate of both of these viewpoints.

McKenna focuses on the notion of *constant change* and argues that speed and innovation matter more than consistency. Furthermore, customers adapt faster than firms, so companies must "turn not on a dime but a pixel" just to keep pace. The well-received contributions of Don Peppers and Martha Rogers in terms of one-to-one marketing and mass customization lend substantial credence to McKenna's real-time concept.

Does real-time marketing necessarily imply "chaos and complications"? Does the growth of "keep-in-touch" tools like the Internet, e-mail, customer call centers, and the simultaneous decline of broadcast budgets imply the importance of real-time service? The "simple" camp might argue the importance of keeping these tools as user-friendly and uncomplicated as possible so that average customers are not confused. The users might demand something that is consistent in format and easy to read. In 1999 many major retailers (e.g., Toys 'R' Us) did not do well with e-commerce, since most of their customers were unable to easily navigate through their Web sites.

Suggested Readings

Gerrard Macintosh and James W. Gentry, "Decision Making in Personal Selling: Testing the KISS Principle," *Psychology and Marketing* (August 1999)

"Make It Simple," *Business Week* (September 9, 1996)

From *Taking Sides: Marketing.* Copyright © 2000 by The McGraw-Hill Companies, Inc. All rights reserved. Reprinted by permission of McGraw-Hill/Dushkin Publishing.

Regis McKenna, "Real Time Marketing," *Harvard Business Review* (July–August 1995)

Rachel McLaughlin, "Marketing in Real Time," *Target Marketing* (March 1999)

Christopher Meyer, *Fast Cycle Time* (Free Press, 1993)

Richard O. Oliver, Ronald T. Rust, and Sanjeev Varki, "Real-Time Marketing," *Marketing Management* (Fall 1998)

Don Peppers and Martha Rogers, *Enterprise One to One: Tools for Competing in an Interactive Age* (Doubleday/Currency, 1997)

Rosser Reeves, *Reality in Advertising* (Alfred A. Knopf, 1960)

Al Reis and Jack Trout, *Positioning: The Battle for Your Mind* (Warner Books, 1982)

Sarah Schaefer, "Have It Your Way," *Inc.* (November 18, 1997)

"Simple Marketing Hits the Mark," *Discount Store News* (October 1999)

"The Simple New Year's Eve: Why We're Saying No to the Hype and Opting for a Quiet, Meaningful Evening," *Time* (November 29, 1999)

George Stalk, Jr., and Thomas M. Hout, *Competing Against Time* (Free Press, 1990)

Michael Treacy and Fred Wiersema, *The Discipline of Market Leaders: Choose Your Customers, Narrow Your Focus, Dominate Your Market* (Addison-Wesley, 1997)

ISSUE 4

Is Relationship Marketing a Tenable Concept?

YES: Jennifer Bresnahan, from "Improving the Odds," *CIO Enterprise Magazine* (November 15, 1998)

NO: James R. Rosenfield, from "Whatever Happened to Relationship Marketing? Nine Big Mistakes," *Direct Marketing* (May 1999)

Issue Summary

YES: Law student Jennifer Bresnahan describes the new era of information technology, which enables marketers to serve every consumer, one at a time, and develop long-term mutually beneficial relationships.

NO: James R. Rosenfield, chairperson and CEO of Rosenfield & Associates, maintains that relationships in marketing are not always like those between human beings; customers want more of a one-way street. He shares "nine big mistakes" that impede successful development of marketing relationships.

Roger Dow, vice president of Marriott Hotels, has stated, "It takes five times the effort to attract a new customer as it does to keep an old one." In the context of our current information-rich empowered consumer, this claim is now likely to be terribly understated. The loss in profits from defecting customers is a revolutionary concern for marketers, and it has served as a wake-up call for relationship marketing. No longer does the average consumer habitually buy from the same car dealer. Recent reports reveal that almost 50 percent of all auto purchasers have searched the Internet for the greatest deal.

Most sources associate Leonard Berry with the first published works on relationship marketing, and in the last two decades the field has received significant attention by academicians as well as marketing practitioners. Although varied definitions of relationship marketing have been provided, it basically consists of attracting, developing, and retaining customers. The guiding principle of relationship marketing is to increase the value of a company's customer base by indentifying, tracking, and interacting with individuals and then reconfiguring products/services to meet specific needs. Thus, it is rooted in the idea of establishing a "learning relationship" with each customer—starting with those that are most valuable. An important question is, How feasible is this today? Is it really possible to build strong customer relationships when consumers are now "armed to the teeth" with competitive information and can gain alternative access to major providers at the click of a mouse?

From *Taking Sides: Marketing*. Copyright © 2000 by The McGraw-Hill Companies, Inc. All rights reserved. Reprinted by permission of McGraw-Hill/Dushkin Publishing.

While there is an apparent need and urgency for relationship marketing, its actual implementation and successful program maintenance is another question. Can every company adequately identify its end-user customers and gather the relevant information essential for the marketing plan? It is essential to differentiate customers based on their value to the company and their unique needs. The ability and willingness for customers to interact is an important consideration. Can the company actually customize its products and services based upon the available information? Finally, are customers sure to respond—will they care enough to adopt the modified offering? Certainly the development of a customer relationship program is a complex and highly integrated task. Yet the "lifetime value" of consumers over the short-term profits of building new ones serves as an important goal. The crucial tools to create these relationship opportunities are interaction and information technologies. It is fair to presume that the trend toward consumer use of these technologies will continue to experience exponential growth.

As Jennifer Bresnahan contends, marketing was the last great holdout of the technology revolution, but it has embraced this major vehicle for accomplishing new goals. She offers several examples of successful relationship marketing programs—within companies such as Charles Schwab, British Airways, Dell computers, and Eddie Bauer—and illustrates the necessity of implementing database techniques.

Unfortunately, companies can fall into the trap of collecting data only because the technology is available and then fail to analyze and apply the information in a meaningful way. *Frequency buying programs* are often misused as a tool for relationship building. The strength of the database is only as good as the marketing strategists capable of developing it into a viable and innovative marketing plan.

Another question relates to the *profitability* of maintaining customer relationships. Consumers by nature keep consistently increasing demands on their provider to at least match, if not exceed, the competition's prices, services, or added incentives to switch brands. Companies risk being forced into reacting to every new gimmick that hits the market, losing control of their own unique identity.

Despite the benefits, relationship marketing demands diligent management and perpetual caution. In the following selections, Bresnahan expresses optimism about the future of relationship marketing. In contrast, James R. Rosenfield identifies the potential hazards of pursuing this strategy, which, he argues, have resulted in the premature death of relationship marketing.

Jennifer Bresnahan **YES**

Improving the Odds

Get with the program. E-commerce, ERP [enterprise resource planning] and other temporary fashions that have recently hogged our attention are yesterday's news. The next big thing has arrived. Call it "Customer Relationship Management," "One-to-One Marketing," "Enterprise Marketing Automation" or any of the other catch phrases that have cropped up, but the coming competitive frontier is about finding, knowing and delighting customers. In the past, businesses competed by making stellar products and later by meeting the needs of the average customer. Today the goal is to know and serve every consumer, one at a time, and to build long-term, mutually beneficial relationships.

Information technology (IT) is the key to achieving customer intimacy. But the people who need to wield the key are, ironically, in the one department that hasn't yet been flattened and reshaped by the IT thumbprint: marketing. Until recently, marketing was the last great holdout of the technology revolution because technology didn't seem to address marketing's imprecise, creative mandate. In addition, marketers and IT people tended to regard each other with distrust, misunderstanding and misgivings about one another's priorities. "If you had one of these continuums on a circle, marketing and IS would probably be 180 degrees opposite each other," says John Boushy, senior vice president of IT and marketing services at the Memphis, Tenn.-based casino and entertainment company Harrah's Entertainment Inc.

But that's all changing now as marketing takes a dominant role in shaping organizations' interactions with consumers. Marketing thus becomes the company's darling and the information systems (IS) department's new best friend. Together, marketing and IS are finding innovative ways to understand and reach customers. In the process, they are discarding their ancient enmity and fundamentally reinventing the relationships between businesses and their customers. "Marketing is about designing things that meet the needs and wants of customers, and today the use of information is how you meet some of those needs," says Boushy. "So IT very much becomes the means to the marketing ends. It's like you must join these entities with Velcro."

All Grown Up: Database Marketing

The root of all IT-enabled marketing is the common database. Marketing outfits have been using databases for years to get a picture of their customers, either working with IS to leverage a companywide, huge data warehouse or creating their own simple, stovepipe database. Using data mining tools, companies can figure out which of their customers are most likely to buy a given product, respond to a certain communication medium or defect to the competition. Companies can even gauge which of their competitors' customers are ripe for the taking. This is all basic stuff. But now that IT and marketing are making a concerted effort to know and please customers, databases are becoming more strategic and even a little sexy.

Marketers have many new windows available to them for viewing the customer, and warehouses are jampacked with the additional information this provides. Besides the ubiquitous telemarketing center and direct mail campaign, companies can communicate new products, services or promotions to consumers via e-mail, Web-based product registration or customer service and

From *CIO Enterprise Magazine*, November 15, 1998 by Jennifer Bresnahan. Copyright © CIO Communications, Inc. Reprinted by permission.

community forums on the Internet. Hitachi Semiconductor (America) Inc. notes the interests and needs of its corporate customers electronically through cookies [a message given to a Web browser by a Web server, containing user information] that track their comings and goings on the site. British Airways uses basic observation as a path to customer intimacy. According to Bob Dorf, president of the Stamford, Conn.-based marketing consultancy Marketing 1 to 1/Peppers and Rogers Group, British Airways flight attendants notice what their most valuable passengers choose and then enter that into a laptop computer onboard so that the next time the passenger in seat 3B flies with the airline, she automatically receives an extra pillow or a Diet Coke with no ice, as she prefers.

Marketers are also becoming more sophisticated in their use of data warehouses, applying their results of data mining in the pursuit of customer intimacy. For example, Mary H. Kelley, vice president of database and relationship marketing at Charles Schwab & Co. Inc. in San Francisco, told the audience at the July 1998 DCI Marketing Automation conference in New York City that Charles Schwab is striving to use its data warehouse to discover how much money a customer isn't investing with Charles Schwab. "If a customer invests $10,000, we want to know if he has a million dollars elsewhere that he isn't investing with us and why not," Kelley says. Spiegel Inc.'s Redmond, Wash.-based Eddie Bauer Inc. subsidiary uses catalog sales information in its data warehouse to determine the best sites for new stores and to eliminate duplicate retail mailings to customers who shop at both retail and catalog channels, says CIO [chief information officer] Jon K. Nordeen. The $14 billion Dallas-based consumer products company Kimberly Clark Corp. uses its data warehouse in the business-to-business sector to market to its customers' customers. The company identifies individuals its distributors market to, such as the building manager of a particular company, and targets that person with mailings about the benefits of Kleenex, Scott towels and other Kimberly Clark products, says Tom Ahonen, director of business systems.

One to One

The next evolutionary step in database marketing is targeting one customer at a time. BMG Direct, the New York City-based direct marketing division of BMG Entertainment, uses its data warehouse to coordinate the 50 variations of a single promotion that are mailed out to its 8 million club members in any given period. BMG's customers are classified into 14 different musical genre preferences and further divided by length of membership. Based on those factors, each member receives different promotional offers, lists of music titles on sale and monthly featured music selections. The longer customers have been in the club, the bigger the discounts they receive. "Our entire business is dependent on our ability to segment our customers so that members receive catalogs and offers with the right kind of music, a featured selection we think they would like and at a discount level in line with their membership in the club," says Elizabeth Rose, vice president of strategic planning and electronic commerce. "There's virtually nothing we can do as marketers that doesn't have systems implications. For me, there are certain people whose phone calls I will pick up every time, and they include the top three systems guys I work with."

Harrah's is also mastering the art of one-to-one marketing. In 1997 it launched its Total Gold national guest-recognition program, which rewards loyal customers with points and complimentary offerings. When a customer swipes her Total Gold identification card at a slot machine or presents it when checking into a Harrah's hotel, the account number is transmitted to Harrah's data warehouse in Memphis, Tenn. The data warehouse sends back her detailed history to the casino property and alerts the property employees via an electronic pager or a PC screen that this customer needs to be welcomed. "When an Atlantic City customer who's never been to Las Vegas goes there and inserts a Total Gold card into a slot machine, within seven seconds we know who that customer is and make sure that information is accessible in Las Vegas," says Boushy. The program engenders such loyalty that in its first four months, from September through December 1997, there was a 60 percent increase in customers that chose Harrah's when traveling to a new casino over the same time period before the Total Gold card program was started and has continued through August 1998. The Vegas property almost doubled its cross-market visitation (Atlantic City customers going to Las Vegas and vice-versa) revenue, and cross-market play overall increased by more than $16 million, says Boushy.

Cleveland-based KeyCorp uses its data warehouse to cross-sell new products to existing customers, says former Vice President of Direct Marketing Jonathan T. Hill. For example, if the warehouse "notices" that a customer is buying a lot of home improvement products, it may suggest to a customer service representative that he offer the customer a low-interest-rate home equity loan. This capability in itself isn't particularly new. But Key has taken it a step further and now generates customer leads without any human intervention. At the end of a customer call to the bank's voice response unit, the system automatically informs the customer that she's been approved for a home equity loan and asks if she'd like to receive an application. "I was afraid they'd hear [the voice response unit] and hang up, but that's not what's been happening at all," says Allen J. Gula, chairman and CEO of Key Services, the IS arm of KeyCorp. "We've had better success than we ever thought we would."

Enter the Internet

More than anything, the Internet has precipitated the trend toward one-to-one marketing. It is certainly the most economical way to communicate with customers, says Tom Haas, vice president of consulting at Hunter Business Direct Inc., because it only costs about 5 cents to e-mail a customer, compared with as much as $5 for direct mail, $8 to $24 for telephone sales and $40 to $400 for a field call from a sales rep. And it's definitely faster. Planning and executing a traditional marketing campaign used to take three months; today it can be done over the Internet in four hours, says Hal Steger, vice president of marketing at enterprise marketing-automation vendor Rubric Inc. in San Mateo, Calif.

The $15.2 billion computer giant Dell Computer Corp. of Round Rock, Texas, uses the Internet to provide key customers with personalized Premier Web pages. Sitting inside Dell's firewall, the pages contain product, technical and industry information of interest to the particular customer. By taking advantage of this innovation, the customer doesn't have to waste time trying to find what it needs among Dell's reams of information, and Dell gets a more loyal customer, says Joe Marengi, senior vice president and general manager of the relationship group at Dell. Customers can communicate with their Dell account team and buy additional products online. Dell even coordinates discounted employee purchase programs through the customized page. Executives on the customer side can use the site to look at their company's entire order history.

Hitachi has gone a step further, actually allowing customers to download sample products for use in product simulations. In the past, Hitachi's customers had to buy a semiconductor device and range through mountains of paper documentation to see how it worked in the electronic equipment they were building. But now they will have the ability to download technical "CAE/CAD [computer-aided engineering/computer-aided design] symbols" from Hitachi's extranet that summarize how the product works, and they can use that information for testing in computer simulations. "In the past you would have to buy it, have some administrative people put in those footprints manually and then import it into your CAD system," says Jim Rey, director of marketing communication. "Now it's a matter of going to your Web site and downloading it." The result may be fewer actual purchases upfront, but in the long run Rey expects this capability to win Hitachi more customers. Eventually, Hitachi will expand this extranet offering to the public Internet, he says.

The BMG Music Service Web site is linked to its data warehouse. As soon as a customer logs onto the site, the page automatically reconfigures to reflect the customer's musical preferences and account history. BMG music customers receive different prices and music selections and can use the Web site to refuse a featured selection, which otherwise is automatically sent. Customers can also search 12,000 titles of music (20 times as many as listed in BMG's paper catalogs), listen to sound samples, view account history, submit customer service transactions, change listening preferences and, for classical club members, submit questions to BMG's music editors. In addition to the customer loyalty it fosters, BMG's Web site enables the company to learn from and react to customer preferences in a timely manner, says Rose. Prior to the site, by the time marketing received a comment or knew how well a particular musical selection or promotion did, it was already working on several mailings down the line. But now they can analyze response rates and individual preferences for each marketing campaign and make adjustments more quickly to upcoming mailings.

Internal Affairs

To rise to the challenge of leading the rest of the company into the new customer-centered paradigm, marketing must get itself in shape. Many software vendors have created programs that automate such basic internal marketing tasks as lead generation and campaign management.. . . And marketing is increasingly turning to IS to integrate its various data sources to yield a complete picture of the customers. The Internet is also helping marketers coordinate as teams. For example, Charles Schwab's Schweb intranet allows 300 Schwab marketers around the country to access the company's aggregate customer information from the data warehouse and perform simple point-and-click customer queries. They can find out who their best customers are and offer discounts, for example, or generate lead lists for a particular campaign. In the past, when marketers wanted to draw up a list of suitable customer leads, they had to put in a request to the data analysis department. Now they can simply use their browser, says Kelley.

Unlike some of its younger competitors, Hewlett-Packard Co. (HP) of Palo Alto, Calif., enters this era of customer intimacy with baggage from the old way of thinking. Until a few years ago, HP's more than 70 business units didn't work together, nor did they care much about understanding the customer. Each operated nearly autonomously with its own marketing budgets and IS projects. Many were targeting the same customers without even knowing it, says J. Andrew Danver, senior consultant in relationship marketing at HP. Changing this mind-set to work together for a 360-degree view of the customer was no easy task. HP's marketing managers worked with IS to create an intranet site to pass the word that customer intimacy was the way to go and the only way to get there was to become more tightly integrated. The intranet, called 1:1/Relationship Marketing, contained best practice commentary, advice from consultants, a bimonthly newsletter, slide presentations, outside research and discussion groups about how and why to adopt a customer-centered mentality. Slowly but surely, the intranet is helping to change attitudes, says Danver. "It takes a long time to turn a Queen Mary around," he says.

Everyone's a Marketer

Perhaps the most important way that IT supports marketing's mission is by helping it transform the entire company into a customer-centered environment. On the front end, marketing must be able to share knowledge with sales and customer support so everybody has a complete picture of the customer. On the back end, the shop floor must be able to respond to customer demands and deliver what marketing promises, be it mass customization or the ability to track packages. Technology makes this level of integration possible.

Hitachi is among those at the forefront of this integrated company-as-marketing-unit mentality. With 33,000 different semiconductor and integrated circuit products, remembering which customer to tell about which semiconductor update is a tall order. Engineers continually come up with new products or upgrade existing ones. But now customers receive information about new products as a matter of course without any human involvement. Customers fill out a profile on the Web highlighting which products they're interested in and the information is automatically linked to Hitachi's engineering or sales departments. As the product design engineers make changes to existing products or create new semiconductor solutions, they use a standard template to enter their work into a document-management system. The system automatically routes the engineer's changes to the appropriate people in the company for approval and then e-mails it to customers who have requested related documentation online, says Rey.

Dell is probably one of the most highly integrated companies today. Starting with sales reps helping customers configure a system from scratch, every process under Dell's roof is integrated, says CIO Jerry Gregoire. First, the order-management system prevents sales reps from offering a product that can't be built. Once the customer places the order, the system immediately sends it to the shop floor to be constructed and simultaneously to Dell's procurement department and Web site. That way Dell's suppliers know a particular part was used, and the customer can track the order's delivery status. Dell's tight integration wins and retains highly lucrative customers, according to Marketing 1 to 1's Dorf. For instance, if a global company such as KPMG Peat Marwick LLP hires five actuaries in Cleveland, two consultants in Bahrain, Saudia Arabia, and one executive in Paris, each of them will receive new, uniquely configured computers that will be shipped the very next day, provided the order gets to Dell by 4 p.m. The fact that the computers arrive already loaded with the programs that each employee needs saves KPMG from having to employ an additional dozen IS employees, and the employees can be up and running faster. These extra benefits make Dell almost irreplaceable to its customers, says Dorf—the ultimate goal of customer relationship management. Or enterprise marketing automation. Or one-to-one marketing.

Whatever you call it, customer intimacy is the name of the game. And marketing is an organization's coach and clutch player all at once. Companies that figure out how to leaverage IT to build loyal, lasting relationships with consumers will be tomorrow's winners.

NO

James R. Rosenfield

Whatever Happened to Relationship Marketing? Nine Big Mistakes

Looking at my mailbox, thinking about the companies I do business with, making my consulting rounds, a thought occurs to me:

Whatever happened to relationship marketing?

Boomtown America . . . is all about getting rick quick. Customer churn seems to be regarded as a quite acceptable cost of doing business. Customer service is at an all-time low—just think about your own life as a customer. Consumers are battered, bothered, and bewildered.

None of this was supposed to happen. People like me used to predict that by the end of the century relationship marketing, abetted by information technology, would rule the world. Instead, mass marketing seems to prevail, to the point that direct mail itself has turned into a mass marketing medium.

When you look at relationship marketing efforts, the bad and the ugly seem to be driving out the good, in a sort of crazed variation of Gresham's Law. Amazon.com begins to mess up a good thing by "selling" favorable reviews, a practice it quickly backed down on, but not without some brand equity damage. The airlines beat up their best customers—on a recent three-hour Delta flight that left at 8:00 p.m., THERE WAS NO FOOD! A whole panoply of things keeps going wrong. Here are nine of them:

Mistake #1: Assuming Customers Want a Relationship

Relationships in private life are always two-way streets. But customers want more of a one-way street, with the company doing the work of nurturing and maintaining things. They don't want a relationship with us unless we make it worth their while, and unless the basis of the relationship is on the customer's terms. This becomes especially important as loyalty and frequency programs multiply, competing for the same finite pocketbooks and attention spans.

We want relationships, because we know relationships make us money. But what does the customer want?

The customer wants *solutions*. Providing solutions, rather than merely products, creates the basis for a true customer relationship.

As it stands right now, there are too many products, too few solutions. The average suburban supermarket had 8,000 products in 1978, according to the Food Marketing Institute, and over 30,000 10 years later! No one needs 30,000 products, and in fact the sheer number of choices in itself becomes a problem.

The manufacturers are taking notice. A few years back, Procter & Gamble [P&G] stunned the world by de-extending some of its product lines, a radical departure from the epidemic line extension and product proliferation of the last generation. P&G is beginning to understand that customers want solutions, and that simplification is part of the solution process.

Suggestion: Provide solutions, rather than products, and your customers will be willing to have a relationship with you.

From *Direct Marketing*, May 1999 by James R. Rosenfield. Copyright © 1999 by James R. Rosenfield. Reprinted by permission of the author.

Mistake #2: Assuming Customers Are Willing to Work

About 20 percent of American consumers seem to be addicted to the gamelike minutiae of loyalty and frequency programs. These are the same people who transfer credit card balances and switch long-distance carriers. They know how to work the system.

But the other 80 percent of consumers . . . are already working hard enough, and have no desire to put in extra work for you.

What does this mean? It means that the overly complex, difficult-to-figure-out awards schemes that now abound are beginning to turn people off. Customers are dropping out of the game, because the rules are too complicated (or have been changed in midstream—see Mistake #7).

The consumer is sending this message loud and clear: "I've lived without your rewards up until now, and I'm not willing to put in the work to master your complications."

Another example: Have you taken a good look lately at your frequent flyer statements? Most of them were designed by the Marquis de Sade. Awards are often printed in light grey mousetype, guaranteed to be unreadable, especially by the middle-aged frequent flyers who comprise the airlines' single most profitable customer segment.

Suggestion: Relationship marketing programs need to be engineered so that simplicity is built into them, and so that simplicity remains. The customer wants solutions, and simplicity is a solution.

Mistake #3: Assuming Customers Will Be Fair

You can get things right 900 times, but if you make a mistake on the 901st transaction, you'll get a quick lesson in the highly contingent nature of customer relationships. Customers will not be fair. They'll key in on the last event, which will subsume all the good things that came before. It's human nature: That terrible meal you had last night at a once favorite restaurant obviates the 20 excellent meals you had there previously.

Even worse, dissatisfied customers talk. Dissatisfied customers tell as many as 15 other people about their experience, naturally exaggerating the story with each re-telling.

However, customers' lack of fairness gives you a sterling opportunity for relationship building. The most loyal customer is a customer who complains in the first place (light users don't bother to complain, they merely go away), and who then gets the problem fixed expeditiously. This not only re-cements the bond, it makes it stronger than ever before.

Who's good at this these days? Not many companies, since customer abuse seems to be the . . . standard. But you might audit MBNA, the credit card issuer, for whom customer service is the core competency.

Suggestion: You don't have to be perfect, but your customer service does. Otherwise, you will pay the price . . . at some point.. . . Relationship marketing is impossible without excellent customer service, and customer service must be regarded as one of the most essential marketing functions of the millennial period.. . .

Mistake #4: Assuming Customer Satisfaction Is Enough

Most customers polled in surveys claim to be satisfied. Worldwide, in fact, about 82 percent of all customers everywhere say they're satisfied. Yet everyone suffers from customer defections. What's going on here?

What's going on is that satisfaction is not enough. All satisfaction means is "You're doing OK." And in fact the . . . American consumer actually has diminished expectations, because quality and service really have declined in so many categories. Businesses need to strive for customers who claim to be "very satisfied." When companies ratchet themselves up from "satisfied" to "very satisfied," customer attrition decreases significantly.

More important than offering frequent flyer miles or rebates is making sure that customers are "very satisfied." In fact, another hidden danger of relationship marketing is to substitute rewards for satisfaction. A dissatisfied participant of a frequency/loyalty program will find some other program to join.

Suggestion: Don't be seduced by customer surveys showing "satisfaction." It's the "very satisfied" customer who creates your most significant long-term profits.

Mistake #5: Tier Inflation

In order to reach its potential, relationship marketing has to be predicated on a good marketing database.

The database allows companies to identify the small percentage of customers who account for the majority of profits (the famous Pareto Principle), and then to launch relationship building programs at these customers.

But like all technologies, the database is filled with temptations. One temptation: segmentation without intelligence.

Case in point: American Airlines is certainly a pioneer in database-driven relationship marketing, via its famous AAdvantage Program. In the early 1990s, the airline spotted a segment of its Gold AAdvantage customers who were superfrequent flyers. Voila! These customers became Platinum AAdvantage customers, with all the rights and privileges appertaining thereto.

The problem was that there were no rights and privileges! The only important tangible benefit, in fact, was the ability to get first-class upgrades 72 hours in advance of the flight, rather than the mere 24 hours allowed to Gold customers. But even this benefit was subverted, because at the same time that the marketers launched the Platinum program American's accountants evidently tightened up the availability of first-class upgrades. In other words, things got worse, rather than better, when customers got their Platinum cards. Their expectations had been raised, and then disappointed. Result: less brand loyalty, rather than more, among American's most profitable customers.

American has long since fixed this problem, but now has a new problem: Me!

I'm now Executive Platinum, one step up from mere Platinum, and I'm nearing 4 million miles. I want a segment all to myself.

Will this be cost-effective? Probably not. The big question: At what point does tier inflation stop paying off. Stay tuned for this one.

Suggestion: Be careful about tier inflation, and avoid the fatal mistake of good marketing followed by poor product.

Mistake #6: Accidental Disenfranchisement

This can be another unfortunate consequence of "infinite tiering upwards." What happens to the Gold people when you add a Platinum tier? Loyalty/frequency programs revolve not only around rewards, but also special courtesies, prestige, and status: not having to stand in line, a private toll-free number, etc. A Gold person who has been perfectly content to wait in line might resent the fact that a Platinum customer has no queue.

Every aspect of relationship marketing has to be looked at in terms of strategic downsides, as well as upsides. Failure to do this has been endemic in relationship marketing programs to date. Remember the Chinese military theorist who pointed out that strategy necessitates sacrifice? Think through what you're potentially sacrificing before committing yourself to the possible dangers of accidental disenfranchisement.

Suggestion: When the database tells you what you *could* do, make sure your marketing intelligence tells you what you *should* do.

Mistake #7: Changing the Rules

Relationship marketing programs based on frequency rewards have run into problems due to their very popularity. Airlines, for example, were carrying billions of dollars of free trip liability on their books. In an effort to please the accountants and eliminate the liabilities, the airlines changed the rules in the mid-1990s, typically by introducing expiration dates and upping the ante for trips and upgrades.

The result? Customer mistrust, customer disillusionment, and an erosion in the relationships the airlines have tried so hard to build. No one likes unexpected, unilateral rule changes. It's vital to build in rational expiration dates at the inception of a program, so that disappointment doesn't ensue later.

Suggestion: Get the rules right at the beginning. Remember what Thomas Aquinas said: A small mistake at the start can be a big mistake at the end.

One More Suggestion: When you have bad news for a customer, be direct, be honest, be reassuring. And see if there's something you can give customers (better service, for example) at the same time that you're taking something away.

Mistake #8: Incrementality vs. Cannibalization

From a profitability standpoint, this is the crux of the relationship marketing issue. Are you simply cannibalizing yourself by rewarding customers for doing what they would do anyway, or are you truly achieving incremental results?

A bank in New Zealand earlier this year offered an incentive to customers who used their credit card three times in a month. Problem was, customers were already using the card an average of three and a half times per month. The bank was actually rewarding customers for using the card less!

Suggestion: Think and evaluate before launching a program. Make sure that your efforts are incremental otherwise you're merely getting bogged down in a zero-sum game.

Mistake #9: Confusing Necessity With Loyalty

I have close to 4 million miles on American Airlines, but American doesn't know whether that's because I'm loyal or because I have no choice: I live in San Diego, but I base my working life in the U.S. out of New York. American runs the only nonstop between San Diego and New York.

If you need to travel through the booming cities of the Southeast—Charlotte, for example—it's hard not to travel on USAirways. But I've yet to meet a frequent business traveler who actually prefers USAirways (although I think they're getting better). Anyone traveling back and forth between Charlotte and New York will rack up the miles, but out of necessity, not because of loyalty.

This has some serious implications. Loyalty builds barriers against competition. Necessity, on the other hand, can make competition welcome indeed. Loyalty leads to long-term profits. Necessity can simply lead to customer defections, once they have a competitive choice.

Suggestion: Survey your frequent users to ascertain who is loyal and who uses you out of necessity. Launch cultivation programs at the "necessity" people, in order to convert them to "loyalists."

When all is said and done, the truth is that "relationship marketing" is a misleading term. In fact, if I ran the buzzword factory, I'd try to come up with better stuff.

Why is it misleading? Because the underlying metaphor of the term isn't really appropriate to the situations that marketers address. After all, when do you use the term "relationship?"

You use it when you're talking about your spouses, your children, your bosses, or your employers and clients—all of the people who require energy to deal with.

Relationships, by their nature, are energy-intensive on both ends. And as pointed out earlier, the stressed-out, overloaded and overworked . . . consumer typically doesn't have any leftover energy these days. And certainly doesn't want to work at maintaining a relationship with your company.

POSTSCRIPT

Is Relationship Marketing a Tenable Concept?

In their seminal 1998 *Harvard Business Review* article, Susan Fournier et al. cite an Oxford University study on rules of friendship: "Provide emotional support, respect privacy, preserve confidence and be tolerant of other friendships." If companies violate these rules, how can they show consumers that they are valued partners—gaining their trust—for a chance to build intimacy?

Seth Godin and Don Peppers have introduced an interesting concept in their book *Permission Marketing: Turning Strangers into Friends, and Friends into Customers* (Free Press, 1999). They argue that businesses can no longer rely completely on traditional forms of "interruption advertising" in magazines, mailings, and TV commercials. Once they get the consumer's attention, they must reward that attention and be receptive to interaction with the firm. This appears to be the real imperative for developing successful relationship marketing.

The key is to establish an easy way to make purchases automatic and to position the provider as a source for solving problems and providing solutions to the consumer. It is important to understand how to send a message and establish a communication system whereby the customer is willing to accept the message and is open to communication. Does every message encourage and reward a consumer response? What kinds of firms or market situations are most appropriate for relationship marketing to be successful? Firms have to consider the economics of using such a strategy. The lifetime value of a customer is of paramount importance. A recent study showed that the lifetime revenue stream from a loyal pizza customer can be $8,000; from a Cadillac car customer it can reach $332,000; and, in the case of a corporate purchaser of commercial aircraft, lifetime revenue can amount to billions of dollars.

Understanding the motivations of customers is crucial to the success of this strategy. Are customers primarily concerned with their own personal economic benefits or do they also have an emotional bond with the company? Certainly, with the incredible growth of potential promotional sources because of advancement of technology and communication tools, the few relationships we make in life are meaningful and welcomed. Focusing on relationship marketing may not be a new concept but it may be more important than ever before.

Finally, the importance of the appropriate use of technology to manage customer relationships should never be overlooked. Application of "Customer Relationship Management" (CRM) software has grown by leaps and bounds in the last couple of years, but does the emphasis on technology enhance or undermine such relationships?

Suggested Readings

Gary Abramson, "Seen the Light: Companies Learn the Hard Way That Over-Emphasis on Technology Can Undermine Customer Strategies," *CIO Enterprise Magazine* (June 15, 1999)

M. J. Baker, "Relationship Marketing in Three Dimensions," *Journal of Interactive Marketing* (Autumn 1998)

From *Taking Sides: Marketing*. Copyright © 2000 by The McGraw-Hill Companies, Inc. All rights reserved. Reprinted by permission of McGraw-Hill/Dushkin Publishing.

Jay Curry and Adam Curry, *The Customer Marketing Method: How to Implement and Profit from Customer Relationship Management* (Free Press, 2000)

Merly Davids, "How to Avoid the Ten Biggest Mistakes in CRM," *The Journal of Business Strategy* (November-December 1999)

Susan Fournier, Susan Dobscha, and David Glen Mick, "Preventing the Premature Death of Relationship Marketing," *Harvard Business Review* (January-February 1998)

Thomas W. Gruen, "Relationship Marketing: The Route to Marketing Efficiency and Effectiveness," *Business Horizons* (November-December 1997)

Laura Mazur, "Dotcoms Place CRM Staff Skills in High Demand," *Marketing* (March 9, 2000)

Frederick Newell, *The New Rules of Marketing: How to Use One-to-One Relationship Marketing to Be the Leader in Your Industry* (McGraw-Hill, 1997)

Don Peppers, Martha Rogers, and Bob Dorf, "Is Your Company Ready for One-to-One Marketing?" *Harvard Business Review* (January-February 1999)

Don Peppers and Martha Rogers, *The One-to-One Manager: Real-World Lessons in Customer Relationship Management* (Currency/Doubleday, 1999)

John V. Petrof, "Relationship Marketing: The Wheel Reinvented," *Business Horizons* (November-December 1997)

CRM-Forum. http://www.crm-forum.com

RealMarket Research. http://www.realmarket.com

Relationship Marketing Systems. http://www.smart-marketing.com

CRM Guru.com. http://www.crmguru.com

Andersen Consulting. http://ac.com/services/crm/crm_thought.html

Product Policy and Its Origins

A. P. Sloan, Jr.

After the two great expansions of 1908 to 1910 and 1918 to 1920 — perhaps one should say because of them — General Motors was in need not only of a concept of management but equally of a concept of the automobile business. Every enterprise needs a concept of its industry. There is a logical way of doing business in accordance with the facts and circumstances of an industry, if you can figure it out. If there are different concepts among the enterprises involved, these concepts are likely to express competitive forces in their most vigorous and most decisive form.

Such was the case in the automobile industry in 1921. Mr Ford's concept of a static model at the lowest price in the car market, expressed in the Model T, dominated the big-volume market then as it had for more than a decade. Other concepts were present, such as the one implied in about twenty makes of cars calculated to have low volume and very high price, and those behind the various cars in intermediate price brackets. General Motors then had no clear-cut concept of the business. It is true, as I have shown, that Mr Durant had established the pattern of variety in product expressed in seven lines: Chevrolet (in two very different models with different engines, the '490' standard, and a higher-priced 'FB'), Oakland (predecessor of the Pontiac), Olds, Scripps-Booth, Sheridan, Buick, and Cadillac. Of these, only Buick and Cadillac had clear divisional concepts. Buick with its high quality and fairly high volume in the high middle-price bracket, and Cadillac with its permanent endeavour to present the highest quality at a price consistent with a volume that would make a substantial business; and in fact Cadillac and Buick had long been the industry leaders in their price classes.

Nevertheless, there was then in General Motors no established policy for the car lines as a whole. We had no position in the low-price area, Chevrolet at that time being competitive with Ford in neither price nor quality. In early 1921, the Chevrolet was priced about $300 above the Model T (when an adjustment is made for comparable equipment), hence, out of sight from the viewpoint of competition. The fact that we were producers of middle- and high-price cars, so far as I know, was not a deliberate policy. It just happened that no one had figured out how to compete with the Ford, which had then more than half the total market in units. It should be observed, however, that no producer at that time presented a full line of cars, nor did any other producer present a line as broad as General Motors' line.

The spacing of our product line of ten cars in seven lines in early 1921 reveals its irrationality. Our cars and their prices at that time (priced from the roadster to the sedan, F.O.B. Detroit) were as follows:

Chevrolet '490' (four-cylinder)	$ 795–$1375
Chevrolet 'FB' (four-cylinder)	$1320–$2075
Oakland (six-cylinder)	$1395–$2065

© 1963 by Alfred P. Sloan. Reprinted by permission of the Harold Matson Co., Inc.

Olds (four-cylinder 'FB')	$1445–$2145
(six-cylinder)[1]	$1450–$2145
(eight-cylinder)	$2100–$3300
Scripps-Booth (six-cylinder)[1]	$1545–$2295
Sheridan (four-cylinder 'FB')	$1685
Buick (six-cylinder)	$1795–$3295
Cadillac (eight-cylinder)	$3790–$5690

Superficially this was an imposing car line. In the previous year, 1920, we had sold 331,118 US produced passenger cars, of which Chevrolet accounted for 129,525 and Buick for 112,208, the remaining 89,385 being distributed among the other cars in the line. In total output of vehicle units and in dollar sales, General Motors in 1920 was second to the Ford Motor Company. In the United States and Canada we sold 393,075 cars and trucks as compared with Ford's production of 1,074,336. The total industry sales were about 2,300,000 cars and trucks. Our net sales totalled $567,320,603 as compared with Ford's total of $644,830,550.

From the inside the picture was not quite so good. Not only were we not competitive with Ford in the low-price field — where the big volume and substantial future growth lay — but in the middle, where we were concentrated with duplication, we did not know what we were trying to do except sell cars which, in a sense, took volume from each other. Some kind of rational policy was called for. That is, it was necessary to know what one was *trying* to do, apart from the question of what might be imposed upon one by the consumer, the competition, and a combination of technological and economic conditions in the course of evolution. The lack of a rational policy in the car line can be seen especially in the almost identical duplication in price of the Chevrolet 'FB', Oakland, and Olds. Each division, in the absence of a corporation policy, operated independently, making its own price and production policies, which landed some cars in identical price positions without relationship to the interest of the enterprise as a whole.

The presence of Sheridan and Scripps-Booth in the line was, to my mind, without any justification. Neither car had its own motor. The Sheridan, assembled in a single plant in Muncie, Indiana, had the four-cylinder 'FB' motor. The Scripps-Booth, made in Detroit, had an Oakland six-cylinder motor, which, I might add, was then no attraction. Both had only modest dealer organizations. Singly or together they added nothing but excess baggage to the General Motor car line. Why then were they there? Scripps-Booth stock had come into the corporation with the acquisition of Chevrolet's assets in 1918. But the car had not developed important volume (about 8000 in 1919 and the same in 1920) and had no reasonable place in General Motors' line. The presence of the Sheridan is a mystery to me. Mr Durant caused General Motors to acquire it in 1920, doubtless with something special in mind. I am uncertain what. It did not have a strong organization or demand or recognizable purpose in our line.

As for Oakland and Olds, not only were they competing at nearly identical prices, but both of them were growing rapidly obsolescent in design. Take the Oakland. At a meeting in my office on 10 February 1921, Mr Pratt described the problem of this car as follows:

> Oakland is spending [its] efforts in trying to improve [its] product. Some days they produce ten cars and some days they produce fifty cars. The situation is this — they turn out a lot of cars that are not what they should be and then they have to fix them up . . . The power plant has been the great trouble . . .

---

[1] Six-cylinder engine made by Oakland.

At the same meeting I said:

> There is a lot that enters into this problem. At the present time we are getting 35 to 40 h.p. out of the Oakland motor and the crankshaft is too light for this rate of speed [power], and we have had a lot of poor workmanship together with other things, and the Oakland Motor Car Company over a year ago decided that they would put in a new motor. A new motor plant was authorized a year ago but we had to hold it up when we curtailed our development programme... It is really a question of management to get this motor in the Oakland so it will pass inspection and be right...

Oakland had sold its high of 52,124 cars in the boom year, 1919; it sold 34,839 in 1920, and, as it turned out, was to sell only 11,852 cars in 1921.

So much for Oakland.

Olds was only a little better off. It had sold 41,127 vehicles in 1919, 33,949 in 1920, and would sell 18,978 in 1921. It would take a new design just to save it.

Cadillac made 19,790 unit sales in 1920. In 1921 it would sell 11,130, and with the big price deflation that had taken place in the United States it would have to find a new optimum of cost, price, and volume.

The hard fact was that all the cars in the General Motors line, except Buick and Cadillac, were losing money in 1921. The Chevrolet Division that year lost about half of its 1920 volume. Its dollar losses at one point in 1921 reached approximately $1 million a month, and for the year as a whole it lost nearly $5 million. So strongly did I feel about the situation that, when someone proposed making changes in Buick's management, where Harry Bassett was successfully carrying on Walter Chrysler's old policy, I wrote to Mr du Pont: 'It is far better that the rest of General Motors be scrapped than any chances taken with Buick's earning power.' If that seems like an overextended argument, consider Buick's position. Its sales dropped only moderately from 115,401 in the 1919 boom to 80,122 in the 1921 slump, and what's more, it continued to produce an income. It was Buick that made any kind of General Motors car line worth talking about.

This situation reflected in good part the poor quality and unreliability of the other cars in the line, as compared with the high quality and reliability of Buick and Cadillac; the effect of these factors was intensified by the stress of the general economic slump. Given the fact of the slump and the unavoidability of a general decline in sales, the relative decline of one division as compared with another was a question of management.

The slump had the effect of showing up all kinds of weaknesses, as slumps usually do. General Motors in 1920 had enjoyed 17 per cent of the US car and truck market; in 1921 we were on our way down to 12 per cent. Ford, on the other hand, was in the course of rising from 45 per cent of the market in units in 1920 to 60 per cent in 1921. In other words, Mr Ford, whom no one had dared seriously to challenge in the low-price field since 1908, was tightening his grip while we were losing in unit volume as well as in the profitability of most of our divisions. All in all, with no position in the big-volume, low-price field and no concept to guide our actions, we were in a bad situation. It was clear that we needed an idea for penetrating the low-price field, and for the deployment of the cars through the line as a whole; and we needed a research-and-development policy, a sales policy, and the like, to support whatever we did.

In view of these circumstances, it is hardly surprising that on 6 April 1921, the Executive Committee set up a special committee of the Advisory Staff, made up of experienced automobile men in management, to look into our product policy. This task was to be one of the most significant in the evolution of the corporation. The members of the committee were C. S. Mott, then group executive for car, truck, and parts operations; Norval A. Hawkins, who had been chief of Ford sales before joining General Motors; C. F. Kettering of General Motors research; H. H. Bassett, general manager of Buick; K. W. Zimmerschied, newly appointed general manager of Chevrolet, and myself from the Executive Committee. Since I was in charge of the Advisory Staff when the special committee was formed and the senior member of the committee, its work came under my jurisdiction. About a month later we had completed our study, and on 9 June I presented our recommendations to the

Executive Committee, where they were approved and became the adopted policy of the corporation. The recommendations outlined the basic product policy of the corporation, a market strategy, and some first principles; all together they expressed the concept of the business.

The general historical circumstances described above had much to do with the nature of the recommendations. And there were other circumstances in the internal situation in General Motors which influenced what we had to say. In the first place the Executive Council had instructed the special committee that the corporation intended to enter the low-price field — that is, that it intended to make a competitive challenge to the dominance of Ford. The Executive Committee asked the special committee for advice on this question, and suggested that cars be designed and built in two low-price ranges, the lower of which would compete with Ford. They also asked for a discussion at some later time of other price areas. They excluded, however, any changes in the successfully established positions of Buick and Cadillac.

The seeds of a great controversy in the corporation had been sown a few weeks earlier when the Executive Committee, led by Pierre S. du Pont, decided that the corporation should make its entrance into the low-price field with a new and revolutionary kind of car. This car appeared to have exciting new potentialities, but I had some reservations about our ability to solve all the engineering problems it raised. Indeed a paramount reason for making a product policy explicit, from my point of view, was to bring the automobile men into the discussion. Other immediate circumstances also had a bearing on that discussion, among them an impending shake-out of the divisions forming the old car line, and a need we all felt for ground rules, that is, for first principles that would be acceptable to all in debate. And in order that the new product policy should be considered not just alone but in its essential relations to the over-all objectives of the corporation, we undertook to draw the whole picture and put all the known pieces into it.

Thus the new management took the opportunity that comes rarely in the initial stage of a business, to stand back and review aims and deal with the matters at hand both in particular and with a considerable degree of generalization. It was not going to be easy to get willing agreement on specific and immediate issues. For example, the idea of the revolutionary car was very much entrenched in the Executive Committee, and I wanted to broaden the concept of the product to the concept of the business. I believe it was for this reason that we on the special committee first idealized the problem. We started not with the actual corporation but with a model of a corporation, for which we said we would state policy standards.

Our aim we said was to chart the true best course for the future operations of this model corporation, recognizing that present actual conditions necessitated sailing off the recommended course temporarily until it became practicable to put any adopted policy standard into full effect. To this end we made the assumptions of the business process itself explicit. We presumed that the first purpose in making a capital investment is the establishment of a business that will both pay satisfactory dividends and preserve and increase its capital value. The primary object of the corporation, therefore, we declared was to make money, not just to make motor cars. Positive statements like this have a flavor that has gone out of fashion; but I still think that the ABCs of business have merit for reaching policy conclusions. General Motors had collected a number of profitless motor cars since 1908, and a few were still being produced. The problem was to design a product line that would make money. The future of the corporation and its earning power, we asserted, depended upon its ability to design and produce cars of maximum utility value in quantity at minimum cost. You can't really simultaneously maximize utility and minimize cost, but it was a manner of speaking for what nowadays we refer to more precisely as the optimizing of conflicting functions. To raise the utility and lower the cost of our cars, one of our first conclusions was that the number of models and the duplication that then existed within the corporation should be limited. By such economizing, which has taken various forms through the years, the corporation, I believe, has rendered the service to the public that all must give in the long run to succeed in business.

The prevailing concept in the Executive Committee was to meet Ford more or less head on with a revolutionary car design. Certainly Ford looked unbeatable by any ordinary means. There may also have been opinion among some in the corporation that to enter the low-price precincts on any basis would waste the resources we had gained elsewhere. In any case, we had given to us in our direction a volume product policy, namely, to sell cars in the low-price area, where there were buyers. The real question for the special committee was how to do it. Our answer was to accept the concept of a new car design but to place it in the perspective of a broad product policy.

The product policy we proposed is the one for which General Motors has now long been known. We said first that the corporation should produce a line of cars in each price area, from the lowest price up to one for a strictly high-grade quantity production car, but we would not get into the fancy-price field with small production; second, that the price steps should not be such as to leave wide gaps in the line, and yet should be great enough to keep their number within reason, so that the greatest advantage of quantity production could be secured; and third, that there should be no duplication by the corporation in the price fields or steps.

These new policies never materialized precisely in this form — for example, we always have had in fact duplication and competition between the divisions — yet essentially the new product policy differentiated the new General Motors from the old, and the new General Motors from the Ford organization of the time and from other car manufacturers. Naturally we thought that this policy was superior to competing policies in the industry and would win over them. Again let me say that companies compete in broad policies as well as in specific products. In the perspective of so many years gone by, the idea of this policy seems pretty simple, like a shoe manufacturer proposing to sell shoes in more than one size. But it certainly did not seem simple at the time, when Ford had more than half the market with two grades (the high-volume, low-priced Model T, and the low-volume, high-priced Lincoln), and Dodge, Willys, Maxwell (Chrysler), Hudson, Studebaker, Nash, and others had substantial positions in the industry and were making or preparing powerful bids with other product policies. For all we knew then, our policy might not have worked best. If the industry had thought it would work, the others would have adopted it at the time. The same policy was available to all, but for a number of years General Motors alone was to pursue it and prove its worthiness.

In drawing the whole picture of the policy we integrated into it other possible valid criteria — possible, that is, in the sense that they might be used as individual criteria. For example, the policy we said was valid if our cars were at least equal in design to the best of our competitors in a grade, so that it was not *necessary* to lead in design or run the risk of untried experiments. Certainly I preferred this concept to an irrevocable commitment to replace the then standard Chevrolet with a revolutionary car. Such a car would be fine if it worked, but I preferred to rest first on a broad business strategy; and, as the policy was adopted, it is evident that Pierre S. du Pont also subscribed to the general concept at least in principle. We of the special committee of course acknowledged that General Motors automobiles could reasonably be expected to be made pre-eminent in all grades. We argued that the breadth of the car line would give us this capability, though of course our then 12 per cent of the market gave us no particular advantage in this respect. We figured that in product line and in quality standards we were, or could become, as good as anybody in whatever they were good at and better at what they were not good at.

The same idea held for production, where of course we had to have Ford in mind. We pointed out that it was not *essential* that, for any particular car, production be more efficient than that of its best competitor, or for that matter that the advertising, selling, and servicing methods in any particular product be better than its competitors. The fundamental conception of the advantage to be secured in this business, we said, was expressed by cooperation and coordination of our various policies and divisions. It was natural to expect that coordinated operation of our plants should result in greater efficiency than was the case when the divisions were working at cross purposes, and the same could be said for engineering and other functions. By raising our own standards in this way, we could reasonably expect to equal the best, in any respect, that our competition in any grade had to offer, and to exceed it in some respects. Under a plan of cooperation, the teamwork could thus attain increased volume at reduced cost. And so, at a time when we sold only a small proportion of all US cars and trucks, we nonetheless believed that, with a federated policy in a business of wide scope, General Motors cars in the future would be made pre-eminent in engineering in all grades, and could similarly achieve unquestioned leadership in production, advertising, selling and other functions.

Having set forth these concepts, we then approved the resolution of the Executive Committee, which had been passed on to us to study, to the effect that a car should be designed and built to sell for not more than $600; and that another car should be designed and built to sell for not more than $900. The special committee further recommended four additional models, each to be kept strictly within the price range specified. It also recommended that the policy of the corporation should be to produce and market only six standard models, and that as soon as practicable the following grades should constitute the entire line of cars.

(a) $450–$600
(b) $600–$900
(c) $900–$1200
(d) $1200–$1700
(e) $1700–$2500
(f) $2500–$3500

This brand-new, hypothetical price structure, when compared with General Motors' actual price brackets listed earlier in this chapter, will be seen to reduce the car lines from seven to six (or ten to six cars if the Chevrolet 'FB' and the Olds '6' and '8' are considered separate cars, as they pretty much were). It opened up one new classification on the low end of the list where we had none. And where we had eight cars in the middle, above the lowest price and below the highest, we now had only four classifications. The new set of price classes meant that the General Motors car line should be integral, that each car in the line should properly be conceived in its relationship to the line as a whole.

Having thus separated out a set of related price classes, we set forth an intricate strategy which can be summarized as follows. We proposed in general that General Motors should place its cars at the top of each price range and make them of such a quality that they would attract sales from below that price, selling to those customers who might be willing to pay a little more for the additional quality, and attract sales also from above that price, selling to those customers who would see the price advantage in a car of close to the quality of higher-priced competition. This amounted to quality competition against cars below a given price tag, and price competition against cars above that price tag. Of course, a competitor could respond in kind, but where we had little volume we could thereby chip away an increase from above and below, and where we had volume it was up to us to maintain it. Unless the number of models was limited, we said, and unless it were planned that each model should cover its own grade and also overlap into the grades above and below its price, a large volume could not be secured for each car. This large volume, we observed, was necessary to gain the advantages of quantity production, counted on as a most important factor in earning a position of pre-eminence in all the grades.

The product policy also took up specifically the problem of penetrating the low-price field, a special case of the general concept. The field for cars of the first grade, we noted, was then practically monopolized by the Ford, and we were trying to invade it. We recommended that General Motors should not attempt to build and sell a car of the precise Ford level, as the Ford sold at the lowest price within the first grade. Instead the corporation should market a car much better than the Ford, with a view to selling it at or near the top price in the first grade. We did not propose to compete head on with the Ford grade, but to produce a car that would be superior to the Ford, yet so near the Ford price that demand would be drawn from the Ford grade and lifted to the slightly higher price in preference to Ford's then utility design.

We observed that the converse of this effect would be produced when the new General Motors low-price car, selling at the top of the lowest price range in the table ($600), was compared with cars of competitors in the next higher grade, selling at $750 or slightly below. Even though the new General Motors low-price car might not have quite the quality of competing cars selling at approximately $750, it should be so near the grade of competing cars selling at the middle of the second price range that prospective buyers would prefer to save $150 and to yield the comparatively slight preference they might have for the competing car if the prices were nearly equal.

The specific competitive aim of the new product policy at that time is evident in the lowest price classification set up for the model corporation. In this classification General Motors did not have a car to offer in April 1921. The only car available in this area was the Ford. Furthermore, in the second-lowest classification only Chevrolet and Willys-Overland offered a car. Thus the policy was directed at supplying a car to be put into competition solely with the chief product of the then leading car manufacturer in the United States and the world.

As it happened, actual car prices in all categories fell rapidly in 1921, collapsing the whole price structure that existed in the market in April, when we formulated the policy. But, while actual levels became different, the aim of the policy remained the same, namely to move into the relatively lower price areas. Indeed, by September 1921 the price of the Chevrolet '490' touring car was down from $820 (January 1921 price) to $525, while the Ford Model T was down from $440 to $355. But the Ford price did not include demountable rims and self-starter, as Chevrolet did, so that on a comparable-equipment basis there was in September only about $90 difference between Ford and Chevrolet. This difference was still relatively considerable, but the Chevrolet was beginning to move in the direction indicated in the product policy. Thus, this policy, by opening up new low-price areas, fore-shadowed the challenge that General Motors was actually to make to the dominance of Ford.

The placement of actual products in these price ranges was made by the committee, from bottom to top as follows: Chevrolet, Oakland, a new Buick 4, Buick 6, Olds, and Cadillac. In 1921 we sold Sheridan and took steps to dissolve Scripps-Booth, and in 1922 we dropped the Chevrolet 'FB'. Only the price-class positions of Chevrolet and Cadillac, as it turned out, were to be permanent.

The core of the product policy lies in its concept of mass-producing a full line of cars graded upward in quality and price. This principle supplied the first element in differentiating the General Motors concept of the market from that of the old, Ford Model T concept. Concretely, the General Motors concept provided the strategy for putting Chevrolet into competition with the Model T. Without this policy of ours, Mr Ford would not have had any competition in his chosen field at that time.

In 1921 Ford had about 60 per cent of the total car and truck market in units, and Chevrolet had about 4 per cent. With Ford in almost complete possession of the low-price field, it would have been suicidal to compete with him head on. No conceivable amount of capital short of the United States Treasury could have sustained the losses required to take volume away from him at his own game. The strategy we devised was to take a bite from the top of his position, conceived as a price class, and in this way build up Chevrolet volume on a profitable basis. In later years, as the consumer upgraded his preference, the new General Motors policy was to become critically attuned to the course of American history.

But although this concept gave us direction, it was, as it turned out, formulated before its time. It took a number of events in the automobile market to give full substance to its principles. Also, a number of events in General Motors, particularly with respect to research and development — that is, the revolutionary car — were to hold up the application of the concept and keep General Motors in suspense for the next couple of years.

Strategies for Mature and Declining Markets

Walker, Boyd & Larréché

Johnson Controls: Making Money in Mature Markets[1]

Jim Keyes, CEO of Johnson Controls in Glendale, Wisconsin, appears to deserve your condolences. After all, his conglomerate's success and future survival depend heavily on four product categories that have experienced little or no growth in recent years. Johnson makes batteries for cars, seats for cars, heating and cooling systems for office buildings and schools, and plastic beverage bottles.

But Mr. Keyes isn't looking for sympathy. Instead, he has developed a successful three-pronged strategy for making money in such mature markets. His strategy involves (1) acquiring weaker competitors to gain share and remove excess capacity. (2) fattening profit margins by improving operating efficiencies, and (3) gaining additional revenue via the development of new technologies, product offerings, and services.

A strong balance sheet and a long-term perspective help Johnson build market share by acquiring competitors. In some cases the company has used such acquisitions to help expand its product offerings in one of its established target markets. For instance, the firm spent $167 million to buy Pan Am's World Services division, a facility management operation that does everything from mow the lawn to run the cafeteria. That acquisition, together with some new products and services developed internally, helped the firm grow from just a manufacturer of heating and cooling systems for new buildings into a full-service facilities operator. Johnson can now manage a client's entire building while offering highly customized heating and cooling systems and controls that save money. This combination of custom products and full service has not only increased Johnson's revenues in the commercial real estate market, it has also generated higher operating profit margins.

In other businesses, Johnson has combined the economies of scale generated through savvy acquisitions with process re-engineering to drive down operating costs. For example, the firm has captured a 40 percent share of the U. S. market for out-sourced automotive seats—and has begun to win a commanding share of the European market as well—by supplying successful lines like the Jeep Grand Cherokee. Says Tom Donoughe, the Chrysler engineer in charge of the interior of the company's Neon compact car. "Johnson is able to completely integrate the design, development, and manufacture of the seats" and does it for less than the auto companies could.

Product development based on new technology is another way that Johnson has managed to increase sales to current customers as well as penetrate new market segments. Until recently, for instance, only glass bottles could safely handle certain fruit juices, including cranberry and apple, that are poured into containers when they are hot. But Johnson's R & D people are among the leaders

From *Marketing Strategy: Planning and Implementation* 2E by Walker et al. Reprinted by permission of The McGraw-Hill Companies.

in developing blow-molded plastic bottles that don't shrivel at high temperatures. Consequently, the firm is winning substantial business from new customers like Ocean Spray and Gatorade.

Despite the maturity of its markets, Johnson's three-pronged strategy is paying off. The firm strung together several years of record sales and profits during the early 1990s. In 1993, for instance, sales advanced 18 percent to more than $5.5 billion and profits rose 30 percent to $130 million.

Strategic Issues in Mature and Declining Markets

Many managers, particularly those in marketing, seem obsessed with growth. Their objectives tend to emphasize annual increases in sales volume, market share, or both. But the biggest challenge for many managers in developed nations in future years will be making money in markets that grow slowly, if at all. The majority of product-markets in those nations are in the mature or decline stages of their life cycles. And as accelerating rates of technological and social change continue to shorten such life cycles, today's innovations will move from growth to maturity—and ultimately to decline—ever faster.

But the situation is not always as depressing as it sounds, as Johnson Controls's recent performance confirms. In many cases managers can find opportunities to earn substantial profits and even increase volume in such markets.

Issues During the Transition to Market Maturity

A period of competitive turbulence almost always accompanies the market transition from growth to maturity in an industry. This period often begins after approximately half the potential customers have adopted the product and the rate of sales growth starts to decline. As the growth rate slows, many competitors tend to overestimate future sales volume and consequently end up developing too much production capacity. Competition becomes more intense as firms battle to increase sales volume to cover their high fixed costs and maintain profitability.

Such transition periods are commonly accompanied by a **shakeout**, during which weaker businesses fail, withdraw from the industry, or are acquired by other firms—as has happened to some of Johnson Controls's competitors in the U. S. and European automotive seat and battery industries. The shakeout period is pivotal in influencing a brand's continued survival and the strength of its competitive position during the later maturity and decline stages of the life cycle. The next section of this chapter examines some common strategic traps that can threaten a firm's survival during an industry shakeout.

Issues in Mature Markets

Businesses that survive the shakeout face new challenges as market growth stagnates. As a market matures, total volume stabilizes; replacement purchases rather than first-time buyers account for the vast majority of that volume. A primary marketing objective of all competitors in mature markets, therefore, is simply to hold their existing customers—to sustain a meaningful competitive advantage that will help ensure the continued satisfaction and loyalty of those customers. Thus a product's financial success during the mature life cycle stage depends heavily on the firm's ability to achieve and sustain a lower delivered cost or some perceived product quality or customer service superiority.

Some firms tend to passively defend mature products while using the bulk of the revenues produced by those items to develop and aggressively market new products with more growth potential. This can be shortsighted, however. All segments of a market and all brands in an industry do not necessarily reach maturity at the same time. Aging brands like Jell-O, Johnson's baby shampoo, and Arm & Hammer baking soda experienced sales revivals in recent years because of creative marketing strategies. Thus a share leader in a mature industry might build upon a cost or product differentiation advantage and pursue a marketing strategy aimed at increasing volume by promoting new uses for an old product or by encouraging current customers to buy and use the product more often. A later section of this chapter examines basic business strategies necessary for survival in mature markets and marketing strategies a firm might use to extend a brand's sales and profits.

Issues in Declining Markets

Eventually, technological advances, changing customer demographics, tastes, or lifestyles, and development of substitutes result in declining demand for most product forms and brands. As a product starts to decline, managers face the critical question of whether to divest or liquidate the business. Unfortunately, firms sometimes support dying products too long at the expense of current profitability and the aggressive pursuit of future breadwinners.

An appropriate marketing strategy can, however, produce substantial sales and profits even in a declining market. If few exit barriers exist, an industry leader might attempt to increase market share via aggressive pricing or promotion policies aimed at driving out weaker competitors. Or it might try to consolidate the industry by acquiring weaker brands and reducing overhead by eliminating excess capacity and duplicate marketing programs. Alternatively, a firm might decide to harvest a mature product by maximizing cash flow and profit over the product's remaining life. The last section of this chapter discusses specific marketing strategies for gaining the greatest possible returns from products approaching the end of their life cycle.

Shakeout: The Transition from Market Growth to Maturity

Characteristics of the Transition Period

The transition from growth to maturity typically begins when the market is still growing but the rate of growth starts to decline, as shown in Exhibit 10–1. This declining growth either sparks or occurs simultaneously with other changes in the market and competitive environment. Such

Exhibit 10–1
The Transition or Shakeout Stage of the Generalized Product Life Cycle

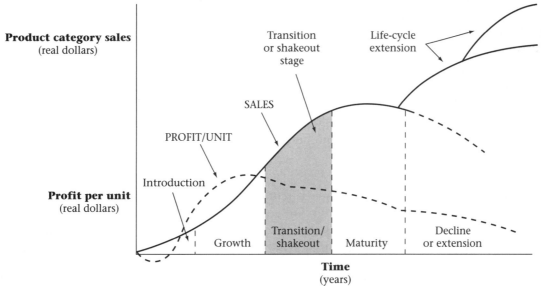

SOURCE: From p. 60 of *Analysis for Strategic Market Decisions*, by George S. Day.

changes include the appearance of excess capacity, increased intensity of competition, increased difficulty of maintaining product differentiation, worsening distribution problems, and growing pressures on costs and profits. Weaker members of the industry often fail or are acquired by larger competitors during this shakeout stage.

Excess Capacity

During a market's growth stage, manufacturers must usually invest heavily in new plants, equipment, and personnel to keep up with increasing demand. Some competitors fail to anticipate the transition from growth to maturity, however, and their expansion plans eventually overshoot market demand. Thus excess production capacity often develops at the end of the growth stage. This leads to an intense struggle for market share as firms seek increased volume to hold down unit costs and maintain profit margins.

More Intense Competition

The intensified battle for increased volume and market share at this stage often leads to price reductions and increased selling and promotional efforts. Firms modify products to appeal to more specialized user segments, make deals to produce for private labels, and take other actions that lower per unit revenues, increase R & D and marketing costs, and put pressure on profit margins.

Difficulty of Maintaining Differentiation

As an industry's technology matures, the better and more popular designs tend to become industry standards, and the physical differences among brands become less substantial. The popularity of the VHS format among video-cassette recorder customers, for example, eventually made it the industry standard, and Sony's alternative Beta format disappeared from the market. This decline in differentiation across brands often leads to a weakening of brand preference among consumers and makes it more difficult for even the market leaders to command premium prices for their products.[2] Such problems have been magnified in recent years as consumers have become more demanding and more willing to objectively evaluate alternatives rather than rely on past loyalty.[3]

Diminishing product differentiation can also increase costs as firms seek differentiation in other ways, such as through improved service. As the products and prices offered by competing suppliers become more similar, many purchasing agents become increasingly concerned with service and its impact on their firm's costs. For instance, they may demand a higher level of delivery reliability (as in just-in-time [JIT] deliveries) to help reduce their cost of capital tied up in inventory.

Distribution Problems

During an industry's transition from growth to maturity, channel members often become more assertive in ways particularly detrimental to smaller-share competitors. As sales growth slows, for example, retailers may reduce the number of brands they carry to reduce inventory costs and space requirements. Much the same can happen at the wholesale/distributor level. Because any reduction in product availability has serious repercussions for a manufacturer, low-share firms often must offer additional trade incentives simply to hold their distribution coverage during this period.

Pressures on Prices and Profits

Prices typically decrease and margins get squeezed during shakeout, which increases the industry's instability and volatility. Given their higher per unit costs, smaller-share businesses often operate at a loss during transition. Some are ultimately forced to leave the industry. This is particularly likely with commodity-type products, when few unique market niches exist in which the firm can main-

---

[2]Neil Gross, Peter Coy, and Otis Port, "The Technology Paradox," *Business Week*, March 6, 1995, pp. 76–84.
[3]Rahul Jacob, "Beyond Quality and Value," *Fortune*, Special Issue, Fall–Winter 1993, pp. 8–11.

tain a competitive advantage and when heavy investments in fixed assets are required and experience curve effects are high.

Firms that enter the transition period with high relative market shares are more likely to survive. Even these firms may experience a severe drop in profits, however. As the shakeout proceeds, the shares held by firms exiting the industry pass to the surviving firms, increasing their volumes and lowering per unit costs. This does not necessarily mean, though, that the leaders' market shares remain stable after shakeout. One study indicates that larger firms tend to lose share during market maturity because they fail to maintain their cost advantage.[4] We will discuss this danger in more detail later in this chapter.

Strategic Traps during the Transition Period

A business's ability to survive the transition from market growth to maturity also depends to a great extent on whether it can avoid some common strategic traps.[5] Four such traps are summarized in Exhibit 10–2.

Exhibit 10-2
Common Strategic Traps Firms Can Fall into During the Shakeout Period

1. Failure to anticipate transition from growth to maturity.
   - Firms may make overly optimistic forecasts of future sales volume.
   - As a result, they expand too rapidly and production capacity overshoots demand as growth slows.
   - Their excess capacity leads to higher costs per unit.
   - Consequently, they must cut prices or increase promotion in an attempt to increase their volume.
2. No clear competitive advantage as growth slows.
   - Many firms can succeed without a strong competitive advantage during periods of rapid growth.
   - However, firms that do not have the lowest costs or a superior offering in terms of product quality or service can have difficulty sustaining their market share and volume as growth slows and competition intensifies.
3. Assumption that an early advantage will insulate the firm from price or service competition.
   - In many cases, technological differentials become smaller as more competitors enter and initiate product improvements as an industry approaches maturity.
   - If customers perceive that the quality of competing brands has become more equal, they are likely to attach greater importance to price or service differences.
   - Failure to detect such trends can cause an early leader to be complacent and slow to respond to competitive threats.
4. Sacrificing market share in favor of short-run profit.
   - A firm may cut marketing or R & D budges or forgo other expenditures in order to maintain its historical level of profitability even though industry profits tend to fall during the transition period.
   - This can cause long-run erosion of market share and further increases in unit costs as the industry matures.

---

[4]Robert D. Buzzell, "Are There 'Natural' Market Structures?" *Journal of Marketing*, Winter 1981, pp. 42–51.

[5]For a more detailed discussion of these traps, see Michael E. Porter, *Competitive Strategy* (New York: Free Press, 1980), pp. 247–49.

The most obvious trap is simply the *failure to recognize the events signaling the beginning of the shakeout period*. The best way to minimize the impact of slowing growth is to accurately forecast the slowdown in sales and hold the firm's production capacity to a sustainable level. For both industrial and consumer durable goods markets, models can forecast when replacement sales will begin to outweigh first-time purchases, a common signal that a market is beginning to mature.[6] But in consumer nondurable markets—particularly those where growth slows because of shifting consumer preferences or the emergence of substitute products—the start of the transition period can be nearly impossible to predict.

A second strategic trap is for a business to *get caught in the middle during the transition period without a clear strategic advantage*. A business may survive and prosper during the growth stage even though it has neither differentiated its offering from competitors nor attained the lowest-cost position in its industry. But during the transition period, such is not the case.

A third trap is the *failure to recognize the declining importance of product differentiation and the increasing importance of price or service*. Businesses that have built their success on technological superiority or other forms of product differentiation often disdain aggressive pricing or marketing practices even though such differentiation typically erodes as markets mature.[7] As a result, such firms may delay meeting their more aggressive competitors head-on and end up losing market share.

Why should a firm not put off responding to the more aggressive pricing or marketing actions of its competitors? Because doing so may lead to a fourth trap—*giving up market share too easily in favor of short-run profit*. Many businesses try to maintain the profitability of the recent past as markets enter the transition period. They usually do this at the expense of market share or by forgoing marketing, R & D, and other investments crucial for maintaining future market position. While some smaller firms with limited resources may have no choice, this tendency can be seriously shortsighted, particularly if economies of scale are crucial for the business's continued success during market maturity.

Business Strategies for Mature Markets

The maturity phase of an industry's life cycle is often depicted as one of stability characterized by few changes in the market shares of leading competitors and steady prices. The industry leaders, because of their low per unit costs and little need to make any further investments, enjoy high profits and positive cash flows. These cash flows are harvested and diverted to other SBUs or products in the firm's portfolio that promise greater future growth.

Unfortunately, this conventional scenario provides an overly simplistic description of the situation businesses face in most mature markets. For one thing, it is not always easy to tell when a market has reached maturity. Variations in brands, marketing programs, and customer groups can mean that different brands and market segments reach maturity at different times.

Further, as the maturity stage progresses, a variety of threats and opportunities can disrupt an industry's stability. Shifts in customer needs or preferences, product substitutes, increased raw material costs, changes in government regulations, or factors such as the entry of low-cost foreign producers or mergers and acquisitions can threaten individual competitors and even throw the en-

---

[6]Fareena Sultan, John U. Farley, and Donald R. Lehmann, "A Meta-Analysis of Applications of Diffusion Models," *Journal of Marketing Research*, February 1990, pp. 70–77.

[7]Ming Jer Chen and Ian C. MacMillan, "Nonresponse and Delayed Response to Competitive Moves: The Roles of Competitor Dependence and Action Irreversibility." *Academy of Management Journal* 35 (1992), pp. 539–70; and Hubert Gatiguon, Eric Anderson, and Kristiaan Helsen, "Competitive Reactions to Market Entry: Explaining Interfirm Differences." *Journal of Marketing Research*, February 1989, pp. 44–55.

tire industry into early decline. Consider, for example, the competitive position of Timex, a brand that dominated the low-price segment of the American watch market in the 1970s. First the appearance of imported digital watches and later a shift in consumer preferences toward more fashionable and prestigious brands buffeted the firm and eroded its market share.

On the positive side, such changes can also open new growth opportunities in mature industries. Product improvements (such as the development of high-fiber nutritional cereals), advances in process technology (for example, the creation of minimills for steel production), falling raw materials costs, increased prices for close substitutes, or environmental changes (such as the increased demand for storm windows in the energy crisis of the 1970s and early 80s) can all provide opportunities for a firm to dramatically increase its sales and profits. An entire industry can even experience a period of renewed growth.

Discontinuities during industry maturity suggest that it is dangerously shortsighted for a firm to simply milk its cash cows. Even industry followers can substantially improve volume, share, and profitability during industry maturity if they can adjust their marketing objectives and programs to fit the new opportunities that arise.[8] Thus success in mature markets requires two sets of strategic actions: (1) the development of a well-implemented business strategy to sustain a competitive advantage and (2) flexible and creative marketing programs geared to pursue growth or profit opportunities as conditions change in specific product-markets.

Strategies for Maintaining Competitive Advantage

Both *analyzer* and *defender strategies* may be appropriate for units with a leading, or at least a profitable, share of one or more major segments in a mature industry. Analyzers and defenders are both concerned with maintaining a strong share position in established product-markets. But analyzers also do some product and market development to avoid being leapfrogged by competitors with more advanced products or being left behind in new application segments. On the other hand, defenders may initiate some product improvements or line extensions to protect and strengthen their position in existing markets, but they spend relatively little on new product R & D. Thus, an analyzer strategy is most appropriate for developed industries that are still experiencing some technological change and may have opportunities for continued growth, such as the computer and commercial aircraft industries. The defender strategy works best in industries where the basic technology is not very complex or is unlikely to change dramatically in the short run, as in the food industry.

Both analyzers and defenders can attempt to sustain a competitive advantage in established product-markets through *differentiation* of their product offering (either on the basis of superior quality or service) or by maintaining a *low-cost* position. Evidence suggests the ability to maintain either a strongly differentiated or a low-cost position continues to be a critical determinant of success throughout both the transition and the maturity stages. One study examined the competitive strategies pursued by the two leading firms (in terms of return on investment) in eight mature industries characterized by slow growth and intense competition. In each industry the two leading firms offered either the lowest relative delivered cost or high relative product differentiation.[9] Similarly, more recent observations by Treacy and Wiersema found that market leaders tend to pursue one of three strategic disciplines. They either stress operational excellence—which typically translates into lower costs—or they differentiate themselves

---

[8]Cathy Anterasian and Lynn W. Phillips, "Discontinuities. Value Delivery, and the Share-Returns Association: A Reexamination of the 'Share-Causes-Profits' Controversy." Distributed working paper (Cambridge, Mass.: Marketing Science Institute, April 1988). Also see Robert Jacobson. "Distinguishing among Competing Theories of the Market Share Effect." *Journal of Marketing*, October 1988, pp. 68–80.

[9]William K. Hall, "Survival Strategies in a Hostile Environment," *Harvard Business Review*, September–October 1980, pp. 75–85.

Exhibit 10–3
Three Strategic Disciplines of Market Leaders and the Traits of Businesses That Implement Them Effectively

Company traits	Disciplines		
	Operational excellence	Product leadership	Customer intimacy
Core business processes	Sharpen distribution systems and provide no-hassle service	Nurture ideas, translate them into products, and market them skillfully	Provide solutions and help customers run their businesses
Structure	Has strong, central authority and a finite level of empowerment	Acts in an ad hoc, organic, loosely knit, and ever-changing way	Pushes empowerment close to customer contact
Management systems	Maintain standard operating procedures	Reward individuals innovative capacity and new product success	Measure the cost of providing service and of maintaining customer loyalty
Culture	Acts predictably and believes "one size fits all"	Experiments and thinks "out-of-the-box"	Is flexible and thinks "have it your way"

SOURCE: Michael Treacy and Fred Wiersema, "How Market Leaders Keep Their Edge," *Fortune*, February 6, 1995, p. 96.

through product leadership or customer intimacy and superior service.[10] These three disciplines are summarized in Exhibit 10–3 together with some of the traits of businesses that are able to implement them effectively.

Generally, it is difficult for a single business to pursue both low-cost and differentiation strategies at the same time. For instance, businesses taking the low-cost approach typically compete primarily by offering the lowest prices in the industry. Such prices allow little room for the firm to make the investments or cover the costs inherent in maintaining superior product quality, performance, or service over time.

It is important to keep in mind, however, that pursuit of a low-cost strategy does not mean that a business can ignore the delivery of desirable benefits to the customer. Similarly, customers will not pay an unlimited price premium for superior quality or service, no matter how superior it is. In both consumer and commercial markets customers seek good *value* for their money—either a solid, no-frills product or service at an outstanding price, or an offering whose higher price is justified by the superior benefits it delivers on one or more dimensions.[11] Thus, even low-cost producers should continually seek ways to improve the quality and performance of their offerings within the financial constraints of their competitive strategy. And even differentiated defenders should continually work to improve efficiency without sacrificing product quality or performance. The critical strategic questions, then, are "How can a business continue to differentiate its offerings and justify a premium price as its market matures and becomes more competitive?" and "How can businesses—particularly those pursuing low-cost strategies—continue to reduce their costs and improve their efficiency as their markets mature?"

---

[10]Michael Treacy and Fred Wiersema. *The Discipline of Market Leaders* (Reading, Mass.: Addison–Wesley, 1995).

[11]Rahul Jacob, "Beyond Quality and Value."

Methods of Differentiation

At the most basic level, a business can attempt to differentiate its offering from competitors' by offering either superior product quality, superior service, or both. The problem is that *quality* and *service* may be defined in a variety of different ways by different customers.

Dimensions of Product Quality[12]

To maintain a competitive advantage in product quality, a firm must understand what *dimensions customers perceive to underlie differences across products* within a given category. One authority has identified eight such dimensions of product quality. These are summarized in Exhibit 10–4 and discussed here.

European manufacturers of prestige automobiles, such as Mercedes-Benz and Porsche, have emphasized the first dimension of product quality—**functional performance**. These automakers have designed cars that provide excellent performance on such attributes as handling, acceleration, and comfort. Volvo, on the other hand, has emphasized and aggressively promoted a different quality dimension—**durability** (and the related attribute of safety). A third quality dimension, **conformance to specifications**, or the absence of defects, has been a major focus of the Japanese automakers. Until recent years American carmakers relied heavily on broad product lines and a wide **variety of features**, both standard and optional, to offset their shortcomings on some of the other quality dimensions.

The **reliability** quality dimension can refer to the consistency of performance from purchase to purchase or to a product's uptime, the percentage of time that it can perform satisfactorily over its life. Tandem Computers has maintained a competitive advantage based on reliability by designing computers with several processors that work in tandem, so that if one fails, the only im-

Exhibit 10-4
Dimensions of Product Quality

• Performance	How well does the washing machine wash clothes?
• Durability	How long will the lawn mower last?
• Conformance with specifications	What is the incidence of product defects?
• Features	Does an airline flight offer a movie and dinner?
• Reliability	Will each visit to a restaurant result in consistent quality?
	What percentage of the time will a product perform satisfactorily?
• Serviceability	Is the product easy to service?
	Is the service system efficient, competent, and convenient?
• Fit and finish	Does the product look and feel like a quality product?
• Brand name	Is this a name that customers associate with quality?
	What is the brand's image?

SOURCE: Adapted from "What Does 'Product Quality' Really Mean?" by David A. Garvin. *Sloan Management Review*, Fall 1984, pp. 25–43.

---

[12]The following discussion is based on material found in David A. Garvin. "What Does 'Product Quality' Really Mean?" *Sloan Management Review*, Fall 1984, pp. 25–43: and David A. Aaker, *Strategic Market Management*. 2nd ed. (New York: John Wiley & Sons, 1988), 11.

pact is the slowing of low-priority tasks. IBM cannot match Tandem's reliability because of its commitment to an operating system not easily adapted to the multiple-processor concept. Consequently, Tandem has maintained a strong position in market segments consisting of large-scale computer users—such as financial institutions and large retailers—for whom system downtime is particularly undesirable.

The quality dimension of **serviceability** refers to a customer's ability to obtain prompt and competent service when the product does break down. For example, Catepillar Tractor has long differentiated itself with a parts and service organization dedicated to providing "24-hour parts service anywhere in the world."

Many of these quality dimensions can be difficult for customers to evaluate, particularly for consumer products. As a result, consumers often generalize from quality dimensions that are more visual or qualitative. Thus, the **fit and finish** dimension can help convince consumers that a product is of high quality. They tend to perceive attractive and well-designed products as generally high in quality, as witnessed by the success of the Krups line of small appliances. Similarly, the **quality reputation of the brand name**, and the promotional activities that sustain that reputation, can strongly influence consumers' perceptions of a product's quality. Indeed, a brand's quality reputation together with psychological factors such as name recognition and loyalty substantially determine a brand's *equity*—the perceived value customers associate with a particular brand name and its logo or symbol.[13] To successfully pursue a differentiation strategy based on quality, then, a business must understand what dimensions or cues its potential customers use to judge quality, and it should pay particular attention to some of the less concrete but more visible and symbolic attributes of the product.

Dimensions of Service Quality

Customers also judge the quality of the service they receive on multiple dimensions. A number of such dimensions of perceived service quality have been identified by a series of studies conducted across diverse industries such as retail banking and appliance repair, and five of those dimensions are listed and briefly defined in Exhibit 10–5.[14]

The quality dimensions listed in Exhibit 10–5 apply specifically to service businesses, but most of them are also relevant for judging the service component of a product offering. This pertains to both the objective performance dimensions of the service delivery system—such as its **reliability** and **responsiveness**—as well as to elements of the performance of service personnel, such as their **empathy** and level of **assurance**.

Exhibit 10-5
Dimensions of Service Quality

• Tangibles	Appearance of physical facilities, equipment, personnel, and communications materials
• Reliability	Ability to perform the promised service dependably and accurately
• Responsiveness	Willingness to help customers and provide prompt service
• Assurance	Knowledge and courtesy of employees and their ability to convey trust and confidence
• Empathy	Caring, individualized attention the firm provides its customers

SOURCE: Valarie A. Zeithaml, A. Parasuraman, and Leonard L. Berry, *Delivering Quality Service: Balancing Customer Perceptions and Expectations* (New York: Free Press, 1990), p. 26.

---

[13]For a more extensive discussion of brand equity, see David A. Aaker, *Brand Equity* (New York: The Free Press, 1991).

[14]Valarie A. Zeithaml, A. Parasuraman, and Leonard L. Berry, *Delivering Quality Service: Balancing Customer Perceptions and Expectations* (New York: The Free Press, 1990).

The results of a number of surveys suggest that customers perceive all five dimensions of service quality to be very important regardless of the kind of service being evaluated. As Exhibit 10–6 indicates, customers of four different kinds of services gave reliability, responsiveness, assurance, and empathy mean importance ratings of more than 9 on a 10-point rating scale. And though the mean ratings for tangibles were somewhat lower in comparison, they still fell toward the upper end of the scale, ranging from 7.14 to 8.56.

The same respondents were also asked which of the five dimensions they would choose as being the most critical in their assessment of service quality. Their responses—which are shown in Exhibit 10–6—suggest that reliability is the most important aspect of service quality to the greatest number of customers. The key to a differentiation strategy based on providing superior service, then, is to meet or exceed target customers' service quality expectations and to do it more

Exhibit 10-6
Perceived Importance of Service Quality Dimensions in Four Different Industries

	Mean importance rating on 10-point scale*	Percentage of respondents indicating dimension is most important
Credit card customers ($n = 187$)		
Tangibles	7.43	0.6
Reliability	9.45	48.6
Responsiveness	9.37	19.8
Assurance	9.25	17.5
Empathy	9.09	13.6
Repair and maintenance customers ($n = 183$)		
Tangibles	8.48	1.2
Reliability	9.64	57.2
Responsiveness	9.54	19.9
Assurance	9.62	12.0
Empathy	9.30	9.6
Long-distance telephone customers ($n = 184$)		
Tangibles	7.14	0.6
Reliability	9.67	60.6
Responsiveness	9.57	16.0
Assurance	9.29	12.6
Empathy	9.25	10.3
Bank customers ($n = 177$)		
Tangibles	8.56	1.1
Reliability	9.44	42.1
Responsiveness	9.34	18.0
Assurance	9.18	13.6
Empathy	9.30	25.1

*Scale ranges from 1 (not at all important) to 10 (extremely important).

SOURCE: From *Delivering Quality Service: Balancing Customer Perceptions and Expectations*, by Valarie A. Zeithaml, A. Parasuraman, and Leonard L. Berry.

consistently than competitors. The problem is that sometimes managers underestimate the level of those customer expectations, and sometimes those expectations can be unrealistically high. Therefore, a firm needs to clearly identify target customers' desires with respect to service quality and clearly define and communicate what level of service they intend to deliver. When this is done, customers have a more realistic idea of what to expect and are less likely to be disappointed with the service they receive.

Improving Customer Perceptions of Service Quality

The major factors that determine a customer's expectations and perceptions concerning service quality—and five gaps that can lead to dissatisfaction with service delivery—are outlined in Exhibit 10–7 and discussed next.

1. *Gap between the customer's expectations and the marketer's perceptions.* Managers do not always have an accurate understanding of what customers want or how they will evaluate a firm's service efforts. The first step in providing good service, then, is to collect information—through customer surveys, evaluations of customer complaints, or other methods—to determine what service attributes customers consider important.

2. *Gap between management perceptions and service quality specifications.* Even when management has a clear understanding of what customers want, that understanding might not get translated into effective operating standards. A firm's policies concerning customer service may be unclear, poorly communicated to employees, or haphazardly enforced. Unless a firm's employees know what the company's service policies are and believe that management is seriously committed to those standards, their performance is likely to fall short of desired levels.

3. *Gap between service quality specifications and service delivery.* Lip service by management is not enough to produce high-quality service. High standards must be backed by the programs, resources, and rewards necessary to enable and encourage employees to deliver good service. Employees must be provided with the training, equipment, and time necessary to deliver good service. Their service performance must be measured and evaluated. And good performance must be rewarded by making it part of the criteria for pay raises or promotions, or by other more direct inducements, in order to motivate the additional effort good service requires.

4. *Gap between service delivery and external communications.* Even good service performance may disappoint some customers if the firm's marketing communications cause them to have unrealistically high expectations. If the photographs in a vacation resort's advertising and brochures make the rooms look more spacious and luxurious than they really are, for instance, first-time customers are likely to be disappointed no matter how clean or well-tended those rooms are kept by the resort's staff.

5. *Gap between perceived service and expected service.* This results when management fails to close one or more of the other four gaps. It is this difference between a customer's expectations and his or her actual experience with the firm that leads to dissatisfaction.

This discussion suggests a number of actions management can take to close the possible gaps and improve customer satisfaction with a company's service. An example of how such actions can be translated into a successful service program that satisfies customers is provided by Hertz's #1 Club Gold program, which is described in Exhibit 10–8. Achieving and sustaining such high levels of service quality can present some difficult implementation problems, however, because it often involves the coordination of efforts of many different employees from different functional departments and organizational levels. Some of these coordination problems are examined later.

Exhibit 10–7
Determinants of Perceived Service Quality

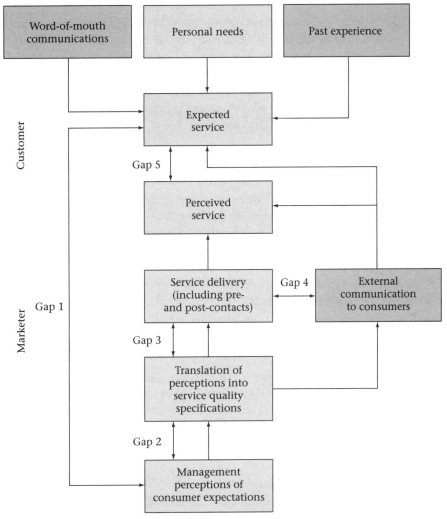

SOURCE: A. Parasuraman, Valarie A. Zeithaml and Leonard L. Berry. "A Conceptual Model of Service Quality and Its Implications for Future Research." *Journal of Marketing*, Fall 1985, p. 44. Published by the American Marketing Association.

Exhibit 10–8
Hertz's Program for Excellent Customer Service

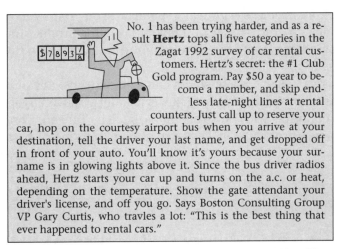

SOURCE: From "Companies That Serve You Best," by Patricia Sellers. *Fortune*, May 31, 1993, p. 76.

Methods for Maintaining a Low-Cost Position

Moving down the experience curve is the most commonly discussed method for achieving and sustaining a low-cost position in an industry. But a firm does not necessarily need a large relative market share to implement a low-cost strategy. The small clone manufacturers in the PC industry, for instance, found other ways to hold their costs well below those of the industry leaders. Other means for obtaining a sustainable cost advantage include producing a no-frills product, creating an innovative product design, finding cheaper raw materials, automating production, developing low-cost distribution channels, and reducing overhead.[15]

A No-Frills Product

A direct approach to obtaining a low-cost position involves simply removing all frills and extras from the basic product or service. Thus Suzuki cars, warehouse furniture stores, legal services clinics, and grocery stores selling canned goods out of crates all offer lower costs and prices than their competitors. This lower production cost is often sustainable because established differentiated competitors find it difficult to stop offering features and services their customers have come to expect. However, those established firms may lower their own prices in the short run—even to the point of suffering losses—in an attempt to drive out a no-frills competitor that poses a serious threat. This was the response of the major airlines to inroads made by People Express. Thus a firm considering a no-frills strategy needs the resources to withstand a possible price war.

Innovative Product Design

A simplified product design and standardized component parts can also lead to cost advantages. In the office copier industry, for instance, Japanese firms overcame substantial entry barriers by designing extremely simple copiers with a fraction of the number of parts in the design used by market-leading Xerox.

Cheaper Raw Materials

A firm with the foresight to acquire or the creativity to find a way to use relatively cheap raw materials can also gain a sustainable cost advantage. For example, Fort Howard Paper achieved an advantage by being the only major papermaker to rely exclusively on recycled pulp. While the finished product was not so high in quality as paper from virgin wood, Fort Howard's lower cost gave it a competitive edge in the price-sensitive commercial market for toilet paper and other such products used in hotels, restaurants, and office buildings.

Innovative Production Processes

Although low-cost defender businesses typically spend little on *product R & D*, they often continue to devote substantial sums to *process R & D*. Innovations in the production process, including the development of automated or computer-controlled processes, can help them sustain cost advantages over competitors.

In some labor-intensive industries a business can achieve a cost advantage, at least in the short term, by gaining access to inexpensive labor. This is usually achieved by moving all or part of the production process to countries with low wage rates, such as Taiwan, Korea, or Mexico. Unfortunately, because such moves are relatively easy to emulate, this kind of cost advantage may not be sustainable.

---

[15] For a more detailed discussion of these and other approaches for lowering costs, see Aaker, *Strategic Market Management*, Ch. 12.

Low-Cost Distribution

When distribution accounts for a relatively high proportion of a product's total delivered cost, a firm might gain a substantial advantage by developing lower-cost alternative channels. Typically, this involves eliminating, or shifting to the customer, some of the functions performed by traditional channels in return for a lower price. In the PC hardware and software industries, for example, mail-order discounters can offer lower prices because they have fewer fixed costs than the retail stores with which they compete. However, they also do not provide technical advice or postsale service to their customers.

Reductions in Overhead

Successfully sustaining a low-cost strategy requires that the firm pare and control its major overhead costs as quickly as possible as its industry matures. Indeed, many U. S. companies learned this lesson the hard way during the 1980s when high costs of old plants, labor, and large inventories left them vulnerable to more efficient foreign competitors and to corporate raiders.

Business Strategy and Performance

Analyzer, and particularly defender, businesses are mostly concerned with protecting their existing positions in one or more mature market segments and maximizing profitability over the remaining life of those product-markets. Thus financial dimensions of performance, such as return on investment and cash flow, are usually of greater interest to such businesses than more growth-oriented dimensions like volume increases or new product success. Businesses can achieve such financial objectives by either successfully differentiating their offerings or by maintaining a low-cost position.

While the primary emphasis in many businesses during the early 1990s was on improving efficiency through downsizing and reengineering,[16] there is substantial evidence that firms with superior quality goods and services also obtain higher returns on investment than businesses with average or below-average quality offerings.[17] The lesson to be learned, then, is that the choice between a differentiation or a low-cost strategy is probably not the critical determinant of success in mature markets. What is critical is that a business *continually work to improve the value* of its offerings—either by improving product or service quality, reducing costs, or some combination—as a basis for maintaining its customer base as its markets mature and become increasingly competitive.

Measuring Customer Satisfaction

In order to gain the knowledge necessary to continually improve the value of their offerings to target customers, firms must understand how satisfied existing and potential customers are with their current offerings. This focus on customer satisfaction is become increasingly important as more firms question whether all attempts to improve the *absolute* quality of their products and services generate sufficient additional sales and profits to justify their cost. This growing concern with the economic "return on quality" has motivated firms to ask which dimensions of product or service quality are most important to customers, and which dimensions customers might be willing to sacrifice for lower prices. For instance, United Parcel Service recently discovered that many of its customers wanted more time to interact with the company's drivers in order to seek advice on their shipping problems, and they were willing to put up with slightly slower delivery times in

---

[16]Ronald Henkoff, "Getting beyond Downsizing," *Fortune*, January 10, 1994, pp. 58–64.

[17]Robert Jacobson and David A. Aaker, "The Strategic Role of Product Quality," *Journal of Marketing*, October 1987, pp. 31–44.

return. Consequently, UPS now allows its drivers an additional 30 minutes a day to spend at their discretion to strengthen ties with customers and perhaps bring in new sales.[18]

As the diagram in Exhibit 10–7 indicates, then, useful measures of customer satisfaction should examine both (1) customers' **expectations and preferences** concerning the various dimensions of product and service quality (such as product performance, features, reliability, on-time delivery, competence of service personnel, and so on) and (2) their **perceptions** concerning how well the firm is meeting those expectations. Any gaps where customer expectations exceed their recent experiences may indicate fruitful areas for the firm to work at improving customer value and satisfaction. Of course, such measurements must be made periodically to determine whether the actions taken have actually been effective.[19]

Improving Customer Retention

As Exhibit 10–9 indicates, maintaining the loyalty of existing customers is crucial for improving a business's profitability as markets mature. The exhibit shows that loyal customers become more profitable over time. The firm not only avoids the high costs associated with acquiring a new customer, but it typically benefits because loyal customers (1) tend to concentrate their purchases, thus leading to larger volumes and lower selling and distribution costs, (2) provide positive word-of-mouth and customer referrals, and (3) may be willing to pay premium prices for the value they receive.[20]

Periodic measurement of customer satisfaction is important, then, because a dissatisfied customer is unlikely to remain loyal to a company over time. Unfortunately, however, the corollary is not always true: Customers who describe themselves as satisfied are not necessarily loyal. Indeed,

Exhibit 10–9

Sources of Increased Profit from Loyal Customers

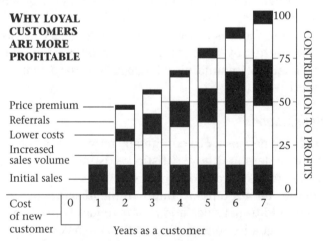

SOURCE: Rahul Jacob, "Why Some Customers Are More Equal Than Others," *Fortune*, September 19, 1994, p. 220.

---

[18]David Greising, "Quality: How to Make It Pay," *Business Week*, August 8, 1994. pp. 54–59.

[19]For a discussion of various approaches to measuring customer satisfaction, see J. Joseph Cronin and Steven A. Taylor, "Measuring Service Quality: A Reexamination and Extension," *Journal of Marketing*, July 1992, pp. 55–68; and Susan J. Devlin and H. K. Dong, "Service Quality from the Customers' Perspective," *Marketing Research* 6 (1994), pp. 5–13.

[20]Frederick F. Reichheld, "Loyalty and the Renaissance of Marketing," *Marketing Management* 2 (1994), pp. 10–21. Also see Rahul Jacob. "Why Some Customers Are More Equal Than Others," *Fortune*, September 19, 1994, pp. 215–24.

one author estimates that 60 to 80 percent of customer defectors in most businesses said they were "satisfied" or "very satisfied" on the last customer survey before their defection.[21] In the interim, perhaps, competitors improved their offerings, the customer's requirements changed, or other environmental factors shifted. The point is that businesses that measure customer satisfaction should be commended—but urged not to stop there. Satisfaction measures need to be supplemented with examinations of customer *behavior*, such as measures of the annual retention rate, frequency of purchases, and the percentage of a customer's total purchases captured by the firm.

Most important, defecting customers should be studied in detail to discover *why* the firm failed to provide sufficient value to retain their loyalty. Such failures often provide more valuable information than satisfaction measures because they stand out as a clear, understandable message telling the organization exactly where improvements are needed. The MicroScan division of Baxter Diagnostics, Inc., provides a good example of the intelligent use of such defector analysis. MicroScan makes instruments used by medical laboratories to identify microbes in patient cultures. In 1990 MicroScan was neck-and-neck with Vitek Systems, Inc., for market leadership, but its management knew they would have to do better to win the race. The firm analyzed its customer base, highlighting accounts that had been lost as well as those that remained active but showed a declining volume of testing. MicroScan interviewed all the lost customers and a large portion of the "decliners," probing deeply for the causes underlying their change in behavior. They found that such customers had concerns about the company's instrument features, reliability, and responsiveness to their problems.

In response, MicroScan's management shifted R & D priorities to address specific shortcomings its lost customers had identified, such as test accuracy and time-to-result. It also redesigned customer service protocols to ensure that immediate attention was given to equipment faults and delivery problems. As a result, MicroScan's sales began to improve and it established a clear market-share lead within two years.[22]

As MicroScan's experience shows, improving customer loyalty is crucial for maintaining market share and profitability as markets mature. As pointed out next, however, simply holding onto current customers may not be the only relevant objective in many mature markets.

Marketing Strategies for Mature Markets

Strategies for Maintaining Current Market Share

Since markets can remain in the maturity stage for decades, milking or harvesting mature product-markets by maximizing short-run profits makes little sense. Pursuing such an objective typically involves substantial cuts in marketing and R & D expenses, which can lead to premature losses of volume and market share and lower profits in the longer term. The business should strive during the early years of market maturity to *maximize the flow of profits over the remaining life of the product-market*. Thus, the most critical marketing objective is to *maintain and protect the business's market share*. In a mature market where few new customers buy the product for the first time, the business must continue to win its share of repeat purchases from existing customers.

We discussed a number of marketing strategies that businesses might use to maintain their market share in growth markets. Many of those same strategies continue to be relevant for holding onto customers as markets mature, particularly for those firms that survived the shakeout period with a relatively strong share position. The most obvious strategy for such share leaders is simply to continue strengthening their position through a *fortress defense*. Recall that

---

[21]Reichheld, "Loyalty and the Renaissance of Marketing."
[22]Reichheld, "Loyalty and The Renaissance of Marketing."

such a strategy involves two sets of marketing actions: those aimed at improving customer satisfaction and loyalty, and those intended to encourage and simplify repeat purchasing. Actions like those discussed earlier for improving the quality of a firm's offering and for reducing costs suggest ways to increase customer satisfaction and loyalty. Similarly, improvements to service quality—such as just-in-time delivery arrangements or computerized reordering systems—can help encourage repeat purchases.

Since markets often become more fragmented as they grow and mature, share leaders may also have to expand their product lines or add one or more *flanker* brands to protect their position against competitive inroads. Thus, Johnson Controls has strengthened its position in the commercial facilities management arena by expanding its array of services through a combination of acquisitions and continued internal development.

Small-share competitors can also earn substantial profits in a mature market. To do so, however, it is often wise for them to focus on strategies that avoid prolonged direct confrontations with larger share leaders. A *niche strategy* can be particularly effective when the target segment is too small to appeal to larger competitors or when the smaller firm can establish a strong differential advantage or brand preference in the segment. For instance, with only 36 hotels worldwide the Four Seasons chain is a small player in the lodging industry. But by focusing on the high end of the business travel market, the chain has grown and prospered. The chain's hotels differentiate themselves by offering a wide range of amenities—such as free overnight shoe shining—that are important to business travelers. Thus, while they charge relatively high prices, they are also seen as delivering good value and rank first in the *Business Travel News* survey of customer satisfaction.[23]

Strategies for Extending Volume Growth

Market maturity is defined by a flattering of the growth rate. In some instances growth slows for structural reasons, such as the emergence of substitute products or a shift in customer preferences. Marketers can do little to revitalize the market under such conditions. But in some cases a market only *appears* to be mature because of the limitations of current marketing programs, such as target segments that are too narrowly defined or limited product offerings. Here more innovative or aggressive marketing strategies might successfully extend the market's life cycle into a period of renewed growth. Thus, *stimulating additional volume growth* can be an important secondary objective under such circumstances, particularly for industry share leaders because they often can capture a relatively large share of any additional volume generated.

A firm might pursue several different marketing strategies either singly or in combination to squeeze additional volume from a mature market. These include an *increased penetration strategy*, an *extended use strategy*, and a *market expansion strategy*. Exhibit 10–10 summarizes the environmental situations where each of these strategies is most appropriate and the objectives each is best suited for accomplishing. Exhibit 10–11 outlines some specific marketing actions a firm might employ to implement each of the strategies, as discussed in more detail in the following paragraphs.

Increased Penetration Strategy

The total sales volume produced by a target segment of customers is a function of (1) the number of potential customers in the segment, (2) the product's penetration of that segment, that is, the proportion of potential customers who actually use the product, and (3) the average frequency with which customers consume the product and make another purchase. Where usage frequency is quite high among current customers but only a relatively small portion of all potential users actually buy the product, a firm might aim at increasing market penetration. This is an appropriate strategy for an industry's share leader because such firms can more likely gain and retain a substantial share of new customers than smaller firms with less well-known brands.

---

[23]Patricia Sellers, "Companies That Serve You Best," *Fortune*, May 31, 1993, p. 80.

The secret to a successful increased penetration strategy lies in discovering why nonusers are uninterested in the product. Very often the product does not offer sufficient value from the potential customer's point of view to justify the effort or expense involved in buying and using it. One obvious solution to such a problem is to enhance the product's value to potential customers by adding features or benefits, usually via line extensions.

Another way to add value to a product is to develop and sell integrated systems that help improve the basic product's performance or ease of use. For instance, instead of simply selling control mechanisms for heating and cooling systems, Johnson Controls offers integrated facilities management programs designed to lower the total costs of operating a commercial building.

Exhibit 10–10

Situational Determinants of Appropriate Marketing Objectives and Strategies for Extending Growth in Mature Markets

Situational variables	Growth extension strategies		
	Increased penetration	**Extended use**	**Market expansion**
Primary objective	Increase the proportion of users by converting current nonusers in one or more major market segments.	Increase the amount of product used by the average customer by increasing frequency of use or developing new and more varied ways to use the product.	Expand the number of potential customers by targeting underdeveloped geographic areas or applications segments.
Market characteristics	Relatively low penetration in one or more segments (a low percentage of potential users have adopted the product); relatively homogeneous market with only a few large segments.	Relatively high penetration but low frequency of use in one or more major segments; product used in only limited ways or for special occasions; relatively homogeneous market with only a few large segments.	Relatively heterogeneous market with a variety of segments; some geographic areas, including foreign countries, with low penetration; some product applications underdeveloped.
Competitor characteristics	Competitors hold relatively small market shares; comparatively limited resources or competencies make it unlikely they will steal a significant portion of converted nonusers.	Competitors hold relatively small market shares; comparatively limited resources or competencies make it unlikely their brands will be purchased for newly developed uses.	Competitors hold relatively small market shares; have insufficient resources or competencies to preempt underdeveloped geographic areas or application segments.
Firm characteristics	A market share leader in the industry; has R & D and marketing competencies to produce product modifications or line extensions; has promotional resources to stimulate primary demand among current nonusers.	A market share leader in the industry; has marketing competencies and resources to develop and promote new uses.	A market share leader in the industry; has marketing and distribution competencies and resources to develop new global markets or application segments.

A firm may also enhance a product's value by offering services that improve its performance or ease of use for the potential customer. Since it is unlikely that people who do not know how to knit will ever buy yarn or knitting needles, for example, most yarn shops offer free knitting lessons.

Product modifications or line extensions will not, however, attract nonusers unless the enhanced benefits are effectively promoted. For industrial goods, this may mean redirecting some sales efforts toward nonusers. The firm may offer additional incentives for new account sales or

Exhibit 10-11
Possible Marketing Actions for Accomplishing Growth Extension Objectives

Marketing strategy and objectives	Possible marketing actions
Increased penetration Convert current nonusers in target segment into users.	• Enhance product's value by adding features, benefits, or services.
	• Enhance product's value by including it in the design of integrated systems.
	• Stimulate additional primary demand through promotional efforts stressing new features or benefits:
	Advertising through selective media aimed at the target segment.
	Sales promotions directed at stimulating trial among current nonusers (such as tie-ins with other products).
	Some sales efforts redirected toward new account generation, perhaps by assigning some sales personnel as account development reps or by offering incentives for new account sales;
	• Improve product's availability by developing innovative distribution systems.
Extended use Increase frequency of use among current users.	• Move storage of the product closer to the point of end use by offering additional package sizes or designs.
	• Encourage larger-volume purchases (for nonperishable products):
	Offer quantity discounts.
	Offer consumer promotions to stimulate volume purchases or more frequent use (for example, multipack deals, frequent flier programs).
	• Reminder advertising stressing basic product benefits for a variety of usage occasions.
Encourage a wider variety of uses among current users.	• Develop line extensions suitable for additional uses or applications.
	• Develop and promote new uses, applications, or recipes for the basic product.

(continues)

assign specific salespeople to call on targeted nonusers and convert them into new customers. For consumer goods, some combination of advertising to stimulate primary demand in the target segment and sales promotions to encourage trial, such as free samples or tie-in promotions with complementary products that nonusers currently buy, can be effective.

Finally, some potential customers may be having trouble finding the product due to limited distribution, or the product's benefits may simply be too modest to justify much purchasing effort. In such cases, expanding distribution or developing more convenient and accessible channels may help expand market penetration. For example, few travelers are so leery of flying that they would go through the effort of calling an insurance agent to buy an accident policy for a single flight. But

Exhibit 10–11 (concluded)

Marketing strategy and objectives	Possible marketing actions
	Include information about new applications/recipes on package. Develop extended use advertising campaign, particularly with print media. Communicate new application ideas through sales presentations to current customers.
	• Encourage new uses through sales promotions (such as tie-ins with complementary products).
Market expansion Develop differentiated positioning focused on untapped or underdeveloped segments.	• Develop a differentiated flanker brand or product line with unique features or price that is more appealing to a segment of potential customers whose needs are not met by existing offerings.
	or
	• Develop multiple line extensions or brand offerings with features or prices targeted to the unique needs and preferences of several smaller potential applications or regional segments.
	• Consider producing for private labels.
	• Design advertising, personal selling, and/or sales promotion campaigns that address specific interests and concerns of potential customers in one or multiple underdeveloped segments to stimulate selective demand.
	• Build unique distribution channels to more effectively reach potential customers in one or multiple underdeveloped segments.
	• Design service programs to reduce the perceived risks of trial and/or solve the unique problems faced by potential customers in one or multiple underdeveloped segments (for example, systems engineering, installation, operator trailing, extended warranties).
	• Enter global markets where product category is in an earlier stage of its life cycle.

the sales of such policies are greatly increased by making them conveniently available through vending machines in airport terminals.

Extended Use Strategy

Some years ago, the manager of General Foods' Cool Whip frozen dessert topping discovered through marketing research that nearly three-fourths of all households used the product, but the average consumer used it only four times per year and served it on only 7 percent of all toppable desserts. In situations of good market penetration but low frequency of use, an extended use strategy may effectively increase volume. This was particularly true in the Cool Whip case: the relatively large and homogeneous target market consisted for the most part of a single mass-market segment. Also, General Foods held nearly a two-thirds share of the frozen topping market, and it had the marketing resources and competencies to capture most of the additional volume that an extended use strategy might generate.

One effective approach for stimulating increased frequency of use is to move product inventories closer to the point of use. This approach works particularly well with low-involvement consumer goods. Marketers know that most consumers are unlikely to expend any additional time or effort to obtain such products when they are ready to use them. If there is no Cool Whip in the refrigerator when the consumer is preparing dessert, for instance, he or she is unlikely to run to the store immediately and will probably serve the dessert without topping.

One obvious way to move inventory closer to the point of consumption is to offer larger package sizes. The more customers buy at one time, the less likely they are to be out of stock when a usage opportunity arises. This approach can backfire, though, for a perishable product or one that consumers perceive to be an impulse indulgence. Thus many super-premium ice creams, such as Hägen-Dazs, are sold in small pint containers; most consumers want to avoid the temptation of having large quantities of such a high-calorie indulgence too readily available.

The design of a package can also help increase use frequency by making the product more convenient or easy to use. Examples include single-serving packages of Jell-O pudding to pack in lunches, packages of paper cups that include a convenient dispenser, and frozen-food packages that can go directly into a microwave oven.

Various sales promotion programs also help move inventories of a product closer to the point of use by encouraging larger volume purchases. Marketers commonly offer quantity discounts for this purpose in selling industrial goods. For consumer products, multi-item discounts or two-for-one deals serve the same purpose. Promotional programs also encourage greater frequency of use and increase customer loyalty in many service industries. Consider, for instance, the frequent flier programs offered by major airlines.

Sometimes the product's characteristics inhibit customers from using it more frequently. If marketers can change those characteristics, such as difficulty of preparation or high caloric content, a new line extension might encourage customers to use more of the product or to use it more often. Microwave waffles and low-calorie salad dressings are examples of such line extensions. For industrial goods, however, firms may have to develop new technology to overcome a product's limitations for some applications. Thus Johnson Controls is working to develop plastic containers that will not shrivel when filled with hot liquids as a means of expanding its potential market.

Finally, advertising can sometimes effectively increase use frequency by simply reminding customers to use the product more often. For instance. General Foods conducted a reminder campaign for Jell-O pudding that featured Bill Cosby asking, "When was the last time you served pudding, Mom?"

Another approach for extending use among current customers involves finding and promoting new functional uses for the product. Jell-O gelatin is a classic example, having generated substantial new sales volume over the years by promoting the use of Jell-O as an ingredient in salads, pie fillings, and other dishes.

Firms promote new ways to use a product through a variety of methods. For industrial products, firms send technical advisories about new applications to the salesforce to present to their customers during regular sales calls. For consumer products, new use suggestions or recipes may be included on the package or in an advertising campaign. Sales promotions, such as including cents-off coupons in ads featuring a new recipe, encourage customers to try a new application. To reduce costs, two or more manufacturers of complementary products sometimes cooperate in running such promotions. A recent ad promoting a simple Italian dinner, for instance, featured coupons for Kraft's Parmesan cheese, Pillsbury's Soft Breadsticks, and Campbell's Prego spaghetti sauce.

In some cases slightly modified line extensions might encourage customers to use the product in different ways. Thus Kraft introduced a jalapeño-flavored Cheese-Whiz in a microwavable container and promoted the product as an easy-to-prepare topping for nachos.

Market Expansion Strategy

In a mature industry with a fragmented and heterogeneous market where some segments are less well developed than others, a market expansion strategy may generate substantial additional volume growth. Such a strategy aims at gaining new customers by targeting new or underdeveloped geographic markets (either regional or foreign) or new customer segments. Once again, share leaders tend to be best suited for implementing this strategy. But even smaller competitors can employ such a strategy successfully if they focus on relatively small or specialized market niches.

Pursuing market expansion by strengthening a firm's position in new or underdeveloped **domestic geographic markets** can lead to experience curve benefits and operating synergies. The firm can rely on largely the same expertise and technology, and perhaps even the same production and distribution facilities, it has already developed. Unfortunately, domestic geographic expansion is often not viable in a mature industry because the share leaders usually have attained national market coverage. Smaller regional competitors, on the other hand, might consider domestic geographic expansion a means for improving their volume and share position. However, such a move risks retaliation from the large national brands as well as from entrenched regional competitors in the prospective new territory.

To get around the retaliation problem, a regional producer might try to expand by acquiring small producers in other regions. This can be a viable option when (1) the low profitability of some regional producers enables the acquiring firm to buy their assets for less than the replacement cost of the capacity involved, and (2) synergies gained by combining regional operations and the infusion of resources from the acquiring firm can improve the effectiveness and profitability of the acquired producers. For example, Heileman Brewing Company grew from the 31st largest brewer of beer in the mid-1960s to the fourth largest by the mid-1980s through the acquisition of nearly 30 regional brands. Heileman took control of strong regional brands such as Old Style, Carling, and Rainier, but because it had no dominant national brand it avoided antitrust opposition to its acquisition program. After acquisition, Heileman maintained the identity of each brand, increased its advertising budget, and expanded its distribution by incorporating it into the firm's distribution system in other regions. As a result. Heileman achieved a strong earnings record for two decades.

In a different approach to domestic market expansion, the firm identifies and develops entirely **new customer** or **application segments**. Sometimes the firm can effectively reach new customer segments by simply expanding the distribution system without changing the product's characteristics or the other marketing mix elements. A sporting goods manufacturer that sells its products to consumers through retail stores, for instance, might expand into the commercial market consisting of schools and amateur and professional sports teams by establishing a direct salesforce. In most instances, though, developing new market segments requires modifying the product to make it more suitable for the application or to provide more of the benefits desired by customers in the new segment.

One final possibility for domestic market expansion is to produce **private-label brands** for large retailers such as Sears or Safeway. Firms whose own brands hold relatively weak positions and who have excess production capacity find this a particularly attractive option. Private labeling allows such firms to gain access to established customer segments without making substantial marketing expenditures, thus increasing the firm's volume and lowering its per unit costs. However, because private labels typically compete with low prices and their sponsors usually have strong bargaining power, producing private labels is often not a very profitable option unless a manufacturer already has a relatively low-cost position in the industry. It can also be a risky strategy, particularly for the smaller firm, because reliance on one or a few large private-label customers can result in drastic volume reductions and unit cost increases should those customers decide to switch suppliers.

Global Market Expansion—Sequential Strategies

For firms with leading positions in mature domestic markets, less developed markets in foreign countries often present the most viable opportunities for geographic expansion. As we shall see in the next chapter, firms can enter foreign markets in a variety of ways, from simply relying on import agents to developing joint ventures to establishing wholly owned subsidiaries—as Johnson Controls has done by acquiring an automotive seat manufacturer in Europe.

Regardless of which mode of entry a firm chooses, it can follow a number of different routes when pursuing global expansion.[24] By *route* we mean the sequence or order in which the firm enters global markets. Japanese companies provide illustrations of different global expansion paths. The most common expansion route involves moving from Japan to developing countries to developed countries. They used this path, for example, with automobiles (Toyota), consumer electronics (National), watches (Seiko), cameras (Minolta), and home appliances, steel, and petrochemicals. This routing reduced manufacturing costs and enabled them to gain marketing experience. In penetrating the U. S. market, the Japanese obtained further economies of scale and gained recognition for their products, which made penetration of European markets easier.

This sequential strategy succeeded: By the early 1970s, 60 percent of Japanese exports went to developed countries—more than half to the United States. Japanese motorcycles dominate Europe, as do its watches and cameras. Its cars have been able to gain a respectable share in most European countries.

A second type of *expansion path* has been used primarily for high-tech products such as computers and semiconductors. For the Japanese it consists of first securing their home market and then targeting developed countries. Japan largely ignored developing countries in this strategy because of their small demand for high-tech products. When demand increased to a point where developing countries became "interesting," Japanese producers quickly entered and established strong market positions using price cuts of up to 50 percent.

A home market–developed markets–developing markets sequence is also usually appropriate for discretionary goods such as soft drinks or candy. Note, for instance, the wide differences in consumption of Coca-Cola shown in Exhibit 10–12. As disposable incomes and discretionary expenditures grow in the markets of Asia and Africa, however, those markets will drive much of Coca-Cola's future growth.

---

[24]The following discussion of sequential strategies is based largely on material found in Somkid Jatusripitak, Liam Fahey, and Philip Kotler, "Strategic Global Marketing: Lessons from the Japanese," *Columbia Journal of World Business*, Spring 1985, pp. 47–53.

Exhibit 10–12

Global Differences in Coca-Cola Consumption

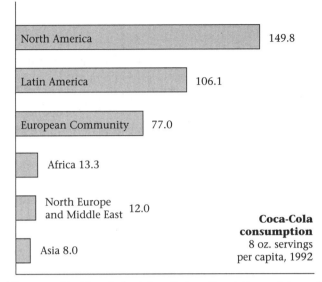

SOURCE: From "The New Global Consumer," by Ricardo Sookdeo, *Fortune*, Special issue, Autumn–Winter 1993, p. 69.

Strategies for Declining Markets

Most products eventually enter a decline phase in their life cycles. As sales decline, excess capacity once again develops. As the remaining competitors fight to hold volume in the face of falling sales, industry profits erode. Consequently, conventional wisdom suggests that firms should either divest declining products quickly or harvest them to maximize short-term profits. Not all markets decline in the same way or at the same speed, however; nor do all firms have the same competitive strengths and weaknesses within those markets. Therefore, as in most other situations, the relative attractiveness of the declining product-market and the business's competitive position within it should dictate the appropriate strategy.

Relative Attractiveness of Declining Markets

Although U. S. high school enrollment declined by about 2 million students from its peak in 1976 through the end of the 1980s, Jostens, Inc.—the leading manufacturer of class rings and other school merchandise—achieved annual increases in revenues and profits every year during that period. One reason for the firm's success was that it saw the market decline coming and prepared for it by improving the efficiency of its operations and developing marketing programs that were effective at persuading a larger proportion of students to buy class rings.[25]

Josten's experience shows that some declining product-markets can offer attractive opportunities well into the future, at least for one or a few strong competitors. In other product-markets, particularly those where decline is the result of customers switching to a new technology (for example, more students buying personal computers instead of portable typewriters), the potential for continued profits during the decline stage is more bleak.

Three sets of factors help determine the strategic attractiveness of declining product-markets: *conditions of demand*, including the rate and certainty of future declines in volume; *exit barriers*, or the ease with which weaker competitors can leave the market; and factors

---

[25]Jaclyn Fierman, "How to Make Money in Mature Markets," *Fortune*, November 25, 1985, p. 47.

affecting the *intensity of future competitive rivalry* within the market.[26] The impact of these variables on the attractiveness of declining market environments is summarized in Exhibit 10–13 and discussed next.

Conditions of Demand

Demand in a product-market declines for a number of reasons. Technological advances produce substitute products (such as electronic calculators for slide rules), often with higher quality or lower cost. Demographic shifts lead to a shrinking target market (for example, baby foods). Customers' needs, tastes, or lifestyles change (consider the falling consumption of beef). Finally, the cost of inputs or complementary products rises and shrinks demand (as can be seen in the effects of rising gasoline prices on sales of recreational vehicles).

The cause of a decline in demand can affect both the rate and the predictability of that decline. A fall in sales due to a demographic shift, for instance, is likely to be gradual, whereas the switch to a technically superior substitute can be abrupt. Similarly, the fall in demand as customers switch to a better substitute is predictable, while a decline in sales due to a change in tastes is not.

As Exhibit 10–13 indicates, both the rate and certainty of sales decline are demand characteristics that affect a market's attractiveness. A slow and gradual decline allows an orderly withdrawal of weaker competitors. Overcapacity does not become excessive and lead to predatory competitive behavior, and the competitors who remain are more likely to make profits than in a quick or erratic decline. Also, when most industry managers believe market decline is predictable and certain, reduction of capacity is more likely to be orderly than when they feel substantial uncertainty about whether demand might level off or even become revitalized.

Of course, not all segments of a market decline at the same time or at the same rate. The number and size of enduring niches or pockets of demand and the customer purchase behavior within them also influence the continuing attractiveness of the market. When the demand pockets are large or numerous and the customers in those niches are brand loyal and relatively insensitive to price, competitors with large shares and differentiated products can continue to make substantial profits. For example, even though the market for cigars has been shrinking for years, there continues to be a sizable number of smokers who prefer premium-quality cigars. Those firms with well-established positions at the premium end of the cigar industry have continued to earn above-average returns.

Exit Barriers

The higher the exit barriers, the less hospitable a product-market will be during the decline phase of its life cycle. When weaker competitors find it hard to leave a product-market as demand falls, excess capacity develops and firms engage in aggressive pricing or promotional efforts to try to prop up their volume and hold down unit costs. Thus exit barriers lead to competitive volatility.

Once again, Exhibit 10–13 indicates that a variety of factors influence the ease with which businesses can exit an industry. One critical consideration involves the amount of highly specialized assets. Assets unique to a given business are difficult to divest because of their low liquidation value. The only potential buyers for such assets are other firms who would use them for a similar purpose, which is unlikely in a declining industry. Thus, the firm may have little choice but to remain in the business or to sell the assets for their scrap value. This option is particularly unattractive when the assets are relatively new and not fully depreciated.

Another major exit barrier occurs when the assets or resources of the declining business intertwine with the firm's other business units, either through shared facilities and programs or

---

[26]Katherine Rudie Harrigan and Michael E. Porter, "End-Game Strategies for Declining Industries," *Harvard Business Review*, July–August 1983, pp. 111–20. Also see Katherine Rudie Harrigan, *Strategies for Declining Businesses* (Lexington, Mass.: D.C. Heath, 1980).

Exhibit 10-13
Factors Affecting the Attractiveness of Declining Markets

	Environmental attractiveness	
	Hospitable	**Inhospitable**
Conditions of demand		
Speed of decline	Very slow	Rapid or erratic
Certainty of decline	100% certain predictable patterns	Great uncertainty, erratic patterns
Pockets of enduring demand	Several or major ones	No niches
Product differentiation	Brand loyalty	Commondity-like products
Price stability	Stable, price premiums attainable	Very unstable, pricing below costs
Exit barriers		
Reinvestment requirements	None	High, often mandatory and involving capital assets
Excess capacity	Little	Substantial
Asset age	Mostly old assets	Sizable new assets and old ones not retired
Resale markets for assets	Easy to convert or sell	No markets available, substantial costs to retire
Shared facilities	Few freestanding plants	Substantial and interconnected with important businesses
Vertical integration	Little	Substantial
Single-product competitors	None	Several large companies
Rivalry determinants		
Customer industries	Fragmented, weak	Strong bargaining power
Customer switching costs	High	Minimal
Diseconomies of scale	None	Substantial penalty
Dissimilar strategic groups	Few	Several in same target markets

SOURCE: Katheyn Rudie Harrigan and Michael E. Porter, "End-Game Strategies for Declining Industries," *Haward Business Review*, July–August 1983, p. 117.

through vertical integration. Exit from the declining business might shut down shared production facilities, lower salesforce commissions, damage customer relations, and increase unit costs in the firm's other businesses to a point that damages their profitability.

Emotional factors can also act as exit barriers. Managers often feel reluctant to admit failure by divesting a business even though it no longer produces acceptable returns. This is especially true when the business played an important role in the firm's history and it houses a large number of senior managers.

Intensity of Future Competitive Rivalry

Even when substantial pockets of continuing demand remain within a declining business, it may not be wise for a firm to pursue them in the face of future intense competitive rivalry. In addition to exit barriers, other factors also affect the ability of the remaining firms to avoid intense price competition and maintain reasonable margins: size and bargaining power of the customers who continue to buy the product; customers' ability to switch to substitute products or to alternative suppliers; and any potential diseconomies of scale involved in capturing an increased share of the remaining volume.

Divestment or Liquidation

When the market environment in a declining industry is unattractive or a business has a relatively weak competitive position, the firm may recover more of its investment by selling the business in the early stages of decline rather than later. The earlier the business is sold, the more uncertain potential buyers are likely to be about the future direction of demand in the industry and thus the more likely that a willing buyer can be found. Thus, Raytheon sold its vacuum-tube business in the early 1960s even though transistors had just begun replacing tubes in radios and TV sets and there was still a strong replacement demand for tubes. By moving early, the firm achieved a much higher liquidation value than companies that tried to unload their tube-making facilities in the 1970s when the industry was clearly in its twilight years.[27]

Of course, the firm that divests early runs the risk that its forecast of the industry's future may be wrong. Also, quick divestment may not be possible if the firm faces high exit barriers, such as interdependencies across business units or customer expectations of continued product availability. By planning early for departure, however, the firm may be able to reduce some of those barriers before the liquidation is necessary.

Marketing strategies for Remaining Competitors

Conventional wisdom suggests that a business remaining in a declining product-market should pursue a harvesting strategy aimed at maximizing its cash flow in the short run. But such businesses also have other strategic options. They might attempt to maintain their position as the market declines, improve their position to become the profitable survivor, or focus efforts on one or more remaining demand pockets or market niches. Once again, the appropriateness of these strategies depends on factors affecting the attractiveness of the declining market and on the business's competitive strengths and weaknesses. Exhibit 10–14 summarizes the situational determinants of the appropriateness of each strategy. Some of the marketing actions a firm might take to implement them are discussed here and listed in Exhibit 10–15.

Harvesting Strategy

The objective of a harvesting or milking strategy is to generate cash quickly by maximizing cash flow over a relatively short term. This typically involves avoiding any additional investment in the business, greatly reducing operating (including marketing) expenses, and perhaps raising prices. Since the firm usually expects to ultimately divest or abandon the business, some loss of sales and market share during the pursuit of this strategy is likely. The trick is to hold the business's volume and share declines to a relatively slow and steady rate. A precipitous and premature loss of share would limit the total amount of cash the business could generate during the market's decline.

A harvesting strategy is most appropriate for a firm holding a relatively strong competitive position in the market at the start of the decline and a cadre of current customers likely to continue buying the brand even after marketing support is reduced. Such a strategy also works best when the market's decline is inevitable but likely to occur at a relatively slow and steady rate and when rivalry among remaining competitors is not likely to be very intense. Such conditions help enable the business to maintain adequate price levels and profit margins as volume gradually falls.

Implementing a harvesting strategy means avoiding any additional long-term investments in plants, equipment, or R & D. It also necessitates substantial cuts in operating expenditures for

---

[27]Harrigan and Porter, "End-Game Strategies," p. 114.

Exhibit 10-14
Situational Determinants of Appropriate Marketing Objectives and Strategies for Declining Markets

Situational variables	Strategies for declining markets			
	Harvesting	**Maintenance**	**Profitable survivor**	**Niche**
Primary objective	Maximize short-term cash flow: maintain or increase margins even at the expense of a slow decline in market share.	Maintain share in short term as market declines, even if, margins must be sacrificed.	Increase share of the declining market with an eye to future profits: encourage weaker competitors to exit.	Focus on strengthening position in one or a few relatively substantial segments with potential for future profits.
Market characteristics	Future market decline is certain but likely to occur at a slow and steady rate.	Market has experienced recent declines, but future direction and attractiveness are currently hard to predict.	Future market decline is certain but likely to occur at a slow and steady rate: substantial pockets of demand will continue to exist.	Overall market may decline quickly, but one or more segments will remain as demand pockets or decay slowly.
Competitor characteristics	Few strong competitors, low exit barriers; future rivalry not likely to be intense.	Few strong competitors, but intensity of future rivalry is hard to predict.	Few strong competitors; exit barriers are low or can be reduced by firm's intervention.	One or more stronger competitors in mass market, but not in, the target segment.
Firm's characteristics	Has a leading share position; has a substantial proportion of loyal customers who are likely to continue buying brand even if marketing support is reduced.	Has a leading share of the market and a relatively strong, competitive position.	Has a leading share of the market and a strong, competitive position; has superior resources or competencies necessary to encourage competitors to exit or to acquire them.	Has a sustainable competitive advantage in target segment, but overall resources may be limited.

marketing activities. This often means that the firm should greatly reduce the number of models or package sizes in its product line in order to reduce inventory and manufacturing costs.

The business should improve the efficiency of sales and distribution. For instance, an industrial goods manufacturer might service its smaller accounts through telemarketing rather than a field salesforce or assign its smaller customers to agent intermediaries. For consumer goods the business might move to more selective distribution by concentrating its efforts on the larger retail chains.

The firm would likely reduce advertising and promotion expenditures, usually to the minimum level necessary to retain adequate distribution. Finally, the business should attempt to maintain or perhaps even increase its price levels to increase margins.

Maintenance Strategy

In markets where future volume trends are highly uncertain, a business with a leading share position might consider pursuing a strategy aimed at maintaining its market share, at least until the market's future becomes more predictable. In such a maintenance strategy the business continues to pursue the same strategy that brought it success during the market's mature stage. This approach

Exhibit 10-15
Possible Marketing Actions Appropriate for Different Strategies in Declining Markets

Marketing strategy and objectives	Possible marketing actions

Harvesting strategy
Maximize short-term cash flow: maintain or increase margins even at the expense of market share decline.
	• Eliminate R & D expenditures and capital investments related to the business.
	• Reduce marketing and sales budgets.
	    Greatly reduce or eliminate advertising and sales promotion expenditures, with the possible exception of periodic reminder advertising targeted at current customers.
	    Reduce trade promotions to minimum level necessary to prevent rapid loss of distribution coverage.
	    Focus salesforce efforts on attaining repeat purchases from current customers.
	• Seek ways to reduce production costs, even at the expense of slow erosion in product quality.
	• Raise price if necessary to maintain margins.

Maintenance strategy Maintain market share for the short term, even at the expense of margins.	• Continue product and process R & D expenditures in short term aimed at maintaining or improving product quality. • Continue maintenance levels of advertising and sales promotion targeted at current users. • Continue trade promotion at levels sufficient to avoid any reduction in distribution coverage. • Focus salesforce efforts on attaining repeat purchases from current users. • Lower prices if necessary to maintain share, even at the expense of reduced margins.
Profitable survivor strategy Increase share of the declining market: encourage weaker competitors to exit.	Signal competitors that firm intends to remain in industry and pursue an increased share. Maintain or increase advertising and sales promotion budgets.

(continues)

often results in reduced margins and profits in the short term, though, because firms usually must reduce prices or increase marketing expenditures to hold share in the face of declining industry volume. Thus a firm should consider share maintenance an interim strategy. Once it becomes clear that the market will continue to decline, the business should switch to a different strategy that will provide better cash flows and return on investment over the market's remaining life.

Exhibit 10-15 (concluded)

Marketing strategy and objectives	Possible marketing actions
	Maintain or increase distribution coverage through aggressive trade promotion.
	Focus some salesforce effort on winning away competitors' customers.
	Continue product and process R & D to seek product improvements or cost reductions.
	• Consider introducing line extensions to appeal to remaining demand segments.
	• Lower prices if necessary to increase share, even at the expense of short-term margins.
	• Consider agreements to produce replacement parts or private labels for smaller competitors considering getting out of production.
Niche strategy Strengthen share position in one or a few segments with potential for continued profit.	• Continue product and process R & D aimed at product improvements or modifications that will appeal to target segment(s).
	• Consider producing for private labels in order to maintain volume and hold down unit costs.
	• Focus advertising, sales promotion, and personal selling campaigns on customers in target segment(s); stress appeals of greatest importance to those customers.
	• Maintain distribution channels appropriate for reaching target segment; seek unique channel arrangements to more effectively reach customers, in target segment(s).
	• Design service programs that address unique concerns/problems of customers in the target segment(s).

Profitable Survivor Strategy

An aggressive alternative for a business with a strong share position and a sustainable competitive advantage in a declining product-market is to invest enough to increase its share position and establish itself as the industry leader for the remainder of the market's decline. This kind of strategy makes the most sense when the firm expects a gradual decline in market demand or when substantial pockets of continuing demand are likely well into the future. It is also an attractive strategy when a firm's declining business is closely intertwined with other SBUs through shared facilities and programs or common customer segments.

A strong competitor can often improve its share position in a declining market at relatively low cost because other competitors may be harvesting their businesses or preparing to exit.

The key to the success of such a strategy is to encourage other competitors to leave the market early. Once the firm has achieved a strong and unchallenged position, it can switch to a harvesting strategy and reap substantial profits over the remaining life of the product-market.

A firm might encourage smaller competitors to abandon the industry by being visible and explicit about its commitment to become the leading survivor. It should aggressively seek increased market share, either by cutting prices or by increasing advertising and promotion expenditures. It might also introduce line extensions aimed at remaining pockets of demand to make it more difficult for smaller competitors to find profitable niches. Finally, the firm might act to reduce its competitors' exit barriers, making it easier for them to leave the industry. This could involve taking over competitors' long-term contracts, agreeing to supply spare parts, service their products in the field, or provide them with components or private-label products. For instance, large regional bakeries have encouraged grocery chains to abandon their own bakery operations by supplying them with private-label baked goods.

The ultimate way to remove competitors' exit barriers is to purchase their operations and either improve their efficiency or remove them from the industry to avoid excess capacity. With continued decline in industry sales a certainty, smaller competitors may be forced to sell their assets at a book value price low enough for the survivor to reap high returns on its investment, as Heileman Brewing Company did on its acquisitions of smaller regional brewers during the 1970s and 80s.

Niche Strategy

Even when most segments of an industry are expected to decline rapidly, a niche strategy may still be viable if one or more substantial segments will either remain as stable pockets of demand or decay slowly. The business pursuing such a strategy should have a strong competitive position in the target segment or be able to build a sustainable competitive advantage relatively quickly to preempt competitors. This is one strategy that even smaller competitors can sometimes successfully pursue because they can focus the required assets and resources on a limited portion of the total market. The marketing actions a business might take to strengthen and preserve its position in a target niche are similar to those discussed earlier concerning niche strategies in mature markets.

Summary

An industry's transition from growth to maturity begins when approximately half the potential customers have adopted the product and, while sales are still growing, the rate of growth begins to decline. As growth slows, some competitors are likely to find themselves with excess production capacity. Other changes in the competitive environment, including a reduction in the degree of differentiation across brands and increased difficulty in maintaining adequate distribution, occur at about the same time. As a result, competition becomes more intense with firms either cutting prices or increasing their marketing expenditures as they battle to increase volume, cover high fixed costs, and maintain profitability. This transition is usually accompanied by a shakeout as weaker competitors fail or leave the industry.

Success during the maturity stage of a product-market's life cycle requires two sets of strategic actions. First, managers should work to maintain and strengthen either the differentiation of the firm's offerings on quality and/or service dimensions or its position as a low-cost competitor within the industry. The second strategic consideration during the maturity stage is to develop meaningful marketing objectives and a marketing strategy appropriate for achieving them. Since maturity can last for many years, the most critical marketing objective is to maintain and protect the business's market share. For share leaders, some variation of the fortress defense, confrontation, or flanker strategies are often appropriate for achieving that objective. Smaller competitors, on the other hand, may have to rely on a niche strategy to hold their position.

Since different market segments may mature at different times and environmental conditions can change over the mature phase of a product's life, firms often find opportunities to extend the growth of seemingly mature product-markets. Thus an important secondary objective for firms in many mature markets is to stimulate additional volume growth. Among the marketing strategies firms might use to accomplish that objective are an increased penetration strategy, an extended use strategy, or a market expansion strategy focused on developing either new geographic territories (including global markets) or new application segments.

Conventional wisdom suggests that declining products should be either divested or harvested to maximize short-term profits. However, some declining product-markets remain attractive enough to justify more aggressive marketing strategies. The attractiveness of such markets is determined by three sets of factors: (1) conditions of demand, including the rate and certainty of future declines in volume; (2) exit barriers, or the ease with which weaker competitors can leave the market; and (3) factors affecting the intensity of future competitive rivalry. When a declining product-market is judged to offer continuing opportunities for profitable sales, managers might consider one of several strategic alternatives to divestment or harvesting. Those alternative strategies include a maintenance strategy, a profitable survivor strategy, and a niche strategy.

Social Relations and Japanese Business Practices

Bradley M. Richardson & Taizo Ueda

The foreign businessman entering into negotiations with Japanese counterparts is entering into another culture, just as the Japanese counterparts themselves are experiencing contact with practices different from their own. Assumptions about proper interpersonal behavior are different, and the whole process of business contacts is predicated upon a different value system. This does not mean that European or American businessmen cannot get along with Japanese. But knowing how Japanese behave, what they believe, and what their expectations are can help a great deal in smoothing interpersonal contacts and business discussions.

As Yoshi Tsurumi points out, friendships in Japan are usually lifelong ties. They are not a casual matter. Nor are they the product of a meeting that lasts only a few minutes such as those after which many Americans immediately proceed into a first-name basis "fictive friendship" with their counterparts in business. Friendships for Japanese more often than not begin with shared experiences during youth. These ties of an almost brotherly nature go on through life and are renewed through sustained contact and socialization at various points in time. To be a friend in Japan involves a commitment to support each other when there are problems and stress on the job or in home life. The bond is deep and ideally is selfless. Because of the deeper and more permanent nature of friendship in Japan—which is not totally unlike that in Europe, despite the obvious differences in culture—foreigners in Japan or meeting Japanese should not assume that acquaintanceships will develop with the same speed they do in one's native culture. Still friendships can and do form between Japanese and foreigners where both partners are understanding and not explotive in their approach and where the foreigner recognizes the slower time dimension involved in Japanese social ties.

Negotiating with Japanese counterparts involves some of the sensitivities appropriate to making friends Japanese style. Japanese business negotiations are ideally conducted on the basis of long-standing relationships of mutual trust. They are not legalistic and formalistic. They involve understanding of both semantic subtleties, wherein real motivations may be concealed behind overt behavior and talk that could imply other substance. They also involve adjustment to the time-consuming Japanese process of talking things over slowly until full mutual understanding of all parties' motivations and assumptions emerges. These and other aspects of business negotiations with Japanese counterparts are discussed by Tsurumi in terms of a series of "dos" and "don'ts" to be avoided in such relationships.

Negotiation with businessmen in Japan inevitably involves after-hours social contact where Japanese practices may be somewhat different than those in the foreigner's home country. Japanese usually do not bring their wives to social events involving other businessmen, and the foreigner in Japan who brings his spouse to evening parties with Japanese counterparts may face some embarrassing situations. Drunkenness and flirting with bar hostesses is condoned among some Japanese businessmen to a degree probably not typically accepted in Europe or the United States (perhaps American convention behavior is the best point for comparison)! There are also certain protocols in Japan that must be kept in mind for relationships to go smoothly: tipping is much less common in Japan than in the United States and Europe, and is done only where extraordinary services are rendered or a long-term relationship exists, such as at a restaurant or bar normally frequented by the Japanese host. Japanese are also great gift givers in most social relationships, including those

From *Business and Society in Japan* edited by Richardson and Ueda, 1981. Reproduced with permission of Greenwood Publishing Group, Inc., Westport, CT.

between businessmen, and reciprocal gift giving demonstrates extra thoughtfulness on the part of both partners and often helps provide the warmth and trust necessary to effective relationships in Japan.

Negotiations with Japanese Firms

Some Western businessmen say it is very hard to negotiate with Japanese. There are many subtle things which Westerners don't understand. Just what are some of the major "rules" of negotiations Japanese style and some of the areas of misunderstanding of these matters between Japanese and Westerners?

There is nothing mysterious about negotiating with Japanese businessmen. All of the rules you would normally apply in negotiations with your fellow American businessmen would be equally applicable in doing business in Japan. However, I have been investigating for some time the causes of the dismal failures of some business negotiations between Japanese and foreign (American) businessmen and have found that those failures stemmed overwhelmingly from eight principal points of miscommunication between Japanese and foreign negotiators. But the end result is the same: negotiations were not concluded successfully.

Cause #1: Slicing the Pie before It Is Baked

The uneasiness of foreigners regarding the hidden intentions of their Japanese counterparts is heartily reciprocated by the Japanese themselves. These hidden suspicions make for a predisposition by both parties from the outset to become preoccupied with safeguarding their respective control over the dividing up and resultant shares of the economic pie that both sides are supposedly meeting to bake together but has not yet been produced. Once this sort of adversary relationship enters into the negotiations, little hope remains for reaching a successful conclusion. Even when a fragile agreement is reached formally, it may be doomed to failure if it lacks the mutual trust between the two parties that is vital for an amicable implementation of the agreement.

The remedy for this is simple. Foreign negotiators can easily maintain the initiative in the negotiations while at the same time enhancing their personal trust with their Japanese counterparts by first concentrating on working together with the Japanese to arrive at a clear-cut understanding of what they can achieve only by working together and not on their own. The rest falls into place as both parties grow more aware of each other's contribution to their joint deal.

Cause #2: Selling the Deal, and Not the Seller

No American would enter into an agreement with a fellow American who seemed to be untrustworthy. This rule of human relations needs to be expanded by an order of ten when negotiating with the Japanese. The Japanese must be convinced that you are trustworthy, just as you have the right to expect the Japanese to prove themselves to you.

Unlike in the United States, where legalistic and contractual bondings are prevalent in business relationships, personal trust between negotiators is one major guarantee in Japan that business agreements will be honored by each firm. Accordingly, Japanese negotiators instinctively attempt to assess whether their foreign counterparts are well respected by peers and superiors within their firm and whether their foreign counterparts are individually trustworthy to do business with.

Haste on the part of a foreigner to sell a specific deal before selling himself is often interpreted by the Japanese as the sign of a small person with whom dealing would be too risky. To avoid this unfortunate stereotyping by the Japanese, foreigners should at least take the following two precautions. First, they should obtain a very good introduction to the executives of their targeted Japanese firms, preferably by Japanese or foreign executives who have successfully done business with the targeted firm in the past. Japanese banks and trading companies can often provide such introductions. Second, before they explain the specific business deal they have in mind, they should first take time to introduce themselves, their educational and vocational background, their family heritage (perhaps even including who their grandfathers were), and their position and functions within their firm. The tone of this personal "sales pitch" could be likened to that which is often employed at social gatherings in the United States in getting to know an interesting stranger of the opposite sex on a personal basis.

The Japanese attitude toward the business negotiation is very personal in that the negotiation is merely one process to test their counterparts' trustworthiness. On the other hand, the American attitude toward the negotiation tends to be very legalistic in that the negotiation process is a legal sparring to make as many points as possible with their opponents. Thus, Americans often assume that nothing is binding until the final signing of the detailed legal documents. Any agreements that are reached in the process of negotiations are assumed to be subject to subsequent changes as the new phases of the negotiation unfold new circumstances.

This is why Japanese negotiators often see American counterparts try to change promises and agreements reached the day before. To most Japanese who are not familiar with the American legalistic attitude toward the business negotiation, this sudden reversal of American positions unfortunately signals the untrustworthiness of American negotiators. The only way to avoid such unfortunate misunderstandings would be to set the negotiation rule from the outset that permits both parties to change any interim promises and agreements until the final agreement. Please do not assume that the other side would understand your position and rule.

Cause #3: Ignoring the Hidden Economics of Japanese Business Relationships

When American managers attempt to sell their products or services, they are prone to speak to their prospective customers only in narrow economic terms of such product- or service-specific variables as price, delivery, quality, or sales promotion. This narrow view of things will suffice in simple over-the-counter deals. But in negotiating with Japanese businesses, they should be more sensitive to such hidden but nevertheless vital economic factors as whether the deal in question will require Japanese businessmen to alter their business relationships with other Japanese firms.

What to an uninitiated foreigner might seem a simple supplier-client relationship often masks important considerations such as an outside supplier's cumulative favors to its client through its hiring of surplus or retired employees of the client firm. As a result, a narrow economic advantage such as price or quality differences between your product and that of a Japanese competitor may have to be extremely distinctive to motivate your prospective Japanese clients to forego the hidden benefits associated with their existing relationships with other Japanese firms.

Cause #4: Letting Lawyers in on Your Negotiations

Of course, some lawyers are superb practicing business executives. But with the exception of a case in which a foreign businessman who happens to be a lawyer is acting as a bona fide business executive, lawyers should be kept out of business negotiations in Japan. You can consult with them privately to check on the legal parameters of your business deals. But the presence of a lawyer in the negotiations will convey the unfortunate message that you do not trust your Japanese counterpart and that you are not sure of yourself as a negotiator.

In Japan, lawyers become involved only in those serious civil or criminal disputes that are beyond normal resolution by reasonable-minded adults. The feeling an ordinary Japanese might have in consulting a lawyer is akin to the sense of guilt and shame he might feel in consulting a dermatologist for treatment of certain unmentionable social diseases.

Besides, lawyers are trained to anticipate and defuse potential problems that their clients might encounter. Accordingly, their advice could be likely to steer you into the kind of adversary bargaining we have already identified as Cause #1 for the frequent failures of American negotiations in Japan.

Cause #5: Lack of Semantic Sensitivity

Unfortunately, there are still too few American business executives who possess even a rudimentary knowledge of the Japanese language, not to mention a crucially important sensitivity to the Japanese mode of interpersonal relationships and communication. American firms desiring to establish lasting business relations with Japan would benefit considerably from the development of a cadre of their own managers and specialists who are well versed in the Japanese language and culture. Until this happens, however, American business managers or government officials who negotiate with Japanese firms or government ministries should stay alert for three typical areas of miscommunication between Japanese and American negotiators.

First, the implied meaning of the Japanese phrase which is translated as "in principle" (*gensoku to shite*) is the opposite of the English meaning. If your Japanese negotiators agree to a certain point "in principle" that is tantamount to their declaring that they will abide by it 90 percent of the time (the remaining 10 percent being subject to acts of God). I have seen situations in which American negotiators nearly blew an entire deal merely because of their mental block against the Japanese use of the phrase "in principle." Second, the same holds true for the Japanese interpretation of "gentleman's agreement." In a society in which one's trustworthiness (gentlemanliness) carries high social and economic value, a gentleman's agreement—especially one which is witnessed by a respected third party—is, again, almost unbreakable. Third, Japanese have a tendency to say "*hai, hai*" (yes, yes), or the equivalent of "I understand," or even "I agree," while they are listening to you. These phrases merely mean that they are listening to you and that they understand your positions. Semantic miscommunication is often compounded by an innate Japanese propensity to avoid saying "no" directly. Instead of saying "no," they prefer to say "I will consider it." This makes it difficult for you as a negotiator to distinguish between their actual, serious intention to consider your proposal and a polite, but firm refusal. At a time like this you might rely on a trustworthy third party to find out for you. The judicious use of a third party is a basic skill you will need to master. Often, the individuals who gave you a good introduction to your prospective Japanese clients are able to act as a third party for you.

Cause #6: Insisting on Detailed Discussions with High-Level Executives

In Japanese firms, the degree to which de facto authority to formulate strategic decisions is delegated to middle-echelon executives is usually far greater than in American firms. High-level executives in Japanese firms are often present at negotiations only to arbitrate various decisions recommended by their middle-level management personnel, and often do not carry overly impressive formal job titles. Many American negotiators overlook this factor and insist upon negotiating on details with their "formal" Japanese counterparts, to the latter's inordinate sense of discomfort.

Cause #7: Rushing the Negotiations

With the exception of instances in which a sense of urgency is already shared by your Japanese counterparts, there is no use in rushing through the negotiation process. Americans often complain that it takes an eternity for the Japanese to make up their minds on something. In turn, Japanese often complain that it takes Americans forever to implement decisions once they have been mutually agreed upon. It is standard Japanese business practice not to finalize a decision unless its implementation is also ensured and prepared for in advance. This is why your Japanese counterparts often need time to contact key bases within their firm and prepare their colleagues to help implement the deal emerging between you and them.

At the same time, you need to educate your Japanese negotiating counterparts so that they will fully understand that decision making is often separated from implementation in American firms. To avoid any distrust that may arise through mutual ignorance of respective corporate cultures, you should budget ample time for concluding negotiations with Japanese firms. You cannot hope to wrap it all up in just a few days. As your negotiation makes positive progress, it would be advisable to work out a timetable with your Japanese counterparts for implementation of the deal. In this way you would also ascertain what will need to be done to prepare your colleagues back home so that they can help you implement the new business decisions.

Cause #8: Assuming Lasting Stability of the Agreement

Even in a marriage, it cannot simply be assumed that the relationship between husband and wife will always be peaceful, loving, or, least of all, everlasting. Neither can one take another for granted. If a marriage is to be long-lasting and mutually gratifying, one must work at it and be on guard to resolve any difficulties as they arise.

It is therefore rather strange for Japanese and foreign negotiators to enter into a business agreement without working out in advance the procedures and criteria by which their mutual relationship will be reviewed on a periodic basis. Some liken joint-venture agreements to marriage. Actually, they are more akin to contractual cohabitation. The needs of the parties change over time. According to my research findings on questions of stability in joint ventures, I have to conclude that there are inherent instabilities in any joint venture, let alone one between Japanese and foreign business partners.

In order to ensure the stability of your business agreements with Japanese partners, you would be well advised to agree on procedures and criteria for periodic review of the arrangement once the initial agreements for your business deals are concluded. With the establishment of formal procedures for such reviews, you can also handle your own corporate politics that might at least imply an evaluation of your predecessors who were involved in the initial agreements pertaining to the business deals.

The eight above-mentioned causes are quite commonsensical and straightforward. And yet, one American negotiator after another ignores them. This is often because they program themselves mentally for failure by convincing themselves that there are certain "mysterious" tricks to negotiating with the Japanese. They forget to act sensibly, thus sowing the seeds of their own eventual failure.

Yoshi Tsurumi

Bibliography

Tsurumi, Yoshi. *Multinational Management.* Cambridge, Mass.: Ballinger, 1977.

Dos and Don'ts of Japanese Etiquette

> Any country has its "dos" and "don'ts" of social etiquette. If a foreigner wants to observe Japanese customs in his relations with Japanese business counterparts what are some of the things he should keep in mind as far as everyday etiquette is concerned?

Since 1868, Japan has transformed herself from an agrarian and feudalistic society to a leading industrial and democratic country. This transformation has been brought about by Japan's successful assimilation and adaptations of legal, political, educational, economic, cultural and social institutions and mores that Japan transplanted selectively from England, Germany, France, and the United States. Japanese businesses of the post-World War II period have carefully studied American business practices, in particular, and adapted them to the Japanese scene so thoroughly that American business managers today find their Japanese counterparts following much of the same business and social etiquette that Americans follow.

In order to impress Japanese businessmen, therefore, foreigners only have to behave the same way as they would behave in dealing with well-educated and cultured American, British, and European businessmen. The social values that are still strongly held among Japanese businessmen, young and old, are the time-honored Japanese versions of values such as "frugality," "diligence," and "social respectability," and these are much akin to similar values in the Judeo-Christian tradition. In fact, one can make a strong case that Japan's assimilation of many Western forms of legal, economic, and other institutions and mores was facilitated by Japan's sharing similar social values as her Western mentors.

Of course, the Japanese are not without their own subtle idiosyncrasies, idiosyncrasies that occasionally baffle and embarrass foreigners dealing with their Japanese business counterparts in informal social settings. The following pointers might be useful to foreigners doing business in Japan.

Point #1: Stag Outing

Although much American socializing is done in male-and-female paired couples, the Japanese definitely practice "stag only" or "business-relations only" rules for social activities. Japanese and foreign female professionals are included in "stag" outings or dinners but they are also expected to come without their dates, as equally individualistic and independent professionals should.

This tends to create problems for foreign businessmen who bring their wives with them on their business trips to Japan. As more and more Japanese become aware of the "pairing culture" of western society, they often gladly extend dinner and other social invitations to the wives of foreign businessmen. But the Japanese hosts will come stag almost invariably. If the social occasions are likely to digress or expand into informal business shop talk, foreigners would be well advised to go without their spouses or dates. Also, after-hours socializing in Japan often extends well into the night, in seemingly endless hoppings from one dining and wining spot to another.

Your Japanese hosts are simply displaying the typical behavior of the all-male "night tribe" (*gozensama*), a "tribe" composed of businessmen who return home only in the wee small hours of the morning. Their wives often sit up late waiting for the return of their past-midnight husbands. In Japan, the notion that business is very much a male domain is still unchallenged. Foreigners who insist on getting together socially with their "Mr. and Mrs. Japanese counterparts" are often politely evaded.

Point #2: Dining Out

Unlike American homes, Japanese homes are usually exclusively for family members, relatives, and close friends. Accordingly, Japanese businessmen would rather invite their foreign counterparts out to restaurants and clubs for social entertainment. In addition, very few Japanese businessmen feel that their homes are worthy to show to important foreign visitors. They are being honest when they humbly apologize for not inviting you to their homes, even though their excuses usually sound rather lame.

Knowing that Americans particularly appreciate being invited to private homes, some Japanese take pride in bringing their foreign guests home. However, foreign guests are likely to discover the host's wife spending almost the entire time either in the kitchen or in serving foods and drinks to the guests and host alike. There is no use appealing to the host and his wife that both of them should join the party for this is often the way things are done in Japan.

Point #3: Gift Exchange

Japanese hosts often shower foreigners with many personal gifts. Chances are that foreigners will be presented with gifts specifically meant for their spouses back home. Many Westerners feel put on the spot by this Japanese generosity and wonder if they are obligated to reciprocate. Furthermore, often gifts turn out to be awkward. They may be too big to fit into an already packed suitcase or the special color and style of a gift for a businessman's wife might not be the sort that appeals to American women.

Well, you do not need to feel embarrassed about such gifts. Your Japanese hosts reap sufficient psychological rewards when they see their important foreign guests genuinely appreciate the gifts.

All you have to do is send your Japanese hosts sincere notes of thanks once you return home. As your personal acquaintance with your Japanese hosts grows, and as you have a chance to visit them again in Japan, you might pick up, at the airport duty-free shop, a bottle of whiskey or a carton of cigarettes as your personal gift to them. If your Japanese hosts happen to come and visit you in your home country, that might be a good time to reciprocate their generosity, not necessarily by expensive gifts but by entertaining them the same way you would entertain your own good friends.

Point #4: No Tipping

Japan is one of the few countries where tipping has not yet contaminated the masses. Neither Japanese nor foreigners are expected to leave tips for any service personnel including taxi driver, doormen, hotel bellboys, waiters, hairdressers, and others. Your Japanese hosts prefer to retain their practice of no tipping. Foreigners' cooperation would be appreciated.

Likewise, foreigners cannot hope to grease their ways around through heavy tipping or suggestions of personal kickbacks to their Japanese business counterparts. Nor can they hope to wiggle their way out of traffic violations or other infractions by paying off policemen. Recently one American businessman was arrested and jailed in Tokyo when he attempted to bribe a traffic policeman into forgetting the small traffic violation committed by the foreigner's cab driver. The bewildered foreigner bemoaned, "Back home, that's the way we fix traffic tickets."

Section 3

Illustrations

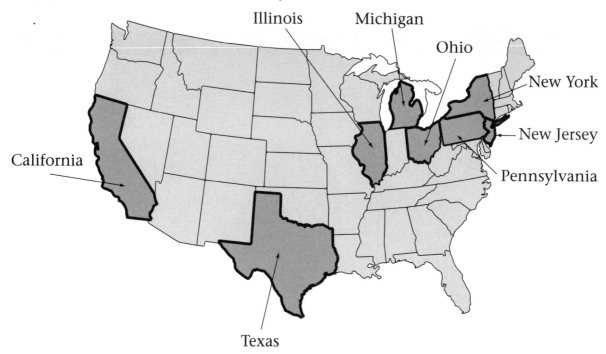

Geographical Concentration of Industrial Buyers

Alternative Shapes for Territories

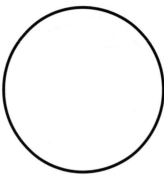
CIRCLE

CLOVERLEAF

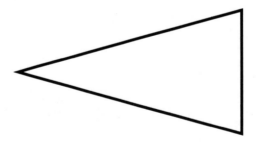
WEDGE or TRIANGLE